Advances in the Management and Treatment of Depression

With compliments of
Eli Lilly and Company Limited and Boehringer Ingelheim

Advances in the Management and Treatment of Depression

Edited by

John Potokar MD
Senior Lecturer in Psychiatry
Department of Psychopharmacology
School of Medical Sciences
University of Bristol
Bristol

Michael E Thase MD
Professor of Psychiatry
University of Pittsburgh Medical Center
Western Psychiatric Institute and Clinic
Pittsburgh PA
USA

Taylor & Francis
Taylor & Francis Group

LONDON AND NEW YORK

A MARTIN DUNITZ BOOK

© 2003 Taylor & Francis, an imprint of the Taylor & Francis Group

First published in the United Kingdom in 2003
by Taylor & Francis, an imprint of the Taylor & Francis Group, 2 Park Square,
Milton Park, Abingdon, Oxon OX14 4RN

Tel.:   +44 (0)20 7017 6000
Fax.:   +44 (0)20 7017 6699
E-mail: info@dunitz.co.uk
Website: http://www.dunitz.co.uk

Reprinted 2005

Although every effort has been made to ensure that all owners of copyright
material have been acknowledged in this publication, we would be glad to
acknowledge in subsequent reprints or editions any omissions brought to our
attention.

A CIP record for this book is available from the British Library.

Library of Congress Cataloging-in-Publication Data
Data available on application

ISBN 1 84184 582 5

Distributed in North and South America by
Taylor & Francis
2000 NW Corporate Blvd
Boca Raton, FL 33431, USA

Within Continental USA
Tel: 800 272 7737; Fax: 800 374 3401
Outside Continental USA
Tel: 561 994 0555; Fax: 561 361 6018
E-mail: orders@crcpress.com

Distributed in the rest of the world by
Thomson Publishing Services
Cheriton House
North Way
Andover, Hampshire SP10 5BE, UK
Tel.:   +44 (0)1264 332424
E-mail: salesorder.tandf@thomsonpublishingservices.co.uk

Composition by Wearset Ltd, Boldon, Tyne and Wear
Printed and bound in Great Britain by the Cromwell Press, Trowbridge

Contents

Contributors

Spilios V Argyropoulos MSc MB MRCPsych
Lecturer in Psychiatry
Division of Psychiatry
Psychopharmacology Unit
University of Bristol
UK

Mathias Berger MD
Professor of Psychiatry and Head,
Department of Psychiatry and
Psychotherapy
University of Freiburg
Germany

Nick Craddock PhD MB MRCPsych
Professor of Psychiatry
Neuropsychiatric Genetics Unit
Tenovus Building
University of Wales College of
Medicine
Heath Park, Cardiff
UK

Subodh Dave MD MRCPsych
Honorary Clinical Lecturer in
Psychiatry
Molecular Psychiatry Group
Division of Neuroscience
University of Birmingham
Queen Elizabeth Psychiatric
Hospital, Birmingham
UK

Mary Amanda Dew PhD
Departments of Psychiatry,
Psychology and Epidemiology
University of Pittsburgh School of
Medicine and Graduate School of
Public Health
Western Psychiatric Institute and
Clinic
Pittsburgh PA
USA

Mark S George MD
Distinguished Professor of
Psychiatry, Radiology and
Neurology
Director, Brain Stimulation
Laboratory, and Center for
Advanced Imaging Research
Medical University of South
Carolina (MUSC)
IOP
Psychiatry Department
Charleston SC
USA

Meghan M Grady BA
Editorial Assistant
Neuroscience Education Institute
Carlsbad, CA
USA

Martica Hall PhD
Department of Psychiatry
University of Pittsburgh School of
Medicine
Western Psychiatric Institute and
Clinic
Pittsburgh PA
USA

Jeremy Holmes MD
Senior Clinical Lecturer
Peninsula Medical School
Visiting Professor Psychoanalysis
Unit, University College London
Department of Mental Health
University of Exeter
Wonford House Hospital
Exeter
UK

Ian Jones PhD MB MRCPsych
Senior Lecturer in Psychiatry
Molecular Psychiatry Group
Division of Neuroscience
University of Birmingham
Queen Elizabeth Psychiatric
Hospital
Birmingham
UK

F Andrew Kozel MD
Instructor in Psychiatry
Imaging Research Fellow
Medical University of South
Carolina (MUSC) and
Ralph H Johnson
VA Medical Center
Psychiatry Department
Charleston SC
USA

Lynn M Martire PhD
Department of Psychiatry
University of Pittsburgh School of
Medicine
Western Psychiatric Institute and
Clinic
Pittsburgh PA
USA

David Mischoulon PhD MD
Assistant Professor of Psychiatry
Harvard Medical School;
Depression Clinical and Research
Program
Massachusetts General Hospital
Boston, MA
USA

Charles Montgomery MBBS
Consultant Psychiatrist
Devon Partnership Trust
Department of Mental Health
University of Exeter
Wonford House Hospital
Exeter
UK

**Jon R Nash MB MRCP
MRCPsych**
Lecturer in Old Age Psychiatry
Division of Psychiatry
Psychopharmacology Unit
University of Bristol
UK

Robert Niculescu MD
Neurosciences Research Center
8899 University Center Lane
Suite 130
San Diego
CA 92122
USA

Andrew A Nierenberg MD
Associate Professor of Psychiatry
Harvard Medical School;
Associate Director,
Depression Clinical and Research
Program
Department of Psychiatry
Massachusetts General Hospital,
Boston, MA
USA

Claus Normann MD
Department of Psychiatry and
Psychotherapy
University of Freiburg
Germany

John Potokar MD MRCPsych
Senior Lecturer in Psychiatry
Psychopharmacology Unit
University of Bristol
UK

Stephen M Stahl PhD MD
Chairman, Neuroscience
Education Institute;
Adjunct Professor
Neuroscience Education Institute
San Diego, CA
USA

Introduction

Sir Winston Churchill was recently voted the 'greatest Briton ever' by the British public in a television poll that captured large media attention. His achievements were many and his determination in the face of enemy threat stands as a lasting icon of the bulldog spirit that stood firm against invasion by Nazi Germany. However in his later years he endured episodes of severe depression which brought great darkness to his life and which he named his 'black dog'. He exemplifies the fact that depression is not a weakness of character, something that can be overcome with willpower, but an illness that causes immense suffering. His death in 1965 occurred at a time when new treatments were emerging for depressive illnesses and since that time there has been a considerable development in our understanding of both the aetiology and management of depression. The 1990s were designated the decade of the brain in a proclamation by the then President of the United States, George Bush. Although now over, the waves of progress that have resulted from research into brain disorders continues gathering momentum. This is particularly true for depressive disorders, which are common and as such have a major impact on the health of our population. Although the majority will not necessarily have personal experience of depression, there are few of us who do not know a close friend or relative who has not at some time suffered a depressive illness. Depression is associated with increased mortality not only from suicide (approximately 20 times greater risk compared to the expected population death rate) but also from non suicidal violent deaths, deaths defined as resulting from unnatural versus natural causes and death from all causes. The huge impact of this illness is underlined by the World Health Organization which ranks major depression as the fourth most important cause of global disease burden and the leading cause of disability measured in years lived with disability.

The aim of this book is to provide a user-friendly update on current research findings in depression covering the major areas of importance. We wanted this to be a practical book in a readable format and have therefore tried to avoid long reference lists although major findings are cited. The authors, all experts in their field, were asked to provide a state-of-the-art essay on current developments in their specialized areas.

The science and art of clinical research depends not only on defining the problem, but also putting it into a societal context, ie what is the extent of the problem? In the first chapter Mary Amanda Dew and colleagues from the University of Pittsburgh describe this wider context by looking at epidemiological and risk factors for depressive disorders. They highlight the fact that scores on self-report symptoms scales do not necessarily correlate with the diagnosis of a psychiatric disorder and emphasize the fact that standardized diagnostic criteria are essential if meaningful conclusions are to be drawn from studies into causation. They look at both prevalence and incidence rates and emphasize the huge global burden of depressive illness. The main disorders that are co-morbid with the major depressive syndromes are discussed together with the relationship with physical illness. In terms of the latter, the amount of co-morbidity depends on the nature of the physical illness and this may lead primary care physicians to under diagnose depressive disorders especially in older patients and amongst those with chronic physical illnesses. The role of co-morbid alcohol and substance misuse is critical and may give insights into the underlying neurobiology of depressive disorders. Cocaine, for example, is associated with a greatly increased risk of subsequent bipolar 1 disorder.

Given this huge burden, it is essential to explore factors that underpin this illness. In chapter 2 Claus Normann and Mathias Berger from the University of Freiburg discuss recent advances in the neurobiology of depression. They describe recent work demonstrating loss of hippocampal volume in depression and the relationship between this and the effects of stress, including activation of the HPA axis. Stress also appears to play a role in inhibiting neurogenesis, which is now a clear phenomenon, although it may be limited to specific brain regions. They also discuss the intriguing findings that suggest that antidepressants may both enhance self-survival and stimulate neurogenesis possibly via serotonergic influences on the 5-HT$_{1A}$ receptor. This seems likely to be an area of important future research. Other active areas of research include study of the relationship between early adverse experiences and adult onset depression and there is emerging evidence of the neurobiology that may underpin this. The HPA axis may mediate some of the longer lasting effects of early adversity and recent developments of the dexamethasone suppression tests, combining it with a CRF stimulation test can differentiate between normal and depressed patients with a sensitivity of over 80%.

The nature/nurture debate continues but few would argue that genetic factors do not have a role in a persons susceptibility to developing depression. In chapter 3 Subodh Dave et al from the University of Birmingham highlight recent advances in our understanding of the genetics of unipolar depression. There is very active research in this area which may not only help explain the increased relative risk of developing depression in first degree relatives of probands with the illness, but also through identifying susceptibility genes help elucidate the biochemical pathways involved in pathogenesis. There are many questions that need addressing including the fact that pre pubertal onset depression may be a distinct illness (with less genetic causation). The interaction between genes and environment is complex as exemplified by the fact that it seems that those who are genetically vulnerable are more likely to experience depressogenic life events!

In chapter 4 Stephen Stahl and colleagues from the Neuroscience Education Institute, San Diego discuss developments in antidepressants. In this chapter noradrenaline deficiency and serotonergic deficiency states are discussed together with the current mainstay of treatment, the SSRIs. Although there are many similarities in these medications, there are significant differences which may be important in individual situations, including side-effect profiles. Dual action antidepressants are more effective than single action especially in more severe forms of depression. More innovative approaches including the use of transdermal patches (selegiline) and injectable preparations (netamiftide) are also discussed. Mood stabilisers are also promising agents especially in bipolar depression and atypical antipsychotics may also have a role, particularly in treatment resistance. For a long time it has been known that in some forms of severe depression cortisol levels are raised and CRF antagonists may have a role with recent work focussing on the morning after pill, RU486, which acts as a blocker of CRF receptors. Other hormones probably also play a role and women over 50 appear to have lower response rates to SSRIs but not to the SNRI venlafaxine.

In chapter 5 Mark George and Andrew Kozel from the Medical University of South Carolina discuss minimally invasive brain stimulation techniques. Light therapy is effective in seasonal affective disorder but interestingly mean daily hours of sunshine prior to each visit is associated with response and remission. There have also been recent advances in the use of ECT including the use of shorter pulse widths and inducing the seizure with a magnet. These techniques may offer the real advantage of reducing side-effects whilst maintaining efficacy. Another treatment, transcranial magnetic stimulation has been shown to be as effective as ECT and is approved in some countries for the treatment of depression. It does not appear to cause cognitive deficits and thus may have advantages over ECT in severe depressive illness. The authors also discuss vagal nerve stimulation which has shown some efficacy particularly in patients with low to moderate, but not extreme antidepressant resistance. Deep brain stimulation, which is less invasive than ablative surgery may also have some role although a recent study showed that it produced depressogenic effects when stimulation was at the level of the subthalamic nucleus.

The long term treatment of depression is of critical importance but despite this most studies only cover the acute phase. In chapter 6 Jon Nash and colleagues, from the Psychopharmacology Unit, University of Bristol, highlight the evidence for recurrence of depression and factors that help the clinician decide whether such recurrence is likely. Some interesting facts emerge including residual subsyndromal depression being a stronger predictor of relapse than multiple previous episodes. It is essential to screen for other mental disorders since co-morbidity is common and in itself predicts longer and more severe episodes of depression. It has been estimated that less than 10% of depressed patients receive adequate medication regimes and less than half of patients adhere to the treatment plan agreed with their doctor. Strategies include thorough assessment, psychoeducation and regular review. Once weekly preparations may also help and 'Prozac Weekly' has recently been licensed in the US for continuation and maintenance treatment of depression. Psychological treatments are also effective in preventing recurrence and the combination of medication with eg CBT or IPT is more effective than either treatment alone.

Jeremy Holmes and Charles Montgomery from the University of Exeter discuss the role of psychological therapies in chapter 7. A tripartite biopsychosocial framework is emphasized with different therapies focussing on each component. Thus psychological approaches focus on intrapsychic conflicts eg guilt, anger (often suppressed) and low self esteem, whereas a social approach emphasizes eg absence of, or disturbance in, interpersonal relationships. Vulnerability may relate to early painful experiences occurring at times when the capacity to control the external environment is limited and the parallel is drawn between receptor kindling and seizure threshold. The main goals of generic therapies eg psychoanalytical psychotherapy and psychodynamic interpersonal therapy, modified generic therapies (eg CBT) and specific antidepressant therapies (interpersonal therapy and interpersonal–social rhythm therapy) are all discussed. Finally the authors look at the evidence for psychological therapies including four major studies that have looked at brief therapies in a rigorous manner. Patient preference is probably key, together with availability of resources and combination therapy (psychotherapy and medication) probably represents the most effective treatment, especially where depression is chronic.

In the last chapter, David Mischoulon and Andrew Nierenberg from Harvard discuss the evidence for complementary medications, an increasingly important area given that up to 25% of people in the US are using some form of alternative treatment. St Johns Wort is perhaps the best known and although recent studies have questioned its effectiveness in severe depression, there is evidence for a beneficial effect in mild/moderate depression. It is important to be aware of its interactions with prescribed medication, especially since it induces the cytochrome P450 enzyme 3A4. S-Adenyosyl methionine, omega fatty acids and inositol are other agents that have also been used with some effect in depression. Further studies are needed with these agents, not only for efficacy but also to establish their exact modes of action since this may help us to improve our understanding of the pathophysiology of depression.

We have certainly learned a lot in assembling these contributions and what is clear is that there has been much happening in the field of depression research in the last decade. It is hoped that this update will not only help guide holistic treatment of patients with this illness but also stimulate interest in asking the research questions that are so necessary if our knowledge of depression is to deepen and treatments are to improve.

John Potokar
Michael E Thase

chapter 1

Depression: Epidemiology and risk factors

Mary Amanda Dew, Lynn M Martire and Martica Hall

Considerable strides have been made in the past several decades in understanding the epidemiology of depression. Although the aetiology of depressive illness remains largely unknown, the risk factors identified through epidemiologic studies suggest avenues for prevention and for early intervention, as well as potential directions for aetiologic study. In this chapter, we will address several basic issues regarding the nature and distribution of depression in community-based, primary care, and specialty medical populations. We will consider its association with other psychiatric disorders and with other health outcomes, including suicide and mortality from other causes. Finally, we will summarize current information on key risk factors for depressive illness across the lifespan.

Depression: Definition and case identification

What conditions are encompassed by the term, 'depression'? Epidemiologic research requires a clear definition of caseness—whether that definition relies on individuals scoring above a certain threshold on a self-report symptom rating or whether an individual is required to meet criteria specified in formal diagnostic systems such as the Diagnostic and Statistical Manual for Mental Disorders—4th edition (DSM-IV) (APA, 1994) or the International Classification of Diseases—Mental Disorders, 10th edition

(ICD-10) (WHO, 1992). With respect to depressive illness, both the symptom-based threshold approach and the diagnostic approach have been used when epidemiologists have attempted to determine the total number of cases in a given population during a particular time-frame.

From the standpoint of understanding the magnitude of an individual's current distress level, or the average level of distress in a population, it can be very informative to obtain symptom ratings directly from self-report. After all, when an individual consults a treatment provider because they 'feel depressed', they are probably evaluating their mood along a subjective continuum of bad to good. Yet, feeling that one's mood is depressed may or may not be related to the other signs and symptoms that health care professionals have come to define as an episode of depression. In fact, there is considerable empirical evidence that elevated scores on self-report symptom scales are not necessarily highly related to a diagnosis of psychiatric disorder in general, or highly specific for the psychiatric disorder (for example, a depressive disorder), that they were designed to assess (Fechner-Bates et al, 1994). The clinical significance of the distress levels obtained with scales, such as the Beck Depression Inventory or the Zung Depression Scale, is also clouded by the fact that scales of this sort do not routinely establish duration or temporal variability of symptoms. Finally, rating scales generally treat depression as essentially a unidimensional, homogeneous illness, rather than as a cluster of disorders that share similarities regarding mood but differ widely in other respects.

Thus, in terms of establishing depression incidence and prevalence rates, estimating general mental health services needs at the community level, or making treatment decisions for specific patients, use of a diagnostic approach which defines and distinguishes between the different clinical manifestations of depression is often the optimal approach. In the present review, we will therefore focus on the epidemiologic evidence regarding diagnosed depressive disorders, as opposed to elevated depressive symptomatology. The five depressive disorders that have been examined in community-based populations will be considered: major depression, dysthymia, bipolar disorders (bipolar I and II in the DSM-IV), and cyclothymia.

As recognized in current diagnostic systems, depressed mood is an essential feature of all depressive disorders. Yet this symptom may be expressed in ways other than feelings of being sad or 'blue'. As shown in Table 1.1, which lists DSM-IV and ICD-10 criteria for the most common depressive disorder, major depression, the core element of depressed mood may be expressed as a lack of interest or as a sense of excessive fatigue or loss of energy. An episode is also typically characterized by the presence of additional symptoms that are affective, cognitive or somatic in nature. These symptoms represent a change from the individual's usual state and must be present daily for at least two weeks. The DSM also requires that the individual experience impaired functioning in work, social, or other important life domains during this period. While the ICD does not require functional impairment, it is noted that impairment will usually be present. The ICD further differentiates among mild, moderate, and severe depressive episodes. (The DSM includes a category of minor depressive disorder that is similar to ICD-10 mild depression. However, it is listed as a provisional diagnosis that may be considered for research purposes but is not part of the current clinical diagnostic system.) The vast majority of epidemiologic studies of depressive disorders have focused on (DSM-defined) major depression, and we have a clearer understanding of the risk factors for this condition than for the remainder of depressive disorders.

Some individuals with depressed mood may not meet even the criteria for mild (or minor) depression. However, if the mood state endures for an extended period of two years or more, and if two other depressive symptoms of the sort listed in Table 1.1 continue to be present for more days than not during this period, a diagnosis of dysthymia may be assigned under the DSM-IV and ICD-10 systems. While the symptoms and mood state may wax and wane to some degree, the diagnosis is appropriate only when the individual reports no period as long as a month in which at least some of the symptoms were not present. Dysthymia, which overlaps with the older diagnoses of 'depressive neurosis' and 'neurotic depression', may be exacerbated by stressful situations. While such exacerbations may continue to be subthreshold for major depressive disorder, some individuals may develop full-blown episodes

Table 1.1 Criteria for the diagnosis of unipolar depression

DSM-IV major depressive disorder[a]	*ICD-10 depressive disorder*[b]
1 At least 1 of the following: • depressed mood • loss of interest or pleasure	**1** At least 2 of the following: • depressed mood • loss of interest or pleasure • fatigue or loss of energy
2 Additional symptoms from the following list to give a total (with symptoms above) of at least 5: • significant weight change when not dieting, or change in appetite • insomnia or hypersomnia • psychomotor agitation or retardation • feelings of worthlessness or excessive or inappropriate guilt • fatigue or loss of energy • diminished ability to think or concentrate, or indecisiveness • recurrent thoughts of death, passive or active suicidal plans	**2** Additional symptom(s) from the following list to give a total (with symptoms above) of at least 4 for mild depression; 5 for moderate depression; 6 for severe depression: • significant weight change when not dieting or change in appetite • sleep disturbance of any type • psychomotor agitation or retardation • loss of confidence and self-esteem • excessive or inappropriate feelings of self-reproach or guilt • diminished ability to think or concentrate, or indecisiveness • recurrent thoughts of death, passive or active suicidal plans
3 Duration of 2 weeks or more, with the above symptoms present most of the day, nearly every day	**3** Duration of 2 weeks or more, with the above symptoms present most of the day, nearly every day
4 The symptoms are not due to the direct physiological effects of a substance or a general medical condition	**4** The symptoms are not due to the direct physiological effects of a substance or a general medical condition
5 The symptoms cause distress and/or impairment in social, occupational or other important areas of functioning	

[a]APA (1994). [b]WHO (1992).

of major depression superimposed on an underlying dysthymia. This combination has sometimes been referred to as 'double depression' (Keller and Boland, 1998). While some epidemiologic work has examined the prevalence of dysthymia, no studies have precisely determined the frequency of double depression in community or patient groups.

Depressed individuals who meet the criteria in Table 1.1 but who have experienced hypomania or mania at any point in their life are considered to have bipolar illness ('manic-depression'). Hypomania and mania are characterized by an elevated mood that may be expressed as euphoria or expansiveness, or by irritability. The mood change (of several days duration for hypomania, and at least one week for mania) is accompanied by symptoms such as grandiosity, decreased need for sleep, increased talkativeness, and increased activity or agitation. Although the presence of a single episode of mania is sufficient for a diagnosis of bipolar disorder (bipolar I in the DSM), the majority of individuals with mania are likely to have had depressive episodes previously or will develop them in the future (Kessler et al, 1997). Recurrent hypomanic episodes (without intercurrent depressive symptoms) qualify for a diagnosis of bipolar disorder Not Otherwise Specified (NOS) under DSM. However, hypomania in an individual with a history of major depressive episodes is captured by DSM-IV bipolar II disorder, formerly referred to as atypical bipolar disorder.

Just as a diagnosis of dysthymia may apply to individuals in a chronic, subsyndromal depressive state, individuals with subsyndromal bipolar features may be assigned a diagnosis of cyclothymic disorder. This disorder is characterized by at least two years of numerous periods of hypomanic symptoms, and numerous periods of depressive symptoms that do not meet criteria for major depression. Bipolar and cyclothymic disorders, perhaps because they are relatively less common compared to major depression and dysthymia, have not been considered in as fine detail in epidemiologic studies and their risk factors are less well understood.

Before summarizing information on prevalence and incidence rates, an additional issue must be considered with respect to establishing caseness in epidemiologic work. We know that even in specialty mental health settings, differentiating among the depressive disorders, and between them and other psychiatric conditions can be challenging. In the primary care setting, where physical comorbidities are the norm, the difficulties in diagnostic assignment are often compounded. For example, primary care physicians are likely to ascribe somatic aetiologies to depressive symptoms, and they thus tend to underdiagnose depressive conditions, especially in older patients and among those with chronic physical illnesses (Mulsant and Ganguli, 1999). If this difficulty is common in clinical settings with highly trained physician assessors, how can we expect epidemiologic studies to ascertain rates of these problems in the community or in any other setting? Fortunately, with the development of several systematic clinical interviewing tools employing standard diagnostic criteria, large-scale epidemiologic studies of rates of depressive illness have become feasible. Many of the standardized diagnostic assessments developed for epidemiologic studies—including, for example, the Structured Clinical Interview for DSM-IV, the Diagnostic Interview Schedule, the Composite International Diagnostic Interview, and the Structured Clinical Assessment for Neuropsychiatric Disorders—have also become routine components of basic clinical research. All of the studies summarized below utilized standardized assessment interviews to assign diagnoses according to DSM or ICD criteria.

Epidemiology of depression

What is the distribution of depressive illness in various populations? Is depressive illness becoming more common? Since depression is composed of several diagnostic entities, the epidemiology of depression—and therefore the answers to these questions—must be considered in terms of the set of disorders that comprise this spectrum. Reaching conclusions about the distribution of depressive disorders requires considering both the prevalence rates and incidence rates of each disorder (Lilienfeld and Stolley, 1994).

- A *prevalence rate* is a ratio of the number of existing cases during a given time period to the number of persons in the defined population.

- An *incidence rate* is a ratio of newly diagnosed cases during a given time period to the number of persons in the population at risk for developing a first episode of an illness. The population at risk is defined as those individuals who have not yet had an episode of the illness.

Each of these rates is calculated for a specified time-frame: for example, incidence during a 12-month period, prevalence at one point in time (point prevalence), or prevalence during a given period. When examining whether a possible risk factor or aetiologic factor is related to the development of a depressive illness, incidence rates are generally the most useful. This is because incidence rates directly estimate the likelihood of developing the illness during a specific time period; it is thus possible to examine whether individuals with and without a possible risk factor differ in developing the disorder during that period.

Prevalence rates, on the other hand, are particularly useful for evaluating the need for mental health services because they count both new and recurrent cases of depressive illness (Lilienfeld and Stolley, 1994). In the absence of incidence rates, they are useful for generating hypotheses about risk and possibly aetiologic factors. But they are limited in terms of firmly establishing that a given factor or correlate *is* specifically a *risk* factor. For example, if major depression is found to be more prevalent among women than men during a given time period, this finding could mean *either* that women are at increased risk for depression, *or* that women's episodes of depression last longer than men's, *or* that women experience more recurrences of depression than do men. Unfortunately, since the field of psychiatric epidemiology is relatively young and because many mental disorders are relatively rare, very few true incidence studies have been conducted to date. For some depressive disorders, the only epidemiologic information available concerns prevalence rates, and it is therefore these rates on which we focus below.

Lifetime prevalence rates for bipolar I disorder, bipolar II disorder, dysthymia, and major depression are shown in Figure 1.1. (There are no data on lifetime prevalence of bipolar NOS or cyclothymia.) For each disorder, Figure 1.1 shows the range of rates obtained across available

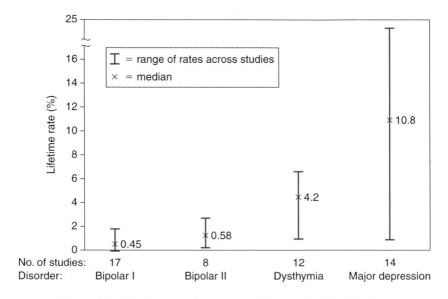

Figure 1.1 *Lifetime prevalence rates of depressive disorders from epidemiologic studies.*

studies, and the median rate across those studies. Bipolar I disorder is the least common disorder. Across the 17 published studies of community-based populations to date the median lifetime rate is 0.45, ranging from 0 to 1.8. (A complete reference list of all reports summarized in Figure 1.1 is available from the first author.) Thus, relying on the median, about 4 to 5 out of every 1000 persons would be expected to develop this disorder at some point in their lives. The 17 studies represent a wide range of countries and cultures, although North American and European sites predominate. There does not appear to be any marked association between country and specific lifetime rate of bipolar I disorder. The lifetime rate of bipolar II disorder is slightly higher than bipolar I disorder, with a median of 0.58, and a range of 0.20 to 3.0 across the eight available studies. The majority of these studies were conducted in the United States.

Both dysthymia and major depression are considerably more common: the median lifetime rate for dysthymia is 4.2 (ranging from

1.1 to 6.4) across 12 studies, while the median for major depression is 10.8 (ranging from 9.0 to 24.4) across 14 studies. As for bipolar disorders, these studies have been conducted in a variety of countries, although North American and European countries predominate. For all of the disorders in Figure 1.1, and for major depression in particular, estimates of lifetime prevalence show considerable variability across studies. There are a number of possible reasons for this variability:

- While all of the epidemiologic studies summarized in Figure 1.1 used standardized diagnostic assessments and applied DSM or ICD criteria, they varied in the specific assessment instrument that they used as well as in the specific criteria for diagnosis (depending on which version of the DSM or ICD was being applied).
- The studies varied in the age range of adults studied; some, for example, limited sampling to adults under age 60, while others included adults of all ages.
- The studies were conducted across a 20-year period from 1978 (when the first standardized instrument and set of diagnostic criteria became available) to 1998. The true rates of the disorders may have changed over time, as we discuss further below.

Despite these differences, the essential ordering of disorders from most rare (bipolar I and II) to most common (major depression) is consistent.

Figure 1.2 shows 12-month and point prevalence rates for these disorders. As would be expected, since these disorders are largely episodic and recurrent, the 12-month and point prevalence rates are lower than the lifetime rates in Figure 1.1. However, fewer studies have examined these rates, compared to investigations of lifetime rates, especially for the bipolar disorders. Thus, confidence in the accuracy of these period and point estimates must be more restrained. Nevertheless, the ordering of disorders from most rare to most common remains similar to that in Figure 1.1, with the bipolar disorders having lower prevalences (eg point prevalence medians of 0.3 and 1.05 for bipolar I and bipolar II, respectively) than unipolar disorders (point prevalence medians of 0.8 and 3.1 for dysthymia and major depression, respectively). The one study that examined cyclothymia found a 12-month rate and a current rate of 0.4%.

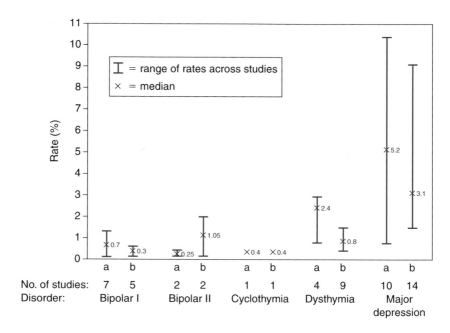

Figure 1.2 *12-month (a) and point prevalence (b) rates of depressive disorders from epidemiologic studies.*

Compared to information on prevalence rates, we have scant data on how likely it is that new onsets of depressive disorders will occur in previously well individuals. Indeed, no incidence studies have been conducted for bipolar II disorder, cyclothymia or dysthymia. One investigation has examined the 12-month incidence of bipolar I disorder, reporting no cases during the study period (Lewinsohn et al, 1993). The 12-month incidence of major depression has been examined in three reports, and has been estimated at 1.6%, 2.8%, and 5.7%, respectively (Eaton et al, 1989; Lewinsohn et al, 1993; Newman and Bland, 1998). These incidence studies were all conducted in North America; generalizability elsewhere has not been examined.

While the epidemiology of depressive illness in community-based populations is critical for determining the broad scope of the problem, it is also important to consider rates of these disorders in segments of the population that seek health care services. In fact, the rates appear to climb as one moves from community-based samples to primary care (ambulatory) and specialty medical care populations. However, the evidence is based virtually exclusively on studies of major depression and dysthymia; clinical epidemiologic studies of bipolar and cyclothymic disorders remain rare in populations seeking non-psychiatric medical treatment.

Point prevalence rates of major depression, already the highest of any depressive disorder in community-based populations, become even more elevated in primary care populations, where 5% to 17% of patients have been observed to meet diagnostic criteria (for reviews, see Katon and Schulberg, 1992; Dew, 1998; Wittchen et al, 1999). In the largest study to date, the World Health Organization (WHO) examined the point prevalence of major depression in primary care settings in 15 countries and found a median rate of 9.1% (ranging from 2.6% in Japan to 29.5% in Chile; Goldberg and Lecrubier, 1995).

In clinical epidemiologic studies of patient populations seen in specialty medical settings (eg for cancer treatment, heart disease, etc), the rates of major depression are often even higher, ranging from approximately 4% to as high as 60% (see Dew, 1998). As shown in Figure 1.3, median rates (which are better estimates of central tendency than the raw range of rates) go from 4% across studies in patients with lung diseases to 25% in individuals who have suffered a stroke. Rates of dysthymia are similarly elevated, with the bulk of reports showing median point prevalences between 6% and 20% across these illness populations (Dew, 1998). To date, the information available on bipolar disorders is almost exclusively based on small case series, especially in individuals seen in specialty medical settings. One study, focused on a primary care population, reported point prevalence rates of 0.95 for bipolar I disorder and 1.18 for bipolar II disorder (Coyne et al 1994).

A frequent observation in recent years is that rates of depressive illness seem to be on the increase, no matter what sector of the population—community-based or treatment-seeking—is being considered (Cross-National Collaborative Group, 1992). This conclusion was supported initially by findings from the Epidemiologic Catchment Area (ECA)

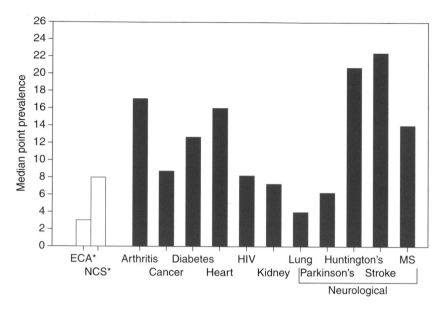

Figure 1.3 *Prevalence of major depression across patient samples in specialty medical settings (N = 32 reports, see also Dew, 1998). *Comparison data (1-month prevalence) from the Epidemiologic Catchment Area Study (ECA; Robins and Regier, 1991) and the National Comorbidity Survey (NCS; Kessler et al, 1994).*

study in the US, and later buttressed by epidemiologic studies in other countries, all of which indicated that younger generations (or birth cohorts) showed higher lifetime rates of major depression than did older generations (Robins and Regier, 1991). A similar pattern was noted for bipolar illness in the ECA study. Explanations for these data have centred on the potential impact of social, demographic, or historical events, which have been hypothesized to lead to younger ages of first onset of depressive illness. However, since the bulk of the studies relied on a single retrospective interview to establish lifetime prevalence, many alternative explanations are possible. For example, apparently lower rates in older adults may be a function of memory effects, selective mortality, or differential reporting of depression by older individuals.

Moreover, as we noted earlier, prevalence rates—especially *lifetime* rates—can be difficult to interpret because they are influenced not only by initial onset cases but by duration and recurrence of illness. It is note-worthy, then, that studies of the point prevalence and the incidence of depression yield a more complex picture. For example, two longitudinal follow-up studies found stable point prevalence rates over periods of 5 to 40 years (Lehtinen et al, 1991; Murphy et al, 2000a). While one report found evidence of rising incidence rates over time (Hagnell et al, 1982), another found incidence rates to be stable (Murphy et al, 2000b).

Can these various findings about different sorts of rates of depression be reconciled? As Murphy and colleagues (2000a) point out, 'a stable current prevalence rate is not necessarily incompatible with increasing lifetime rates. If most of the disorders registered in the lifetime rates were short-lived, either because of their nature or because of effective treatment, their increase would have only small influence on current prevalence. Thus, at least theoretically, rising lifetime rates of acute depression and steady prevalence of chronic depression can occur together.' They note, further, that while their current prevalence rates and their incidence rates were stable over time, there was a significant redistribution of cases by gender and age within these rates: in more recent years, younger women have come to represent a greater propor-tion of all incident and point prevalence cases (Murphy et al, 2000a, b). They suggest, then, that their findings, combined with studies showing increasing lifetime depression rates, indicate that depression *has* become more common. But the increase is specific to younger women, and World War II appeared to act as the key landmark for this change. We will return to the roles of gender, age, and birth cohort as risk factors for depression below.

Patterns of comorbidity between depression and other psychiatric disorders

Are individuals with depressive disorders at increased risk of having additional psychiatric disorders? The answer to this question has import-ant practical and conceptual implications (Robins and Regier, 1991). In terms of clinical evaluation and treatment, depressed individuals who meet criteria for other psychiatric disorders—either concurrently or at varying points in their lifetimes—may require unique intervention and maintenance care strategies relative to individuals with simpler diagnostic profiles. Conceptually, comorbidity of depression with other psychiatric disorders may hold clues about the direction and nature of risk of one disorder given the presence of the other, about whether the multiple disorders may share a common aetiology, as well as about the severity and chronicity of illness course for the disorders.

From an epidemiologic perspective, comorbidity of depressive illness with other psychiatric disorders can first be considered in terms of lifetime co-occurrence. This perspective gives information about the lifetime burden of all mental illness for the individual with a depressive disorder. Of the various depressive disorders, major depression and dysthymia have been examined most extensively for comorbidity, and it appears that the majority of respondents with lifetime histories of either of these disorders also meet lifetime criteria for at least one other psychiatric disorder. For example, in the two major studies in the US, 74% (National Comorbidity Survey; NCS) and 75% (ECA) of individuals with major depression had other lifetime psychiatric diagnoses (Robins and Regier, 1991; Kessler et al, 1996), and 86% of those with dysthymia in the ECA study had other diagnoses. Major depression and dysthymia themselves also frequently co-occurred within the same individual across the lifespan: 42% of individuals with a lifetime diagnosis of dysthymia also had diagnosable episodes of major depression; 28% of all individuals with major depression also met criteria for a lifetime diagnosis of dysthymia.

Two classes of disorders appear particularly prominent in the lifetime histories of individuals with major depression: substance-use disorders and anxiety disorders. Data summarizing the overlap in these disorders from seven independent epidemiologic studies are shown in Figure 1.4 (data from Weissman et al, 1996). The figure presents odds ratios for the two substance-use and the two anxiety disorder diagnoses that were the most frequently comorbid in these studies. Thus, in the US (based on the ECA study), individuals with a history of major depression were twice as likely to also meet lifetime criteria for alcohol abuse and/or dependence. They were over four times as likely to meet criteria for life-time drug abuse/dependence, over five times as likely to meet criteria for obsessive-compulsive disorder, and over nine times more likely to meet criteria for panic disorder. Across the range of sites included in Figure 1.4, anxiety disorders consistently showed higher comorbidity with major depression than did the substance-use diagnoses; in all but one site (Germany), panic disorder was by far the most prominent comorbid lifetime disorder. Additional studies have indicated that, at least in the US, generalized anxiety disorder may be as frequently comorbid with major depression as lifetime panic disorder (Robins and Regier, 1991; Kessler et al, 1996).

There has been relatively little consideration of lifetime comorbidity in the context of bipolar disorders. The NCS has reported very high rates of comorbidity among individuals with bipolar I disorder: Kessler et al (1997) found that for a subset of individuals who had a euphoric-grandiose presentation (the only bipolar I cases that could be reliably diagnosed in the NCS), 100% had one or more other lifetime psychiatric

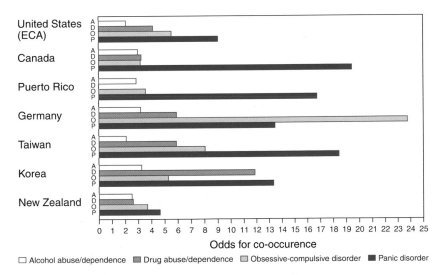

Figure 1.4 *Comorbidity of lifetime major depression with lifetime substance-use and anxiety disorders: Odds ratios* for co-occurrence in adults at 7 sites (from data reported by Weissman et al, 1996). *Standardized to US age/sex distributions and adjusted by age/sex within each site.*

diagnoses, with 93% having an anxiety disorder, 71% a substance-use disorder, and 82% a history of either conduct disorder or adult antisocial behaviour. Compared to NCS participants without this presentation of bipolar I disorder, these bipolar respondents were 5.6 to 22.7 times more likely to have other psychiatric disorders, with anxiety disorders being particularly prominent.

Lifetime comorbidity rates do not necessarily imply that psychiatric disorders occur simultaneously and, since disorders that overlap temporally may require different treatment strategies than those well separated in time, it is also important to examine comorbidity during more narrowly defined time periods. Ignoring the DSM and ICD exclusion criteria that prevent giving a diagnosis if certain other diagnoses are present (and bearing in mind that increasingly few exclusions are being retained as these diagnostic systems continue to develop), the level of comorbidity between depressive disorders and other disorders within 12 months, within 6 months, or even within 1 month prior to diagnostic assessment are quite high (Boyd et al, 1984; Robins and Regier, 1991; Wittchen et al, 1992; Kessler et al, 1996). Data from the ECA study illustrating the increase in likelihood of additional disorders given the presence of bipolar I or major depressive disorder within a 1-month time-frame are shown in Table 1.2. Risk of anxiety and substance-use disorders is increased by 4 to almost 19 times over that of individuals without bipolar or major depressive disorders.

The high levels of overlap between major depression and schizophrenia and schizophreniform disorder in Table 1.2 illustrate an additional important point to consider in evaluating comorbidity: the temporal ordering of onset of depressive disorders relative to other psychiatric disorders. Ordering is important because of its implications for direction of risk and possible aetiology, as well as illness course and sequelae. Most epidemiologic studies, because they rely on cross-sectional assessments, use retrospective age of onset reports to attempt to determine which disorder came first. In the case of schizophrenia and schizophreniform disorder, depressive disorders' onsets appear to follow the development of these other conditions in the majority of cases (ie individuals with schizophrenia are at increased risk of developing

Table 1.2 One-month comorbidity rates of DSM-III disorders in the US among adults in the Epidemiologic Catchment Area (ECA) study, across three sites (N = 11,519)[a]

	Odds ratios	
	Bipolar I	*Major depression*
Alcohol abuse/dependence	14.5	4.1
Drug abuse/dependence	3.4	4.2
Phobic disorders		
• agoraphobia	[b]	15.3
• simple phobia	[b]	9.0
• any phobia	12.7	[b]
Obsessive-compulsive disorder	17.8	10.8
Panic	24.1	18.8
Antisocial personality	6.7	5.1
Schizophrenia	89.1	28.5
Schizophreniform disorder	4.6	33.1
Somatization	11.9	26.8

[a]From data reported by Boyd et al (1994). [b]Odds ratio not reported.

incident depression, but not vice versa). For substance-use and anxiety disorders, however, the proportion of comorbid cases in which depressive disorders—major depression, in particular—antedate the onset of other psychiatric illness is considerably larger. Most importantly, in analyses that go beyond simple age of onset comparisons and attempts to control for disorders' relative prevalences and differences in distributions for pure and comorbid cases, Kessler (1999) has shown that the increased relative odds of the subsequent onset of other disorders associated with prior major depression are generally as large as the relative odds of subsequent major depression associated with prior disorders.

For bipolar I disorder, 59.3% of the NCS sample had other disorders before either the manic or the depressive episodes of the bipolar illness. Anxiety disorders were especially likely to begin in these bipolar respondents before the onset of their bipolar illness. While undifferentiated substance-use disorders did not antedate and predict the onset of bipolar illness, stimulant abuse and dependence were important predictors. Cocaine use, in particular, raised the odds of subsequent onset of bipolar I disorder by a factor of 4.2 (Kessler et al, 1997). These findings are consistent with clinical observations that drugs can precipitate and/or act as inducers of the development of bipolar illness (Weller et al, 1988).

In general, treated samples are well known to show even higher rates of comorbidity of all types of disorders than community-based populations; this is the well-known Berkson's bias in trying to generalize from studies of treated samples to untreated populations. In terms of co-morbidity specifically of depression and other psychiatric disorders in primary care and specialty medical settings, Schulberg et al (1995) found that of a sample of patients with major depression identified in a primary care setting, nearly 75% had suffered at some time during their lives from an additional DSM axis I disorder, most commonly generalized anxiety (62%) or panic disorder (44%). Lifetime substance dependence (alcohol or drug) was also fairly prevalent (28% of the sample). Coyne et al (1994) found similarly high rates for lifetime anxiety and substance-use disorders in a primary care sample, and also reported high current comorbidity rates: 28% met criteria for current anxiety disorders, 5.7% met criteria for current substance abuse, and 42.6% met criteria for lifetime substance abuse. The WHO study of primary care sites world-wide found that current comorbidity of major depression with other disorders was 62% (Ustun and Sartorius, 1995).

In one of the only empirical examinations of comorbidity with personality disorders in a primary care setting, Schulberg et al (1995) found that 68% of their primary care sample with major depression had a DSM axis II personality disorder. This rate is as high as rates reported in patients treated within specialty mental health settings and is disturbing given that personality pathology in the context of depression bodes for poor antidepressant response (Schulberg et al, 1995).

Epidemiology of the complications of depressive illness

In addition to its associations with other psychiatric disorders, what is the epidemiology of potential complications of depressive illness? In this section, we will briefly summarize work concerning two key areas of complications: (a) suicide and mortality from other causes, and (b) disability and reduced quality of life.

Suicide ranks as the ninth to tenth leading cause of death worldwide, averaged across age groups (Murray and Lopez, 1996). Depressive illness, alone or in combination with substance abuse and anxiety disorders, has been estimated to account for as much as 75% of all deaths by suicide (Frank and Thase, 1999). Not only does the rate of suicide increase considerably with age, particularly for men, but the association between depressive illness and suicide also grows stronger across the lifespan (Moscicki, 1995).

Prospective studies of rates of suicide among individuals with depressive disorders are largely limited to patient samples, and hence present difficulties for generalizability to the larger population of depressed persons in the community, at least half of whom do not seek treatment for their depressive episodes (Robins and Regier, 1991). Nevertheless, in combination with the smaller body of epidemiologic reports, a consistent picture emerges regarding the degree to which risk of suicide and suicide attempts is increased in the face of depression. For example, in the ECA study, the lifetime rate of suicide attempts was 7.9% in persons with major depression, and 19.5% in individuals with lifetime co-morbidities of major depression and alcohol abuse/dependence, while it was 1% in individuals without any documented psychiatric illness (Johnson et al, 1990).

The WHO conducted a 10-year follow-up of patients with depressive disorders in five different cultures, reporting that 11% of the sample had died by suicide and 14% had unsuccessful suicide attempts (Thornicroft and Sartorius, 1993). In the most extensive report to date, Harris and Barraclough (1998) completed a series of meta-analyses across all available studies showing that the risk of suicide in the face of major depression was increased by over 21 times (compared to the expected population death rate), and the risk of suicide among individuals with bipolar illness was equally elevated. Figure 1.5 presents these data in terms of standardized mortality ratios (SMRs). The SMR is the observed divided by the expected number of deaths, multiplied by 100. It gives the risk of death compared with the general population of similar age and gender. An SMR of 100 indicates equal degrees of risk between a study group (eg a cohort of depressed persons) and the expected population rate. The first set of bars in Figure 1.5, then, shows average SMRs of 2124 (ie an increased risk of 21.24%) for individuals with major depression, and 1173 for individuals with bipolar illness (bipolar I or II),

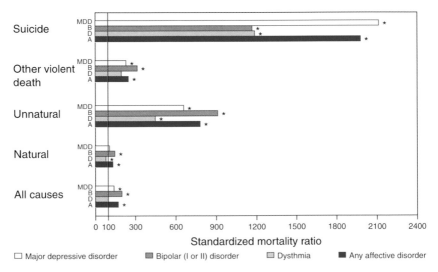

Figure 1.5 *Excess deaths in studies of respondents with major depressive disorder (MDD), bipolar (I or II) disorder, dysthmia, or any affective disorder (from data reported by Harris and Barraclough, 1998). *Statistically significant across all studies.*

based on published studies included in the Harris and Barraclough meta-analysis. Dysthymia was also associated with high SMRs for suicide (averaging 1194), and the SMR for major affective disorders (excluding studies of dysthymia but including studies which did not otherwise differentiate between unipolar and bipolar illnesses) was 1990.

Some follow-up studies have shown that not only suicide, but all-cause mortality rates are increased in psychiatric patients in general and in those with depressive disorders in particular (Newman and Bland, 1991). Analyses of epidemiologic data support this pattern (eg Kouzis et al, 1995; Joukamaa et al, 2001). Figure 1.5 shows that, across all available studies included in the Harris and Barraclough meta-analysis, there are indeed consistent patterns of elevated risk for many categories of causes of death among persons with depressive illness. These data show elevated risks of non-suicidal violent deaths, deaths defined as resulting from 'unnatural' versus 'natural' causes, and death from all causes. Major depression was associated with elevated SMRs for non-suicidal violent death, death from unnatural causes and all-cause mortality. Bipolar illness, interestingly, showed even stronger elevations in risk for these outcomes. Dysthymia, on the other hand, was less reliably associated with elevated SMRs and, in the case of death from natural causes, was associated with fewer than the expected number of deaths. However, because the findings for dysthymia were based on a smaller literature than that available for other depressive illnesses, caution is required in interpreting these latter findings and their generalizability.

Mortality accounts for a relatively small proportion of the total burden of diseases, including mental disorders such as depressive illness. Instead, using other indicators of health impact, such as the reduction of functional status or the reduction in quality of life (QOL) associated with various disease states, it is possible to gain a more complete picture of the degree of disability and potential years of life limited by disability that result from conditions such as major depression and bipolar illness. Examination of these outcomes is one of the most rapidly growing areas of research on mental illness. In the largest-scale investigation of the burden of disease worldwide, Murray and Lopez (1996) used extensive health and economic data to construct indices of years lived with disability (YLD) associated with a large spectrum of diseases, years of life lost due to premature deaths, and a summary measure that combines both of these outcomes to represent the total burden of disease in the population, the disability-adjusted life year (DALY).

While physical illness has long been recognized as a major contributor to worldwide disease burden, results of this study sponsored by the WHO brought the burden associated with mental illness—and depressive illness specifically—into sharp relief. Thus, major depression accounted for 5.1% of the total global burden of disease in 1990 with respect to DALYs lost to the individual and society; it was ranked as the fourth most important cause of global disease burden. Most strikingly, major depression was the leading cause of disability, measured in YLDs. Bipolar illness, primarily due to its lower prevalence than major depression, ranked as the sixth leading cause of disability. This work, which is still underway and will lead to additional reports focused on the sequelae of depressive illness in different regions of the world, has already had an important public health impact. Namely, by establishing the largely hidden impact of these mental illnesses on the overall health status of the world's population, the Murray and Lopez report has clearly shown the limitations of the common practice of judging a population's health and a disease's impact in terms of mortality statistics alone.

Risk factors for depressive illness

What are the key risk factors for depression? Are we getting closer to understanding the aetiologies of depressive illnesses? Psychiatric epidemiologic work has made important contributions to the identification of risk factors for depression, although whether or not these risk factors play an aetiologic role remains largely unknown. However, even in the absence of knowledge of aetiology, risk factor information is valuable in terms of predicting likelihood of onset of particular disorders. Table 1.3 provides an overview and guide to the current state of knowledge regarding major risk factors discussed in this chapter.

Table 1.3 Risk factors for depressive illnesses

	Major Depression	Dysthymia	Bipolar I	Bipolar II	Cyclothymia
Gender, female	+	+	–	–	?
Age, younger	+	+	+	+	?
Ethnicity/race and culture of origin	?	?	?	?	?
Personal history of mental disorder	+	+	+	+	+
Genetics and family history of mental disorder	+	+	+	+	?
Urban residence	+	+	+	+	?
Socioeconomic status, lower	+	+	+	+	?
Marital status, unmarried	+	+	+	+	?
Physical illness	+	+	+	+	?
Community-wide stressors	+	+	?	?	?
Individualized stressors and life events	+	+	?	?	?

+, factor increases risk; –, factor does not increase risk; ?, mixed or little evidence available concerning risk.

Gender

Women have consistently been found to be at greater risk for major depression. This gender difference appears for lifetime and period prevalence rates, as well as for incidence rates. It has been found in general population studies, in studies conducted in primary medical care settings, and in studies of psychiatric patients. In the ECA and NCS studies, for example, women were approximately 1.5 to 3 times more likely to experience major depression (Robins and Regier, 1991; Kessler et al, 1994). These rates have been replicated cross-nationally (Weissman et al, 1996). Rates of dysthymia are elevated to similar degrees in women relative to men (Robins and Regier, 1991; Kessler et al, 1994). Both social and biological factors are likely to contribute to these differences, and women's greater propensity for seeking treatment may elevate the apparent rate differential as well (Robins and Regier, 1991).

In contrast, the prevalence of bipolar I disorder does not differ dramatically by gender (Robins and Regier, 1991; Kessler et al, 1997). Indeed, the finding of a *lack* of any gender difference in rates of bipolar disorders is as consistent cross-nationally as the findings regarding gender effects for major depression and dysthymia. Little is known about gender in relation to cyclothymia. This disorder may be slightly more prevalent in women than in men, although the bulk of studies have examined only treated samples. However, in the single epidemiologic report examining rates of cyclothymia (Faravelli et al, 1990), women were about 1.5 times more likely to meet criteria for this disorder than men.

Age

As noted earlier, prevalence rates for major depression and dysthymia have consistently been found to be higher in younger compared to older individuals. Similar findings appear for bipolar disorders. However, this elevation in younger age groups (eg in adults aged 44 or less) in studies such as the ECA and NCS reports, is not unique to depressive disorders: lifetime and period prevalence rates for *all* psychiatric disorders were generally higher in adults aged 44 or less than in older individuals (Robins and Regier, 1991; Kessler et al, 1994). Nevertheless, as we

discussed earlier, particular attention has focused on the marked elevation of major depression in younger versus older cohorts.

The observation that the generations born since World War II report
earlier ages of onset of major depression, relative to older generations,
has led to speculation regarding various biological, social, or economic
factors that may have resulted in greater risk for younger adults (Cross-
National Collaborative Group, 1992; Paykel, 2000). The picture is com-
plicated by the fact that it is lifetime risk that appears to be elevated in
younger generations, while period prevalence, point prevalence, and
incidence rates do not consistently show an increase across various
investigations. As noted earlier, Murphy et al (2000a,b) argue that the
rising rate of lifetime depression is largely concentrated in younger
women. However, neither they nor others have yet been able to explain
why younger women may be uniquely vulnerable.

A similar association between younger age and increased risk for disorder is also evident for other depressive disorders, although the magnitude of the effect appears to be smaller. Thus, younger age has been
found to be a significant risk factor for bipolar I disorder (Robins and
Regier, 1991; Kessler et al, 1997) and bipolar II disorder (Robins and
Regier, 1991). Most, but not all studies (cf Bland et al, 1988) report a
similar effect for dysthymia. Age has not been examined in relation to
onset of cyclothymia.

Ethnicity/race and culture of origin

In industrialized countries, ethnic/racial differences in prevalence rates
often disappear once the effects of socioeconomic status are taken into
account. When ethnic differences remain, the direction of the relationship with depressive disorders is not consistent across studies. For
example, in the continental US, the ECA study reported that white men
tended to have higher prevalence rates of major depression than black
men, yet black women had higher prevalence rates than white women
(Sommervell et al, 1989). In contrast, the NCS reported that African
Americans had significantly lower prevalence rates of affective disorder
(major depression, dysthymia, bipolar disorder) than white respondents
(Kessler et al, 1994). Comparisons of Hispanic Americans and

non-Hispanic white Americans yield similarly inconsistent results. In the ECA study, with socioeconomic status controlled, Hispanic Americans had lower prevalence rates of major depression than non-Hispanic whites (Burnam et al, 1987), while Hispanics in the NCS had significantly higher rates of affective disorders (major depression, dysthymia, bipolar disorder) than non-Hispanic whites. Differences related to sampling, as well as true changes across the 10 years between the investigations may have contributed to these inconsistencies in findings across the studies.

An issue that overlaps, but is not synonymous, with ethnicity is one's culture of origin. International comparisons of relatively racially homogeneous populations (eg studies of some European countries) often reveal marked differences between countries and/or between cultural groups within a single country (eg Ayuso-Mateos et al, 2001). International comparisons of countries that differ both in racial/ethnic composition and culture (eg European vs Asian countries) also indicate large differences in prevalence rates. One striking finding has been the considerably lower rates of mood disorders (as well as many other psychiatric disorders) in Asian countries (eg Weissman et al, 1996). Whether this effect is due to differences in risk and/or expression of these disorders is not well understood. At any rate, because racial, ethnic, and cultural group definitions overlap, both comparisons of distinct racial/ethnic groups within a given country and comparisons of those groups across cultural and political boundaries are needed in order to understand the role of these potential risk factors for depressive illness.

Personal history of mental disorder

It is well known that a positive history of a disorder is one of the strongest risk factors for new episodes of the disorder (eg Amenson and Lewinsohn, 1981). In the case of depression—both unipolar and bipolar—prior episodes may increase risk through 'sensitizing' the individual. Thus, he/she may become more vulnerable to, for example, major depression in the face of major life stressors, than an individual with no prior history of disorder (Post, 1992). Over time, a 'kindling' process may take place such that lower and lower levels of stress are required to provoke new depressive episodes, and ultimately such episodes may occur spontaneously (Post, 1992). In a related vein, it is also possible that prior episodes of a depressive disorder produce biological or psychosocial 'scarring', that is, residual impairments that constitute additional, new risk factors for future depressive episodes.

As we discussed earlier, individuals with a depressive disorder are also highly likely to have lifetime histories of other disorders, particularly anxiety and substance-use disorders. In the majority of cases of bipolar illness, these disorders antedate the initial onset of the bipolar disorder. While major depression often begins prior to anxiety and substance-use disorders, the opposite pattern is also observed in a large majority of cases. Some illnesses, such as schizophrenia, almost always have onsets before the affected individuals experience their first episode of major depression.

Genetics and family history of mental disorder

Studies of familial aggregation of psychopathology have sought to identify both sociocultural and biological familial risk factors for depressive disorders. Although family, twin, and adoption studies have established that genetic factors are involved in the aetiology of these disorders, the precise degree of heritability and mode of genetic transmission remains to be specified (Merikangas and Swendsen, 1997). Some evidence is now emerging that indicates replicated linkages on several chromosomes for bipolar disorder (Crow and De Lisi, 1998); such work has not yet begun for major depression, dysthymia or cyclothymia.

Reviews of family studies indicate that there is an approximately threefold increase in the disorder in first degree adult relatives of individuals with depressive illnesses (eg Merikangas and Swendsen, 1997). A study of the offspring of depressed patients also found a threefold increase in risk of psychiatric disorder (although not depression *per se*) among these children (Weissman et al, 1984). Twin studies have shown that monozygotic twins have a concordance rate of approximately 67% for affective disorders, ranging from 54% for major depression to 74% for bipolar disorder. In contrast, dizygotic twins have only about a 20% concordance rate for these disorders (Merikangas and Swendsen, 1997).

The most extensive recent studies of twins' risk for a variety of psychiatric disorders has been published by Kendler and colleagues (Kendler et al, 1995). These indicate that genetic factors account for substantial portions of the variability in risk for affective disorders such as major depression.

Marital status

Both marital status and quality of the relationship have been associated with depressive illnesses. In the ECA study, for example, unmarried men and women were approximately 1.5 to 2.5 times more likely to have had a recent episode of major depression or bipolar illness, or to have dysthymia than married participants (Robins and Regier, 1991). Moreover, among unmarried individuals, it is consistently those who are separated or divorced in whom the risk of depression concentrates. This has been reported in North American, European and Asian studies (Weissman et al, 1996). Among married individuals, the risk of depressive illness is substantially higher in those who have a poor relationship with their spouses compared to more happily married persons (Joiner and Coyne, 1999).

The causal direction of these associations remains unclear due to the cross-sectional nature of most studies. However, at least for major depression, a growing body of longitudinal evidence suggests that causality flows in both directions: marriage affects one's mental health which, in turn, influences the future of the marriage (Brown and Harris, 1978; Joiner and Coyne, 1999).

Socioeconomic status (SES)

SES is a complex amalgam of one's level of education, income, occupation, and other social factors. Some epidemiologic research focuses on these components separately; other work integrates them to form broad measures of social class to examine in relation to mental disorders. Across these different measurement approaches, however, SES is generally found to be inversely related to risk for mental disorders in general and for depressive disorders in particular (Canino et al, 1987; Robins and Regier, 1991; Kessler et al, 1997). The relationship of lower SES to increased risk of major depression and dysthymia found in psychiatric epidemiologic studies is consistent with clinical observation of treated cohorts. However, studies of treated cases of bipolar illness have reported that lower SES is related to *lower* risk of bipolar disorder (eg Aro et al, 1995). It is not clear whether this discrepancy between community-based and treated samples of bipolar cases is due to differential access to treatment, or whether it could reflect a relationship between SES and the accuracy of diagnosis of bipolar disorder (Kessler et al, 1997).

Since most studies have focused on depressive disorders' prevalence rates, it has rarely been possible to draw strong inferences about the causal—or even predictive—direction of their relationship with SES. Some have argued for a 'social causation' explanation—that the stressful conditions of being in the lowest class foster illness onset. However, the alternative 'social selection' explanation, that vulnerable people drift downward into the lowest class, is often equally plausible. Examinations of incidence rates indicate that social causation is the more plausible explanation for major depression (eg Dohrenwend et al, 1992). The situation is less clear for bipolar disorder, in which the social causation and social selection hypotheses are only beginning to be longitudinally evaluated.

Urbanicity

Whether an individual resides in an urban versus a rural area has been consistently related to rates of mental illness, including depressive disorders, at least in Western European and North American countries. Rates of major depression, dysthymia and bipolar disorders are elevated in urban areas and lower in very rural areas. Rates for semi-rural and/or suburban areas are either found to be midway between these extremes or closer to the urban rates (Canino et al, 1987; Robins and Regier, 1991; Kessler et al, 1994; Ayuso-Mateos et al, 2001). Whether the increase in risk due to area of residence results from the stresses of living in an urban environment or from ill individuals migrating to an urban environment remains unresolved.

Physical illness

We discussed earlier the fact that major depression becomes more prevalent as one moves from community-based samples to primary care samples and to patients seen in specialty medical settings. In part, this increase across settings and populations is due to a strong association between physical illness and psychiatric disorder. Major depression has received the greatest attention in this regard, but rates of bipolar illness and dysthymia also appear elevated in the presence of physical illness (see Dew, 1998 for a review). In community-based studies, from 23% to 32% of respondents with either self-reported or medically verified physical illnesses met criteria for psychiatric disorders, including major depression, compared to an average of about 15% among physically healthy respondents (Dilling and Weyerer, 1984; Vazquez-Barquero et al, 1987).

Compared to community-based samples, one reason why prevalence rates of depressive disorders are higher among physically ill persons treated in primary care and in specialty medical settings is that the average level of severity of physical illness (or the proportion of the population with severe illness) increases across these sectors. Even among medically ill inpatient groups, for example, rates of mental disorders increase with the severity of the medical condition. However, not only severity but type of physical illness is important to consider, as we discussed earlier in the context of Figure 1.3. Depression and dysthymia, for example, are more common in the presence of diseases such as arthritis, diabetes and heart disease, than in kidney and lung diseases. This between-disease variability in risk for depression is probably due to both psychosocial and biological components of the physical illness. Psychosocially, an illness may elevate risk of mental disorder by affecting body image, self-esteem, and capacity to function at work and socially. Biologically, there is evidence that patients' risk for depression, for example, is elevated by certain endocrine disorders; nutritional or electrolyte abnormalities; some viral disorders; and cognitive impairments (Dew, 1998; Lenze et al, 2001).

Community-wide stressors
The risk factors discussed thus far are largely personal attributes. In contrast, community-wide stressors derive from the environment and expose large numbers of people to uncontrollable events. Both the acute

and long-term mental health effects of many such events have been studied, including natural disasters like volcanic eruptions, floods, and earthquakes (Beiser, 1998). Technological accidents and events related to warfare have also been shown to produce significant mental health effects. Examples include oil spills, nuclear power plant accidents, and terrorist attacks (Beiser, 1998).

Although each disaster has particular characteristics, and studies vary in design and instrument selection, a meta-analysis indicated that disasters increase the prevalence rate of psychopathology by about 17%, on average (Rubonis and Bickman, 1991). Depressive disorders (in addition to anxiety disorders) are by far the most common psychiatric sequelae of such events, with most studies showing two- to three-fold increases in rates of major depression, with or without concurrent post-traumatic stress disorder (eg Bromet et al, 1982; Palinkas et al, 1992) in exposed persons, relative to unexposed comparison samples. Whether or not bipolar illness rates are increased in the face of such stressors remains unknown, given the relative rarity of this illness.

Community-wide stressors vary in intensity and duration, and these elements appear to be among the most critical determinants of mental health effects. Additional features of such events, which also appear to be responsible for inducing psychiatric distress, are their speed of onset; community residents' degree of involvement, in terms of loss of life or property; and whether or not the events were precipitated by human actions (as opposed to being natural disasters) (Bromet and Dew, 1995).

Individual and multiple stressful life events
Single traumatic events, while perhaps as personally devastating as community-wide stressors, typically occur at a more individual level in the population. Thus, life events such as job loss, death of a loved one, and physical injury (Eaton and Dohrenwend, 1998) have been noted to produce changes in mental health, with depressive illness as one prominent outcome. For a majority of individuals, acute episodes of major depression may resolve within 2 to 6 months. However, a significant minority of affected persons—20% to 40%—do not recover fully from depression following a major life stressor, despite the passage of many

months or even years (Kessler et al, 1985). Many of these individuals eventually meet symptomatic and duration criteria for dysthymia and are vulnerable to superimposed new episodes of major depression.

The bulk of work on 'life stressor' effects focuses on the mental health effects of multiple stressors, conceptualized as either acute, discrete life events or chronic strains (or, occasionally, some combination of the two (eg Brown and Harris, 1978; Dohrenwend, 2000). In general, the occurrence of multiple discrete stressful life events is prognostic for major depression and related symptomatology (Brown and Harris, 1978; Kessler et al, 1985). For example, 'fateful' events (stressful events that are unlikely to have been brought about by the individual him/herself) have been found to occur 2.5 to 6.5 times more frequently in persons who then developed depressive illness than in community controls who did not experience such events (Surtees et al, 1986; Shrout et al, 1989).

Adverse life events may play a stronger causal role in the occurrence of major depression in particular individuals already made vulnerable by other factors. For example, Brown and Harris (1978) have shown that threatening life events precipitate episodes of depression in middle to lower class women who already lack a confiding relationship with their husbands, are unemployed, have three or more children under the age of six, and have lost a parent in childhood. Several large literatures have developed around the issues of whether or not factors, such as low social support and poor coping strategies, elevate one's vulnerability to depression in the face of stressful life events (see Kessler et al, 1985; Turner and Turner, 1999 for reviews).

The vast majority of reports in this area pertain to major depression. Although there has been little epidemiologic work to date, the effects of stressful life events may also be important to consider in bipolar illness. At least in treated populations of bipolar patients, new episodes of mania and/or depression can be provoked by the occurrence of multiple major life events (Ambelas, 1987).

Some stressful occurrences are more appropriately characterized as chronic strains, rather than discrete events. There is evidence that strains arising from one's social roles, from marriage, and from occupational demands elevate risk for major depression in community samples (see

Turner and Turner, 1999 for a review). Moreover, the combined effects of multiple discrete life events and ongoing chronic strains dramatically elevates risk for both depressive symptoms and diagnosable disorder. However, causal interpretation of the association of depression with chronic strains remains problematic: most chronic strain measures are based on subjective assessments and thus may sometimes be symptoms of, rather than risk factors for, respondents' depressive illnesses.

Conclusions

This chapter has addressed several major issues for understanding the epidemiology and risk factors for depressive illness. The information is relevant for assessing, in any given individual, the likelihood that he/she will develop one or more depressive conditions, the nature of psychiatric comorbidities that are most common in depressed persons, risk for critical outcomes including suicide and reduced QOL, and factors that significantly elevate the risk for episodes of disorder. We began each section of this chapter with a key question. State-of-the-art 'answers', or at least responses, to these questions can be summarized as follows:

What conditions are encompassed by the term, 'depression'? An understanding of the epidemiology of any illness requires a clear definition of caseness. Use of a diagnostic approach which defines and distinguishes between the different clinical manifestations of depressive illness is also essential for estimating community-based mental health services needs, and making treatment decisions for individual patients. Five diagnosable disorders have been examined in psychiatric epidemiologic studies: major depression, dysthymia, bipolar I disorder, bipolar II disorder, and cyclothymia. These disorders have been found to be reliably distinguished from each other in both treated-related and community-based settings.

What is the distribution of depressive disorders in the population and is depression becoming more common? Across the spectrum of depressive disorder, and considering lifetime prevalence, period prevalence, and incidence, there is clear evidence that bipolar disorders are most rare, followed by dysthymia (and perhaps cyclothymia). Major depression consistently emerges as most common, both in terms of new onsets and point prevalence. Moreover, major depression becomes increasingly prevalent as one moves from community-based populations to primary care and specialty medical populations. There is growing evidence that major depression is becoming more prevalent over time, at least in certain sectors of the population. This appears to be a cohort effect. Thus, for reasons that are not completely understood, younger generations (and young women in particular) appear to be at uniquely elevated risk to experience major depressive illness at one or more points in their lifetimes.

Are individuals with depression at increased risk of having other comorbid psychiatric illnesses? Comorbidity of depressive disorders with other psychiatric disorders seems to be the rule rather than the exception, especially when comorbidity is considered in terms of lifetime co-occurrence of disorders. Lifetime comorbidity rates are particularly high in individuals with bipolar illness. Both bipolar and unipolar depressive illnesses show particularly large associations with anxiety and substance-use disorders. In terms of temporal ordering of disorder onset, bipolar illness by and large begins after the onset of other conditions, while major depression is as likely to occur before as after the onset of other psychiatric disorders.

What is the epidemiology of key complications of depressive illness? Both mortality and burden associated with disability and reduced quality of life are major complications of depressive illness. In terms of mortality, suicide is prevalent in the context of both bipolar disorder and major depression, and death rates from other causes are elevated as well. These encompass 'unnatural' deaths in which life may be ended by careless or hazardous behaviour, as well as 'natural' deaths in which depressive illness may influence risk more indirectly by, for example, effects on lifestyle and exposure to other environmental factors (Harris and

Barraclough, 1998). The burden of depressive illness is more fully realized by considering its role in everyday life: its prevalence, duration and severity combine to produce dramatic increases in the years of 'healthy' life that are lost to individuals and populations. Both major depression and bipolar disorder are among the leading contributors to the worldwide burden of disease.

What are the key risk factors for depression? Excluding cyclothymia for which virtually no risk factor studies exist, the range of depressive disorders considered in this chapter largely share a common set of risk factors. Thus, the risk of major depression, dysthymia and bipolar illness is increased in individuals who are younger, have a positive history of one or more other psychiatric disorders, have a family history of depressive illness, are lower socioeconomic status, unmarried, reside in urban areas and have concurrent physical illnesses. No work has yet examined exposure to community-wide or individualized life stressors in community samples of individuals with bipolar illness, but studies of patient samples suggest similar effects as those noted for unipolar depression. Across all of the depressive disorders, the role of ethnicity, race and culture remains unclear.

The single risk factor which shows a unique profile of risk for some depressive disorders is gender. Female gender is strongly associated with unipolar depression (major depression, dysthymia). There is equally strong evidence that neither men nor women predominate among cases of bipolar illness.

The evidence relevant to each of the questions discussed above continues to amass. Across the spectrum of depressive disorders, the past 20 to 25 years of epidemiologic research has considered major depression in the greatest depth. Major strides are expected within the next decade regarding the epidemiology and risk factors for more rare—but often equally debilitating—depressive disorders.

References

Ambelas A (1987) Life events and mania: A special relationship. *Br J Psychiatry* **150**: 235–240.

Amenson CS, Lewinsohn PM (1981) An investigation into the observed sex difference in prevalence of unipolar depression. *J Abnormal Psychology* **90**: 1–13.

APA (American Psychiatric Association) (1994) *Diagnostic and Statistical Manual of Mental Disorders*. Washington, DC: APA, 4th edn.

Aro S, Aro H, Salinto M, et al (1995) Educational level and hospital use in mental disorders: A population-based study. *Acta Psychiat Scand* **91**: 305–312.

Ayuso-Mateos JL, Vazquez-Barquero JL, Dowrick C, et al; The ODIN Group (2001) Depressive disorders in Europe: Prevalence figures from the ODIN study. *Br J Psychiatry* **179**: 308–316.

Beiser M (1998) Extreme situations. In Dohrenwend BP (ed.), *Adversity, stress, and psychopathology*. New York: Oxford University Press, pp 9–12.

Bland RC, Newman SC, Orn H (1988) Period prevalence of psychiatric disorders in Edmonton. *Acta Psychiat Scand* **77**(Suppl 338): 33–42.

Boyd JH, Burke JD, Gruenberg E, et al (1984) Exclusion criteria of DSM-III: A study of co-occurrence of hierarchy-free syndromes. *Arch Gen Psychiatry* **41**: 983–989.

Bromet EJ, Dew MA (1995) Review of psychiatric epidemiologic research on disasters. *Epidemiol Rev* **17**: 113–119.

Bromet EJ, Parkinson DK, Dunn LO, et al (1982) Mental health of residents near the TMI reactor: A comparative study of selected groups. *J Prev Psychiatry* **1**: 225–275.

Brown G, Harris T (1978) *The social origins of depression: A study of psychiatric disorder in women*. New York: The Free Press.

Burnam MA, Hough RL, Escobar JI, et al (1987). Six-month prevalence of specific psychiatric disorders among Mexican Americans and non-Hispanic whites in Los Angeles. *Arch Gen Psychiatry* **44**: 687–694.

Canino GJ, Bird HR, Shrout PE, et al (1987). The prevalence of specific psychiatric disorders in Puerto Rico. *Arch Gen Psychiatry* **44**: 727–735.

Coyne JC, Fechner-Bates S, Schwenk TL (1994) Prevalence, nature, and comorbidity of depressive disorders in primary care. *Gen Hosp Psychiatry* **16**: 267–276.

Cross-National Collaborative Group (1992) The changing rate of major depression: Cross-national comparisons. *JAMA* **268**: 3098–3105.

Crow TJ, De Lisi L (1998) The chromosome workshops at the International Congress of Psychiatric Genetics—the weight of the evidence from genome scans. *Psychiat Genet* 1998; **8**: 59–61.

Dew MA (1998) Psychiatric disorder in the context of physical illness. In: Dohrenwend BP (ed.) *Adversity, stress, and psychopathology*, New York: Oxford University Press, pp 177–218.

Dilling H, Weyerer S (1984) Prevalence of mental disorders in the small-town–rural region of Traunstein (Upper Bavaria). *Acta Psychiat Scand* **69**: 60–79.

Dohrenwend BP (2000) The role of adversity and stress in psychopathology: Some evidence and its implications for theory and research. *J Hlth Soc Behavior* **41**: 1–19.

Dohrenwend BP, Levav I, Shrout PE, et al (1992) Socioeconomic status and psychiatric disorders: The causation-selection issue. *Science* **255**: 946–952.

Eaton WW, Dohrenwend DP (1998) Individual events. In Dohrenwend BP (ed.) *Adversity, stress, and psychopathology.* New York: Oxford University Press, pp 77–79.

Eaton WW, Kramer M, Robins LN, et al (1989) The incidence of specific DIS/DSM-III mental disorders: Data from the NIMH Epidemiologic Catchment Area Program. *Acta Psychiat Scand* **79**: 163–178.

Faravelli C, Degl'Innocenti BG, Aiazzi L, et al (1990) Epidemiology of mood disorders: A community survey in Florence. *J Affect Disord* **20**: 135–141.

Fechner-Bates S, Coyne JC, Schwenk TL (1994) The relationship of self-reported distress to depressive disorders and other psychopathology. *J Cons Clin Psychol* **62**: 550–559.

Frank E, Thase ME (1999) Natural history and preventative treatment of recurrent mood disorders. *Annu Rev Med* **50**: 453–456.

Goldberg DP, Lecrubier Y (1995) Form and frequency of mental disorders across centres. In: Ustun TB, Sartorius N (eds), *Mental illness in general health care: An international study.* Chichester, UK: Wiley, pp 323–334.

Hagnell O, Essen-Miller E, Lanke J, et al (1990) *The incidence of mental illnesses over a quarter of a century: The Lundby Longitudinal Study of Mental Illnesses in a total population based on 42,000 observation years.* Stockholm: Almqvist & Wiksell.

Harris EC, Barraclough BB (1998) Excess mortality of mental disorder. *Br J Psychiatry* **173**: 11–53.

Johnson J, Weissman MM, Klerman GL (1990) Panic disorder, comorbidity, and suicide attempts. *Arch Gen Psychiatry* **47**: 805–808.

Joiner T, Coyne JC (1999) *Advances in interpersonal approaches: The interactional nature of depression.* Washington, DC: American Psychological Association.

Joukamaa M, Heliövaara M, Knekt P, et al (2001) Mental disorders and cause-specific mortality. *Br J Psychiatry* **1790**: 498–502.

Katon W, Schulberg HC (1992) Epidemiology of depression in primary care. *Gen Hosp Psychiatry* **14**: 237–247.

Keller MB, Boland RJ (1998) Implications of failing to achieve successful long-term maintenance treatment of recurrent unipolar major depression. *Biol Psychiatry* **44**: 348–360.

Kendler KS, Walters EE, Neale MC, et al (1995) The structure of the genetic and environmental risk factors for six major psychiatric disorders in women. Phobia, generalized anxiety disorder, panic disorder, bulimia, major depression, and alcoholism. *Arch Gen Psychiatry* **52**: 374–383.

Kessler RC (1999) Comorbidity of unipolar and bipolar depression with other psychiatric disorders in a general population survey. In Tohen M (ed), *Comorbidity in affective disorders.* New York: Marcel Dekker, pp 1–25.

Kessler RC, Price RH, Wortman CB (1985) Social factors in psychopathology. *Annu Rev Psychology* **36**: 531–572.

Kessler RC, McGonagle KA, Zhao S, et al (1994) Lifetime and 12-month prevalence of DSM-III-R psychiatric disorders in the United States. *Arch Gen Psychiatry* **51**: 8–19.

Kessler RC, Nelson CB, McGonagle KA, et al (1996) Comorbidity of the DSM-III-R major depressive disorder in the general population: Results from the US National Comorbidity Survey. *Br J Psychiatry* **168**: 17–30.

Kessler RC, Rubinow DR, Holmes C, et al (1997) The epidemiology of DSM-III-R bipolar I disorder in a general population survey. *Psychol Med* **27**: 1079–1089.

Kouzis A, Eaton WW, Leaf PJ (1995) Psychopathology and mortality in the general population. *Soc Psychiatry Psychiat Epidemiol* **30**: 165–170.

Lehtinen V, Lindholm T, Veijola J, et al (1991) Stability of prevalences of mental disorders in a normal population cohort followed for 16 years. *Soc Psychiatry Psychiat Epidemiol* **26**: 40–46.

Lenze EJ, Mulsant BH, Shear MK, et al (2001) Comorbidity of depression and anxiety disorders in later life. *Depres Anxiety* **14**: 86–93.

Lewinsohn PM, Hops H, Roberts RE, et al (1993) Adolescent psychopathology: I. Prevalence and incidence of depression and other DSM-III-R disorders in high school students. *J Abnormal Psychology* **102**: 133–144.

Lilienfeld DE, Stolley PD (eds) (1994) *Foundations of epidemiology*. New York: Oxford University Press, 3rd edn.

Merikangas KR, Swendsen JD (1997) Genetic epidemiology of psychiatric disorders. *Epidemiol Rev* **19**: 144–155.

Moscicki EK (1995) Epidemiology of suicidal behavior. *Suicide Life-Threat Behav* **25**: 22–35.

Mulsant BH, Ganguli M (1999) Epidemiology and diagnosis of depression in late life. *J Clin Psychiatry* **60**(Suppl 20): 9–15.

Murphy JM, Laird NM, Monson RR, et al (2000a) A 40-year perspective on the prevalence of depression: The Stirling County Study. *Arch Gen Psychiatry* **57**: 209–215.

Murphy JM, Laird NM, Monson RR, et al (2000b) Incidence of depression in the Stirling County Study: Historical and comparative perspectives. *Psychol Med* **30**: 505–514.

Murray CJL, Lopez AD (1996) *The global burden of disease: A comprehensive assessment of mortality and disability from disease, injuries, and risk factors in 1990 and projected to 2020*. Cambridge MA: Harvard University Press.

Newman SC, Bland RC (1991) Suicide risk varies by subtype of affective disorder. *Acta Psychiat Scand* **83**: 420–426.

Newman SC, Bland RC (1998) Incidence of mental disorders in Edmonton: Estimates of rates and methodological issues. *J Psychiat Res* **32**: 273–282.

Palinkas LA, Russell J, Downs MA, et al (1992) Ethnic differences in stress, coping, and depressive symptoms after the Exxon Valdez oil spill. *J Nerv Mental Dis* **180**: 287–295.

Paykel ES (2000) Not an age of depression after all? Incidence rates may be stable over time. *Psychol Med* **30**: 489–490.

Post RM (1992) Transduction of psychosocial stress into the neurobiology of recurrent affective disorder. *Am J Psychiatry* **149**: 999–1010.

Robins LN, Regier DA (eds) (1991) *Psychiatric disorders in America: The epidemiologic catchment area study*. New York: The Free Press.

Rubonis AV, Bickman L (1991) Psychological impairment in the wake of disaster: The disaster-psychopathology relationship. *Psychol Bull* **109**: 384–399.

Schulberg HC, Madonia MJ, Block MR, et al (1995) Major depression in primary care practice: Clinical characteristics and treatment implications. *Psychosomatics* **36**: 129–137.

Shrout PE, Llink BG, Dohrenwend BP, et al (1989) Characterizing life events as risk factors for depression: The role of fateful loss events. *J Abnormal Psychology* **98**: 460–467.

Sommervell PD, Leaf PJ, Weissman MM, et al (1989) The prevalence of major depression in black and white adults in five United States communities. *Am J Epidemiol* **130**: 725–735.

Surtees PG, Miller PM, Ingham JG, et al (1986) Life events and the onset of affective disorder: A longitudinal general population study. *J Affect Disord* **10**: 37–50.

Thornicroft G, Sartorius N (1993) The course and outcome of depression in different cultures: 10-year follow-up of the WHO Collaborative Study on the Assessment of Depressive Disorders. *Psychol Med* **23**: 1023–1032.

Turner RJ, Turner JB (1999) Social integration and support. In: Aneshensel CS, Phelan JC (eds), *Handbook of the sociology of mental health*. New York: Kluwer, pp 301–319.

Ustun TB, Sartorius N (eds) (1995) *Mental illness in general health care: An international study*. Chichester, UK: Wiley.

Vasquez-Barquero JL, Diez-Manrique JF, Pena C, et al (1987). A community mental health survey in Cantabria: A general description of morbidity. *Psychol Med* **17**: 227–241.

Weissman MM, Prusoff BA, Gammon GD, et al (1984) Psychopathology in the children (ages 6-18) of depressed and normal parents. *J Am Acad Child Psychiatry* **23**: 78–84.

Weissman MM, Bland RC, Canino GJ, et al (1996) Cross-national epidemiology of major depression and bipolar disorder. *JAMA* **276**: 293–299.

Weller MPI, Ang PC, Latimer-Sayer DT, et al (1988) Drug abuse and mental illness. *Lancet* **i**: 997.

Wittchen H-U, Essau CA, von Zerssen D, et al (1992) Lifetime and six-month prevalence of mental disorders in the Munich Follow-Up Study. *Eur Arch Psychiat Clin Neurosci* **241**: 247–258.

Wittchen H-U, Lieb R, Wunderlich U, et al (1999) Comorbidity in primary care: Presentation and consequences. *J Clin Psychiatry* **60**(Suppl 7): 29–36.

WHO (World Health Organization) (1992) *International Classification of Diseases— Mental Disorders 10th edition*. Geneva: WHO.

chapter 2

Recent advances in the neurobiology of depression

Claus Normann and Mathias Berger

Despite the devastating impact that depressive disorders have on the lives of millions worldwide, our knowledge of the basic pathophysiological and aetiological principles of depression is surprisingly limited. The 'decade of the brain' has passed, but theories on the neurobiology of depression still lack convincing evidence and the existence of a common biological correlate of depression is even doubted by part of the psychiatric community, both professionals and patients. The ongoing conflict between adherents of psychological and biological models of psychopathology is far from being resolved.

However, in the past few years, there have been a number of novel thoughts and contributions that may add to our understanding of brain processes involved in depression and other affective disorders. In this chapter, we will try to answer some questions that have arisen, and will review recent trends in the neurobiology of depression.

Depression: A matter of life and death of neurons?

Many hypotheses on the pathophysiology of depression focus on alterations in the chemical communication between neurons. Traditionally, a disturbed regulation of the neurotransmitters serotonin, noradrenaline and, in part, dopamine has been proposed to result in modifications of receptor densities—or vice versa. Most drugs used in the pharmaco-therapy of depression act on these monoamine systems. Novel approaches are emerging that provide evidence for changes in the basic structure and morphology of the brain in contrast to mere neurochemical alterations.

Cell loss

Recent studies have associated depression with regional reductions in brain volume as well as in the number of neurons in discrete areas, and indicate that affective disorders are associated with impairments of structural plasticity and cellular resilience (Duman et al, 1997; Manji et al, 2000, 2001). Recent volumetric neuroimaging studies suggest cell loss or atrophy in certain brain areas. The third and lateral ventricles have been found to be enlarged in depressed patients, whereas the grey matter in certain cortex areas and the frontal lobe volume seems to be reduced. There are strikingly consistent findings of reduced hippocampal volume in major depressive disorder (MDD). The loss of hippocampal volume appears to be correlated with the total lifetime illness duration and may persist for up to decades after the depressive episodes have resolved (Sheline et al, 1999; Bremner et al, 2000).

N-acetylaspartate (NAA) is regarded as a marker of neuronal viability and function and can be assessed via magnetic resonance spectroscopy (MRS). Frye and others (Frye et al, 2000; Winsberg et al, 2000) found decreased NAA levels in the hippocampus and the dorsolateral pre-frontal cortex of bipolar subjects.

Positron emission tomography (PET) studies have revealed numerous abnormalities of regional cerebral blood flow and glucose metabolism, most notably, an increase in the amygdala and a decrease in the hippo-campus and in certain regions of the prefrontal cortex. Blood flow and metabolism do not entirely normalize during symptom remission in many of these areas.

Postmortem brain studies have reported a layer-specific reduction of regional volume, cell numbers or size in the prefrontal cortex, anterior cingulate cortex and hippocampus. Taken together, a variety of *in vivo* and post-mortem studies in depressed humans using multiple techniques support the idea of a reduction in regional central nervous system (CNS) volume which is accompanied by atrophy and loss of cells.

At least part of this reduction in cell number and function seems to be mediated by the effects of stress. In rats, exposure to restraint or long-term social stress leads to atrophy and eventual loss of hippocampal neurons (Sapolsky, 2000). The activation of the hypothalamic-pituitary-adrenocortical (HPA) axis is likely to play a crucial role in mediating the stress-induced neuronal atrophy, which can be mimicked by administration of high levels of glucocorticoids. More 'downstream', an enhanced glutamatergic neurotransmission via NMDA and non-NMDA ionotropic receptors seems to be involved in the induction of cell loss, mainly by elevating intracellular Ca^{2+} to toxic levels.

Changes in cell structure

In addition to neuronal loss, stress might foster structural changes in some brain regions (McEwen, 2000). Chronic stress in rats causes apical dendrites of CA3 pyramidal neurons to atrophy and a dendritic remodelling of CA1 and the dentate gyrus. This remodelling of dendrites could be a factor in the shrinkage of the hippocampus in depressed patients. It is thought to be mediated by glucocorticoids and/or excitatory amino acids. Of note, animal-to-animal stress is much more effective in inducing dendritic remodelling than experimenter-applied stressors; the stress-induced elevation of catecholamines and glucocorticoids in animal-to-animal stress models is more persistent and shows no sign of habituation (Magarinos et al, 1998).

Dysregulation of apoptosis

A dysregulation of apoptosis, or programmed cell death, may further contribute to the loss of neurons observed in a variety of pathological conditions. This might be mediated by the Bcl-2 family of proteins (Adams and Cory, 1998), which maintain a fine balance between apoptotic and anti-apoptotic factors. Moreover, neurotrophic factors (eg brain-derived neurotrophic factor; BDNF) and the MAP kinase pathway inhibit apoptosis.

Therapeutic drugs increase cell survival

Both antidepressants and mood stabilizers may enhance cell survival. Duman et al (2000) have demonstrated that chronic administration of different classes of antidepressants targets factors involved in neuronal atrophy and survival, such as the cAMP-CREB cascade, and more indirectly, BDNF. Both lithium and valproate upregulate the cytoprotective protein Bcl-2 in brain regions where neuronal changes have been observed in mood disorder patients, for example, the frontal cortex, dentate gyrus and hippocampus (Chen et al, 1999, 2000). A growing

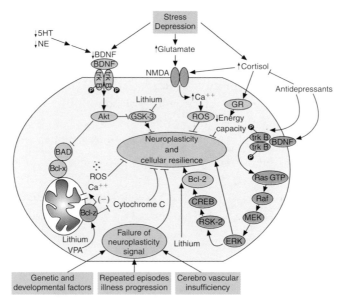

Figure 2.1 *Neuroplasticity and cellular resilience in mood disorders is thought to be modulated by a variety of external parameters and intracellular pathways. Stress might reduce extracellular levels of BDNF and facilitate excitotoxic calcium influx via NMDA receptors. BDNF and other neurotrophic factors enhance cell survival by activating two distinct signaling pathways: the phosphoinositol and the ERK-MAP-kinase pathway which enhances the expression of the major cytoprotective protein Bcl-2. Bcl-2 impairs the release of calcium and cytochrome c, sequesters proforms of caspase-enzymes and enhances mitochondrial calcium uptake. Antidepressants increase the expression of BDNF; lithium and valproate both upregulate Bcl-2 and activate the ERK-MAP-kinase pathway. Reproduced with permission from: Manji et al., 2001,* Nature Medicine *7: 541–547.*

body of evidence supports robust neuroprotective effects of lithium both *in vitro* and *in vivo*. Lithium has been shown to protect neurons against toxic cell damage by the excitatory amino acid glutamate, low potassium, and high levels of anticonvulsants. There is even some degree of protection from ischaemic cell loss by arterial occlusion *in vivo* after chronic lithium application. These cytoprotective properties of lithium might add to its already known modulation of intracellular Ca^{2+} stores via the IP3 pathway.

Adult neurogenesis

Neuronal plasticity is not confined to cell death and regulation of survival. Contrary to long-standing beliefs, there is clear evidence of new neuronal birth throughout life in all mammalian species, including humans (Jacobs et al, 2000). However, adult neurogenesis may be limited to specific brain regions, such as the gyrus dentatus (DG) of the hippocampus and the olfactory bulb (Eriksson et al, 1998). There has been one recent report of neurogenesis in the neocortex of adult primates (Gould et al, 1999b). These new neurons are derived from progenitor cells that have not terminally differentiated and remain in a dormant-like state. It appears that many more cells differentiate in the adult DG than ultimately survive and that the total number of newly produced cells is rather small compared to the total neuronal population.

As is the case for cell death, adult neurogenesis is closely regulated and some distinct entities have been identified that influence the rate of neurogenesis. Factors that increase the birth of new neurons are increased physical activity and novel learning experiences, especially spatial learning tasks in the case of the hippocampus (Gould et al, 1999a). Stress is believed to be the major factor inhibiting neurogenesis (Gould et al, 1998). Stress inhibits proliferative activity in the DG via increased release of glucocorticoid hormones. Therefore, both cell viability and neurogenesis are significantly modulated by stress, which (not surprisingly) is strongly implicated in the aetiology of depression (Kendler et al, 1999). Chronic stress exposure may favour neuronal loss over neurogenesis and may disable throughput in brain circuitry critical for the formation of new cognitions and memory. Thus, people who cannot 'escape' the mood alterations induced by protracted stress might develop a depressed state (Jacobs et al, 2000).

Another substance that stimulates adult neurogenesis is serotonin. Release of brain serotonin by systemic administration of fenfluramine exerts a powerful mitogenic effect in the DG, which is mediated by the 5-HT$_{1A}$ receptor. Moreover, selective serotonin reuptake inhibitors (SSRIs), tricyclic antidepressants and electroconvulsive therapy also increase cell proliferation in the rat DG (Malberg et al, 1999). Thus, enhancement of 5-HT$_{1A}$ neurotransmission may counteract the devastating effects of stress and depression. The time needed for newborn neurons to be integrated within neuronal circuitry may explain the lag of onset of antidepressants.

The neuroplasticity hypothesis of depression

The therapeutic consequences resulting from the neuroplasticity hypothesis of depression are still unclear. It is of note that most classes of antidepressants have been shown to act on certain aspects of cell survival or neurogenesis. Some new approaches focus on the modulation of growth factors, MAP kinase cascades and Bcl-2 proteins. Phosphodiesterase inhibitors increase AMP levels, which (in turn) exert neurotrophic effects via CREB-mediated Bcl-2 upregulation (Finkbeiner, 2000). Capitalizing on this relationship, the phosphodiesterase inhibitor, rolipram, has proceeded to phase 3 clinical testing for its putative antidepressive properties.

The neuroplasticity hypothesis of depression provides an entirely new approach to the understanding of affective disorders, especially more chronic or recurrent depressive states. However, there are major drawbacks that could confound some of the conclusions drawn from the above reports. Significant adult neurogenesis seems to be confined to small brain regions, especially the dentate gyrus of the hippocampus. Not all depressive symptoms can be explained by a pathological state of this brain area. Moreover, the time scale of neuroplasticity may not be entirely congruent to the clinical course of major depressive episodes, where complete recovery occurs in at least a large subset of patients.

Rapid alterations in the patient's affective state can hardly be integrated in this theory (eg instantaneous effect of sleep deprivation, spontaneous recovery, switches and rapid cycling in bipolar disorder). Equally problematic are the difficulties in differentiating primary (aetiological) alterations and secondary (epiphenomenal) modifications in brain structure due to the effects of disease-related changes in sleep, diet or activity, or the effects of medication.

Synaptic long-term plasticity

Another form of plasticity in the CNS is long-term synaptic plasticity [ie long-term potentiation (LTP) and long-term depression (LTD)], which involve activity-dependent modification of synaptic transmission. Synaptic plasticity induces dynamic changes in a neural network and is believed to be a cellular model for learning and memory. Recent findings demonstrate its involvement in fear conditioning in the amygdala (Maren, 1999) and in the brain's response to stress. Stress modulates synaptic long-term plasticity (Rowan et al, 1998). A brief experience of inescapable stress produces significant changes in both the susceptibility to, and the direction of, synaptic plasticity. Stress blocks high frequency-induced LTP, in contrast, low frequency-induced LTD is greatly facilitated by stress (Shors et al, 1997; Xu et al, 1997). These effects of stress are completely blocked by the administration of a glucocorticoid receptor antagonist and, further 'downstream', by inhibitors of protein transcription and translation.

The physiological relevance of the glucocorticoid-mediated modulation of long-term synaptic plasticity is still unclear. It may induce some stress adaptation of learning and memory formation; however, an involvement in the pathophysiology of depression can still be suspected. For example, there is a link between synaptic plasticity and neuroplasticity, as LTP and LTD eventually result in protein synthesis in the process of memory foundation and might be involved in triggering neurogenesis. Moreover, there is preliminary evidence for the involvement of synaptic plasticity in affective regulation and disease states (Normann, 2000; Reid et al, 2001; Popoli et al, 2002). Also, *in vitro* data demonstrate a selective modulation of synaptic plasticity by serotonin favouring LTD over LTP. More data on this topic are forthcoming and may facilitate a unifying hypothesis of affective disorders quite distinct from receptor downregulation theories.

Does the corticosteroid system mediate stress, anxiety or depression?

It is generally recognized that depressed people are 'stressed'. They often display high levels of anxiety and agitation, and their heart rate and blood pressure may be elevated. Moreover, psychological stress is commonly accepted as an underlying factor precipitating the onset of depression. Many patients report a major life event or chronic interpersonal distress. However, the neurobiological basis of stress as a factor in the pathophysiology of affective disorder is poorly understood despite extensive study. Nevertheless, some recent pathophysiological concepts of depression converge on stress as a common pathway.

More than 45 years ago, Board et al (1956) reported elevated plasma cortisol levels in depressed patients. Since then, a compelling number of studies have found several measures indicative of a hyperactive HPA axis in depressed patients, leading to the corticosteroid receptor hypothesis of depression (Arborelius et al, 1999; Holsboer 2000). In the past decade, some studies have added preclinical evidence to this hypothesis and a clinical trial has tested the antidepressive efficacy of a corticotrophin-releasing factor receptor antagonist—one of the first major examples of drug development from bench-to-bedside.

Cortisol, corticotrophin-releasing factor and receptors
Mammalian stress responses are largely mediated through the hypothalamic-pituitary-adrenocortical (HPA) axis. During stress, the synthesis of corticotrophin-releasing factor (CRF) in the hypothalamic paraventricular nucleus is increased and higher amounts of CRF are secreted into the hypothalamo-hypophyseal portal vascular system. CRF binds to receptors in the anterior pituitary gland and releases adrenocorticotrophic hormone (ACTH), which in turn, induces the synthesis of gluco-

corticoids from the adrenal cortex. In healthy states, there are effective feedback autoregulative systems at different levels of this cascade.

CRF, beyond its role as a hormone in the HPA, also serves as a neurotransmitter in the cortex and mediates autonomic and behavioural stress responses. CRF-containing neurons originate in the central nucleus of the amygdala and project to various areas of the brain. They are also directly and indirectly connected to important brainstem nuclei such as the locus coeruleus and the raphé nuclei. Thus, CRF interacts with noradrenergic and serotonergic neurotransmission: CRF increases the firing rate of noradrenergic neurons and inhibits serotonergic neurons in the raphé. When injected directly into the brains of animals, CRF provokes symptoms of acute stress, including autonomic responses, disruption of sleep and facilitation of fear conditioning.

Two different CRF receptors have been described, CRF_1 and CRF_2, both of which are positively coupled to adenylate cyclase. CRF_1 receptors are found in many areas of the brain, whereas CRF_2 receptors are more abundant in the periphery. Their neuroanatomical distribution suggests that they mediate different effects. Studies using antisense probes against CRF_1 and CRF_2 receptor mRNA reported that only reduced CRF_1 receptor levels were associated with anxiolytic effects in stressed rats (Liebsch et al, 1999). These findings were confirmed by mouse mutants lacking specific CRF receptors: only mice lacking CRF_2 receptors displayed increased anxiety-like behaviour (Bale et al, 2000). As observed following direct injection into the brain, overexpression of CRF in mice results in anxiety-like behaviour. However, mice with deletions of the CRF gene exhibit normal stress-induced behaviour, a fact that may suggest that endogenous ligands other than CRF might also bind to CRF receptors to provoke stress responses (Weninger et al, 1999).

At least two types of glucocorticoid receptor have been described in the brain, the mineralocorticoid receptor (MR) and the glucocorticoid receptor (GR). In the hippocampus, MR has a tenfold higher affinity for corticosterone and is almost completely occupied at basal levels of steroid secretion. GRs are only occupied when corticosteroid levels increase under stress conditions or at the peak of circadian rhythm. Basal conditions (where most of the MRs but only a fraction of GRs are occupied) produce a small Ca^{2+} influx and a stable firing rate, whereas increased GR binding under stress results in an increased Ca^{2+} influx and neuronal excitability. This modulation of Ca^{2+} influx may result in a modified pattern of LTP/LTD induction, as discussed above. Stress has been found to facilitate LTD, an effect mediated by glucocorticoids (Xu et al, 1998). A transgenic mouse expressing GR antisense mRNA mainly in neuronal tissue was evaluated as an animal model of depression and showed some biochemical and behavioural features seen in other animal models of depression or depressed humans. Ligand-activated GRs or MRs bind in the cell nucleus to short DNA sequences called glucocorticoid response elements (GRE) in the promoter region of corticosteroid-responsive target genes; a process that is fine-tuned by several activators, inhibitors and other factors (Freedman, 1999).

Early life stress

Evidence from a variety of preclinical and clinical studies suggest that early life stress constitutes a major risk factor for the development and persistence of depression (Heim and Nemeroff, 2001). It can be hypothesized that persistent changes in corticotrophin-releasing factor (CRF) neurotransmission may mediate part of the association between linking stress and depression. Repeated separation of rat pups from their mothers during the neonatal period is a valid animal model of early life stress and induces a sustained release of CRF. These animals also develop marked behavioural abnormalities such as reduced consumption of sweetened fluid (an experimental analogue of anhedonia), increased freezing in an open field, decreased exploration of a novel environment and increased acoustic startle responses; all indicating an increased level of fear (Caldji et al, 2000). As predicted by the CRF-neuron projections, early stress decreases serotonergic cell firing and results in a persistent serotonergic dysfunction (Kirby et al, 2000). Even rats exposed to pre-natal stress show marked increases in fear-related behaviour. Selected aspects of these experiments have been repeated in non-human primates and demonstrate comparable results.

In humans, children who experienced different types of early life stress manifest altered salivary cortisol levels indicative of a disturbed circadian rhythm of the HPA axis. Moreover, urinary noradrenaline and dopamine excretion are elevated and peripheral adrenergic receptors are downregulated in abused children with post-traumatic stress disorder (PTSD). However, some of these results are variable and may be moderated by factors such as age at onset and duration or intensity of the stressful life event. Nevertheless, evidence of the impact of early trauma can still be demonstrated in adulthood. Abused women without depression exhibited increased ACTH responses to CRF similar to non-abused depressed subjects (Heim et al, 2001). Parallel to a finding in abused children, elevated urinary noradrenaline excretion was reported in abused women with PTSD.

The various classes of antidepressants may have differential effects on CRF and HPA axis overactivity and could control or even possibly reverse some abnormalities. Given a decrease in serotonergic neurotransmission following early life stress, the effects of SSRIs on offsetting the neurobiological consequences of early life stress have been of great interest (Hidalgo and Davidson, 2000). In contrast, some of these clinical or animal model disorders are reversed by tricyclic antidepressants (Martin et al, 2000), which might be explained by an already elevated level of noradrenergic neurotransmission. In conclusion, both animal models and findings in humans support a role for early stress in the pathophysiology of depression in vulnerable subjects which might be mediated by a CRF dysfunction.

Dysregulation of the HPA axis

Not only hormone concentrations or receptor structures seem to be disrupted in depression but also regulation mechanisms. It has been known for many years that a single dose of synthetic glucocorticoid dexamethasone suppresses plasma ACTH and cortisol concentrations to a lesser extent and for a shorter time in depressed patients than in healthy nondepressed subjects. Following intravenous injection of CRF, depressed patients also exhibit a blunted ACTH, but normal cortisol response. Holsboer and colleagues have introduced a combination of the dexamethasone suppression test and a CRF stimulation test (Holsboer and Barden, 1996) and found that dexamethasone pre-treated patients show enhanced ACTH and cortisol response to CRF compared to control subjects. In the dex/CRF test, dexamethasone acts primarily on the pituitary to suppress ACTH. Because of its low access to the brain, dexamethasone fails to compensate for the decreased cortisol levels in the neuronal tissue. In response to this situation, the secretion of CRF and other neuropeptides is stimulated. The sensitivity of this test to differentiate between normal and depressed patients is above 80% (Heuser et al, 1994). Normalization of test results after clinical remission from depression has been reported—the dex/CRF test might even be useful as a predictor of increased risk for relapse (Zobel et al, 1999). In those patients where the neuroendocrine abnormalities persisted, the risk of relapse or treatment resistance might be higher. Non-depressed subjects from families with a high genetic load for depression may display abnormal responses to the dex/CRF test (Holsboer et al, 1995; Modell et al, 1998).

Therapeutic options

Derived from preclinical findings, it has been assumed that the suppression of CRF levels by CRF receptor antagonists might have antidepressive efficacy in humans. The CRF_1 receptor antagonist R121919 was tested in an open study and did not compromise the physiological stress coping response. The treatment was well tolerated and resulted in a significant decrease of depression and anxiety ratings (Zobel et al, 2000). However, a subsequent larger double-blind trial had to be terminated due to the compound's hepatotoxicity. It is unclear if CRF receptor antagonists might resolve the entire depressive syndrome or only stress-related symptoms such as anxiety, sleep disturbance and loss of appetite. Moreover, long-term CRF_1 antagonist treatment may result in receptor upregulation and enhanced CRF secretion after cessation of drug treatment, causing withdrawal and rebound problems.

Another alternative focuses on reduction of cortisol either by synthesis inhibitors or receptor antagonists. Metapyrone prevents synthesis of cortisol and corticosterone and has produced antidepressant-like behavioural changes in two animal models of depression (Healy et al, 1999). Ketoconazole blocks adrenal steroid synthesis and has direct inhibitory effects on pituitary cells. In a double-blind study, ketoconazole was superior to placebo in hypercortisolaemic depressed patients (Wolkowitz et al, 1999). Preliminary results suggest that the corticosteroid receptor antagonist mifepristone (RU486) might be a potential antidepressant (Murphy et al, 1993).

Despite the failure of the R121919 trial, controlled clinical trials in the future should evaluate some novel treatment approaches modulating the corticosteroid system. However, it is still unclear if this therapeutic option primarily targets stress-related anxiety or depression. Moreover, it has to be shown if all patients, or only the subset of hypercortisolaemic depressed subjects, might benefit from corticosteroid modulation.

Substance P: Pathogenic, promising or deceptive?

Substance P is another pathophysiological concept apart from monoamine theories and shares a role in the neurobiology of stress (for reviews, see Rupniak and Kramer, 1999; Stout et al, 2001; Lieb et al, 2002).

Substance P ('P' for 'preparation') is a small peptide which belongs to the group of neurokinins (tachykinins) and was discovered in 1931 as a substance that caused intestinal smooth muscle contraction. Substance P (SP) is the most abundant neurokinin and is presumed to be involved in the regulation of many physiological processes. It is found, for example, in the gut, lung, vascular system and CNS. SP binds to the NK1 receptor (neurokinin) and with lower affinity to the NK2 and NK3 receptors. In the CNS, the densest immunoreactivity is localized in the spinal cord and within the substantia nigra, but many other brain regions contain high concentrations of SP.

On the basis of anatomical localization and functional studies, SP has been implicated in the pathophysiology of a diverse range of conditions including asthma, inflammatory bowel disease, pain, psoriasis, migraine, movement disorders, cystitis, schizophrenia, vomiting and anxiety. SP has traditionally been conceptualized as a pain transmitter. However, studies with NK1 receptor antagonists have consistently produced disappointing results in the treatment of different pain conditions. In contrast, NK1 receptor antagonists have been found to be extremely effective antiemetics, especially in the prevention of chemotherapy-induced vomiting. In addition to antiemetic properties and lack of analgesic efficacy, a number of preclinical and behavioural findings have sustained interest in a putative role of NK1 receptor antagonists as antidepressants.

Substance P interacts distinctly with monoamines involved in the pathophysiology of affective disorders. It was already shown more than 20 years ago that brainstem nuclei co-synthesize and co-release 5-HT and SP. This co-localization has been demonstrated for raphé neurons that project to the spinal cord and has been proposed to project to limbic structures and the cortex. Moreover, the raphé nucleus is innervated by SP-containing neurons. The effect of SP receptor activation on serotonergic neurons is unclear and may differ in acute and chronic application. Direct intraventricular injection of SP produces an increase in plasma catecholamine concentrations and is excitatory to the locus coerulus via NK1 receptors. SP appears to play an important role in stress activation of noradrenergic and dopaminergic neurons.

In behavioural animal studies, tachykinin receptor activation in several areas, especially the periaqueductal grey, causes anxiety-like behaviour. However, other behavioural effects of SP are rather non-specific and, at times contradictory. SP neurons are responsive to aversive stimuli; most changes are suggestive of SP neuronal activation by stress. NK1 receptor 'knock-out' mice display very little aggression in threatening social situations. NK1 receptor disruption resulted in a marked reduction of anxiety- and stress-related responses which were paralleled by a desensitization of 5-HT$_{1A}$ inhibitory autoreceptors (Santarelli et al, 2001). In relevant animal models (ie in chronic mild stress and social interaction tests), the NK1 receptor antagonist NKP608 has been shown to exert antidepressant and anxiolytic activity. Preliminary results in the forced swimming test are equivocal. L733 060, another NK1 receptor antagonist, reduced vocalizations of pups after maternal separation, another model for depression and anxiety. Chronic application of lithium in Flinders Sensitive Line rats, an animal model of depressive vulnerability, altered SP immunoreactivity in distinct brain areas (Husum et al, 2001). Measurements of SP in the CSF of depressed patients produced contradictory results and successful treatment of depression did not significantly alter CSF concentrations of SP in these patients. Taken together, preclinical studies and CSF data do not, so far, establish a clear link between abnormal SP neurotransmission and depression. Further studies are needed.

In a randomized clinical trial (Kramer et al, 1998), the NK1 antagonist MK869 showed antidepressive efficacy: 213 depressed patients were randomized to placebo, paroxetine or MK869 and treated for 6 weeks. Clinical improvement was identical in the paroxetine and the MK869 group and superior to placebo. The substance was well tolerated and additionally reduced symptoms of anxiety. The same authors also conducted a follow-up dose-determination study with more than 800 depressed patients. In this study, however, neither MK869 nor the reference antidepressant fluoxetine were superior to placebo (Enserink, 1999). This study caused some confusion concerning the value of NK1 receptor antagonists as antidepressants and stimulated a controversial debate on the effectiveness of placebo formulations in the treatment of depression. Nevertheless, *post-hoc* analyses of this unpublished trial demonstrated antidepressive efficacy of MK869 in a subset of patients with severe depression. In a recently completed, and still unpublished study, MK869 was also effective in the treatment of depression with superior effects as compared to both placebo *and* an SSRI. These promising studies have led to the initiation of several phase II studies to further investigate the effectiveness of NK1 receptor antagonists in the treatment of affective and anxiety disorders.

To summarize, the role of SP in the neurobiology of depression is unclear so far. The clinical trials of the NK1 receptor antagonist MK869 have been promising. However, further studies are needed to arrive at a clear conclusion concerning the role of SP in the neurobiology of depression and the efficacy of NK1 receptor antagonists for treating depression and anxiety.

The relationship between sleep and depression

More than 90% of depressed patients complain of sleep disturbances (Riemann et al, 2001). Depression is one of the most frequent causes of insomnia. In addition to clinical abnormalities, polysomnographic investigations in depressed patients have found numerous indications of disrupted sleep architecture. Sleep in depression is characterized by a reduction of slow wave sleep, a shortening of the interval between sleep onset and the occurrence of the first rapid eye movement (REM) period (REM latency) and an increased intensity of REM sleep (REM density). REM abnormalities tend to normalize in remitted patients, although there is some evidence that disturbances may persist following the acute mood episode or might even precede the onset of depression. The transient antidepressive effects of total sleep deprivation has been confirmed in many trials. The sleep phase advance protocol is based on the assumption that avoidance of sleep during the early morning hours is crucial for the sleep-deprivation effect. A combination of sleep deprivation and sleep phase advance therapy maintains the positive effect of sleep deprivation in 60% to 75% of patients (Berger et al, 1997; Benedetti et al, 2001a).

Recently, a number of studies have addressed the depressogenic effect of sleep and the mechanism of sleep deprivation as an antidepressant. Sleep deprivation is well suited for investigating patients in depressed and non-depressed states, with an interval of one day without pharmacological interventions. David Kupfer's group (Smith et al, 1999) examined brain glucose metabolism by serial PET scans at baseline, after total sleep deprivation, recovery sleep and after two weeks of pharmacotherapy in depressed geriatric patients. They found increased glucose metabolism in the anterior cingulate cortex at pre-treatment. Following treatment, improvement in patients' depressive symptoms was paralleled by a reduction in glucose metabolism in the right anterior cingulate cortex and the right medial frontal cortex. A study using functional MRI methods found similar results and proposed that elevated perfusion in the ventral anterior cingulate and the medial frontal cortex might be predictive for the response to a night of sleep deprivation (Clark et al,

2001). As these findings are in accordance with studies examining standard antidepressants, they suggest a monoaminergic mechanism of action of sleep deprivation. Moreover, Benedetti et al (1999) demonstrated that patients who were homozygotic for the long variant of the 5-HT transporter-linked polymorphic region (5-HTTLPR) showed significant mood amelioration after total sleep deprivation than those who were heterozygotic for the short variant. 5-HTTLPR is a functional polymorphism in the transcriptional control region 'upstream' of the coding sequence of the 5-HT transporter. Similar findings have been reported for serotonergic antidepressants and support a major role for serotonin in the mechanism of action of total sleep deprivation.

Ebert and Berger (1998) have proposed a psychostimulant theory of sleep deprivation based on experimental and clinical similarities between psychostimulant use and sleep deprivation. Both psychostimulants and sleep deprivation show a rapid onset of antidepressant action. However, the effects are short lasting and mania can be provoked in some patients. Psychostimulants and sleep deprivation result in modifications of blood flow and glucose metabolism in functional imaging studies in the limbic area. The positive and psychomotor-activating properties of psychostimulants are linked to dopaminergic neurotransmission. In both animal models and human studies, there are findings of increased dopamine release following sleep deprivation. For example, plasma and urine concentrations of dopamine metabolites are positively correlated with antidepressive efficacy, sleep deprivation decreases prolactin release and the eye-blink rate (a measure of dopaminergic activation) is increased. The dopaminergic antidepressant amineptine has been used to augment the effects of sleep deprivation in depression. However, there have been confounding results. If started 6 days before sleep deprivation, amineptine prevented antidepressive efficacy (Benedetti et al, 1996), whereas it augmented efficacy when started concurrently (Benedetti et al, 2001b). This might be explained by a receptor downregulation following continued administration of amineptine. Taken together, the case for the role of monoamines including dopamine in the mechanism of action of sleep deprivation is still not definitively resolved.

Some aspects of REM sleep disturbance have been explained by the dysregulation of cholinergic neurotransmission (eg cholinergic over-activity or receptor supersensitivity). Pharmacological stimulation of depressed patients with cholinergic drugs has resulted in a more rapid induction of REM sleep as compared to normal controls, or other patients with psychiatric disorders, and the occurrence of sleep-onset REM periods. Recent studies have demonstrated that findings of sleep disturbance following cholinergic stimulation may be a vulnerability marker for major depression. Reduced REM latency and slow wave sleep deficits are familial and associated with an increased risk for major depression (Giles et al, 1998; Krieg et al, 2001). Abnormal polysomno-graphic findings might be helpful in identifying those at high risk for depression within an affected family. Prospective studies are underway to test the predictive value of abnormal sleep patterns.

Serotonin, noradrenaline—and dopamine?

The role of dopamine in the pathogenesis and treatment of depression has received far less attention than that of serotonin or noradrenaline. However, some preclinical and clinical evidence suggest that further research on dopamine in the pathophysiology of affective disorders might be rewarding. D_2 receptor antagonistic neuroleptic drugs are effective in treating mania and are suspected to be depressogenic in some patients. In contrast, drugs that increase dopamine availability, such as amphetamines, induce euphoria that is blocked by dopamine receptor antagonists. Some of the newer antidepressants (eg bupropion and venlafaxine) are thought to be weak to moderate dopamine reup-take inhibitors. Nomifensine, a selective dopamine reuptake inhibitor, is an effective antidepressant but was withdrawn from use after some patients developed severe adverse effects. There are a number of reports on the use of dopamine agonists and amantadine in treatment-refractory depressed patients or when used as adjuncts to standard anti-depressive medication (Nierenberg et al, 1998; Perugi et al, 2001). The novel potent dopamine agonists, pramipexole and ropinirole, have been evaluated for their efficacy in depressed patients. Pramipexole produced a marked improvement in depressive symptoms in a substantial number of patients in one open trial (Szgedi et al, 1997). Also, ropinirole had antidepressive effects in some depressed bipolar II patients (Perugi et al, 2001).

Studies examining central dopaminergic turnover in depression by measuring the CSF concentration of the major metabolite of dopamine, homovanillic acid (HVA), produced mixed results. While some studies found decreased CSF HVA in acutely depressed patients, others have failed to detect a difference, or have even found increased HVA concentrations. Neuroimaging studies have been equally confounding. The serotonin-releasing drug, fenfluramine, acutely modulated dopaminergic systems in a PET study (Smith et al, 1997). Structures that consistently show decreased cerebral glucose metabolism in depressed patients lie within the basal ganglia-thalamocortical circuits where dopamine is an important neurotransmitter. However, there are studies showing unaltered striatal D_2 receptor densities in SPECT examinations and post-mortem binding studies in depressed suicide victims (Allard and Norlen, 2001; Parsey et al, 2001).

Apart from these clinical studies, some pathophysiological concepts involving dopaminergic neurotransmission have evolved. Stress might have a detrimental impact on the normal function of the dopaminergic system (Pani et al, 2000). Stimuli that increase the release of dopamine in the medial prefrontal cortex and the nucleus accumbens (food and sex) are negatively affected by stress. Inescapable shock interferes with the ability of rats to consume a highly palatable diet. The sexual behaviour of male rats is also impaired by long-term stress and even by prenatally experienced stress. Repeated stress reduces the basal locomotor activity of rats. This can be reversed by chronic treatment with antidepressants, an effect that is blocked by pre-treatment with dopamine receptor blockers. Thus, stress might either alter dopaminergic functions as an epiphenomenon or changes in dopamine neurotransmission might be responsible for at least some of the detrimental effects of stress associated with depression.

Serotonergic and dopaminergic systems interact in the brain. In a microdialysis study, the application of serotonin facilitated dopamine release in the nucleus accumbens of rats. This effect was not seen in a rat model of depressive-like behaviour but could be observed following chronic treatment of these animals with antidepressants that also corrected the behaviour deficiencies. Release of dopamine in the nucleus accumbens has been shown to be associated with motivation, reward and hedonia. The inability of serotonin to induce dopamine release in 'depressed' rats may account for the behavioural deficiencies. The impaired serotonergic-dopaminergic interaction in the nucleus accumbens might be an interesting new focus for depression research (Zangen et al, 2001).

The overall evidence for an involvement of dopamine in the pathophysiology of depression is not as strong as that for serotonin and noradrenaline. However, some clinical and theoretical findings point to a putative role of dopamine which might result in future pharmacological treatment options.

Conclusion

The recent contributions on the neurobiology of depression discussed in this chapter converge on some common themes: stress as a central aetiology of depression, not only from a psychological but also from a neurobiological point of view; directions in examining other endogenous substances, in addition to serotonin and noradrenaline; and a focus on neuronal plasticity. These concepts might yield important advances in depression research far beyond monoaminergic receptor downregulation theories.

References

Adams JM, Cory S (1998) The Bcl-2 gene family: arbiters of cell survival. *Science* **281**: 1322–1326.
Allard P, Norlen M (2001) Caudate nucleus dopamine D(2) receptors in depressed suicide victims. *Neuropsychobiol* **44**: 70–73.

Arborelius L, Owens MJ, Plotsky PM, et al (1999) The role of corticotropin-releasing factor in depression and anxiety disorders. *J Endocrinol* **160**: 1–12.

Bale TI, Gontarino A, Smith GW, et al (2000) Mice deficient for corticotropin-releasing hormone receptor-2 display anxiety-like behavior and are hypersensitive to stress. *Nat Genet* **24**: 410–414.

Benedetti F, Barbini B, Campori E, et al (1996) Dopamine agonist amineptine prevents the antidepressant effect of sleep deprivation. *Psychiatry Res* **65**: 179–184.

Benedetti F, Serretti A, Colombo C, et al (1999) Influence of a functional polymorphism within the promoter of the serotonin transporter gene on the effects of total sleep deprivation in bipolar depression. *Am J Psychiatry* **156**: 1450–1452.

Benedetti F, Barbini B, Fulgosi MC, et al (2001a) Sleep phase advance and lithium to sustain antidepressant effect of total sleep deprivation in bipolar depression: new findings supporting the internal coincidence model? *J Psychiat Res* **35**: 323–329.

Benedetti F, Campori E, Barbini B, et al (2001b) Dopaminergic augmentation of sleep deprivation effects in bipolar depression. *Psychiat Res* **104**: 239–246.

Berger M, Vollmann J, Hohagen F, et al (1997) Sleep deprivation combined with consecutive sleep phase advance as a fast-acting therapy in depression: an open pilot trial in medicated and unmedicated patients. *Am J Psychiatry* **154**: 870–872.

Board F, Persky H, Hamburg DA (1956) Psychological stress and endocrine functions. *Psychosomatic Med* **18**: 324–333.

Bremner JD, Narayan M, Anderson ER, et al (2000) Hippocampal volume reduction in major depression. *Am J Psychiatry* **157**: 115–118.

Caldji C, Francis D, Sharma S, et al (2000) The effects early rearing environment on the development of GABAA and central benzodiazepine receptor levels and novelty-induced fearfulness in the rat. *Neuropsychopharmacology* **22**: 219–229.

Chen G, Huang LD, Jiang YM, et al (1999) The mood stabilizing agent valproate inhibits the activity of glycogen synthase kinase 3. *J Neurochem* **72**: 1327–1330.

Chen G, Rajkowska G, Du F, et al (2000) Enhancement of hippocampal neurogenesis by lithium. *J Neurochem* **75**: 1729–1734.

Clark CP, Frank LR, Brown GG (2001) Sleep deprivation, EEG and functional MRI in depression: preliminary results. *Neuropsychopharmacology* **25**: S79–S84.

Duman RS, Heninger GR, Nestler EJ (1997) A molecular and cellular theory of depression. *Arch Gen Psychiatry* **54**: 597–606.

Duman RS, Malberg K, Nakagawa S, et al (2000) Neuronal plasticity and survival in mood disorders. *Biol Psychiatry* **48**: 732–739.

Ebert D, Berger M (1998) Neurobiological similarities in antidepressant sleep deprivation and psychostimulant use: a psychostimulant theory of antidepressant sleep deprivation. *Psychopharmacology* **140**: 1–10.

Enserink M (1999) Can the placebo be the cure? *Science* **284**: 238–240.

Erikson PS, Perfilieva E, Björk-Erikson T, et al (1998) Neurogenesis in adult human hippocampus. *Nat Med* **4**: 1313–1317.

Finkbeiner S (2000) CREB couples neurotrophin signals to survival messages. *Neuron* **25**: 11–14.

Freedman LP (1999) Increasing the complexity of coactivation in nuclear receptor signaling. *Cell* **97**: 5–8.

Frye MA, Bertolino A, Callicott JH, et al (2000) A 1H-MRSI hippocampal study in bipolar patients with a history of alcohol abuse. *Biol Psychiatry* **47**: 260S.

Giles DE, Kupfer DJ, Rush AJ, et al (1998) Controlled comparison of electrophysiological sleep in families of probands with unipolar depression. *Am J Psychiatry* **155**: 192–199.

Gould E, Tanapat P, McEwen BS, et al (1998) Proliferation of granule cell precursors in the dentate gyrus of adult monkeys is diminished by stress. *Proc Natl Acad Sci USA* **95**: 3168–3171.

Gould E, Beylin A, Tanapat P, et al (1999a) Hippocampal-dependent learning enhances the survival of granule neurons generated in the dentate gyrus of adult rats. *Nat Neurosci* **2**: 260–265.

Gould E, Reeves AJ, Graziano MSA, et al (1999b) Neurogenesis in the neocortex of adult primates. *Science* **286**: 548–552.

Healy DG, Harkin A, Cryan JF, et al (1999) Metapyrone displays antidepressant-like properties in preclinical paradigms. *Psychopharmacology* **145**: 303–308.

Heim C, Nemeroff CB (2001) The role of childhood trauma in the neurobiology of mood and anxiety disorders: preclinical and clinical studies. *Biol Psychiatry* **49**: 1023–1039.

Heim C, Newport DJ, Bonsall R, et al (2001) Altered pituitary-adrenal axis responses to provocative challenge tests in adult survivors of childhood abuse: the role of comorbid depression. *Am J Psychiatry* **158**: 575–581.

Heuser I, Yasouridis A, Holsboer F (1994) The combined dexamethasone/CRH test. A refined laboratory test for psychiatric disorders. *J Psychiat Res* **28**: 341–356.

Hidalgo RB, Davidson JR (2000) Selective serotonin reuptake inhibitors in post-traumatic stress disorder. *J Psychopharmacology* **14**: 70–76.

Holsboer F (2000) The corticosteroid receptor hypothesis of depression. *Neuropsychopharmacology* **23**: 477–501.

Holsboer F, Barden N (1996) Antidepressant and HPA regulation. *Endocrinol Rev* **17**: 187–203.

Holsboer F, Lauer CJ, Schreiber W, et al (1995) Altered hypothalamic-pituitary adrenocortical regulation in healthy subjects at high familial risk for affective disorders. *Neuroendocrinology* **62**: 340–347.

Husum H, Vasquez PA, Mathe AA (2001) Changed concentrations of tachykinins and neuropeptide Y in brain of a rat model of depression. Lithium treatment normalizes tachykinins. *Neuropsychopharmacology* **24**: 183–191.

Jacobs BL, van Praag H, Gage FH (2000) Adult brain neurogenesis and psychiatry: a novel theory of depression. *Mol Psychiatry* **5**: 262–269.

Kendler KS, Karkowski LM, Preskott CA (1999) Causal relationship between stressful live events and the onset of major depression. *Am J Psychiatry* **156**: 837–841.

Kirby LG, Rice KC, Valentino RJ (2000) Effects of corticotropin-releasing factor on neuronal activity in the serotonergic dorsal raphe nucleus. *Neuropsychopharmacology* **22**: 148–162.

Kramer MS, Cutler N, Feighner J, et al (1998) Distinct mechanism for antidepressant activity by blockade of central substance P receptors. *Science* **281**: 1640–1645.

Krieg JC, Lauer CJ, Schreiber W, et al (2001) Neuroendocrine, polysomnographic and psychometric observations in healthy subjects at high familial risk for affective disorders: the current state of the 'Munich vulnerability study'. *J Affect Disord* **62**: 33–37.

Lieb K, Treffurth Y, Berger M, et al (2002) Substance P and affective disorders: new treatment opportunities by NK1-receptor antagonists? *Neuropsychobiology* **45**(Suppl 1): 2–6.

Liebsch G, Landgraf R, Engelmann M, et al (1999) Differential behavioral effects of chronic infusion of CRH1 and CRH2 receptor antisense oligodeoxy-nucleotides into the rat brain. *J Psychiat Res* **33**: 153–163.

Magarinos AM, Orchinik M, McEwen BS (1998) Morphological changes in the hippocampal CA 3 region induced by non-invasive glucocorticoid administration: a paradox. *Brain Res* **809**: 314–318.

Malberg JE, Eisch AJ, Nestler EJ, et al (1999) Chronic antidepressant administration increases granule cell genesis in the hippocampus of the adult male rat. *Soc Neurosci Abs* **25**: 1029.

Manji HK, Moore GJ, Rajkowska G, et al (2000) Neuroplasticity and cellular resilience in mood disorders. *Mol Psychiatry* **5**: 578–593.

Manji HK, Drevets WC, Charney DS (2001) The cellular neurobiology of depression. *Nat Med* **7**: 541–547.

Maren S (1999) Long-term potentiation in the amygdala: a mechanism for emotional learning and memory. *TINS* **22**: 561–567.

Martin A, Kaufman J, Charney D (2000) Pharmacotherapy of early-onset depression. Update and new directions. *Child Adolesc Psychiatr Clin N Am* **9**: 135–157.

McEwen B (2000) The neurobiology of stress: from serendipity to clinical relevance. *Brain Res* **886**: 172–189.

Modell S, Lauer CJ, Schreiber W, et al (1998) Hormonal response pattern in combined DEX-CRH test is stable over time in subjects at high familial risk for affective disorders. *Neuropsychopharmacology* **18**: 253–262.

Murphy BEP, Filipini D, Ghadirian AM (1993) Possible use of glucocorticoid receptor antagonists in the treatment of major depression: preliminary results using RU 486. *J Psychiat Neurosci* **18**: 209–213.

Nierenberg AA, Dougherty D, Rosenbaum JF (1998) Dopaminergic agents and stimulants as antidepressant augmentation strategies. *J Clin Psychiatry* **59**: 60–64.

Normann C (2000) Towards a new model for cellular pathophysiology in affective disorder. *Acta Neuropsychiatrica* **12**: 77–80.

Pani L, Porcella A, Gessa GL (2000) The role of stress in the pathophysiology of the dopaminergic system. *Mol Psychiatry* **5**: 14–21.

Parsey RV, Oquendo MA, Zea-Ponce Y, et al (2001) Dopamine D2 receptor availability and amphetamine-induced dopamine release in unipolar depression. *Biol Psychiatry* **50**: 313–322.

Perugi G, Toni C, Ruffolo G, et al (2001) Adjunctive dopamine agonists in treatment resistant bipolar II depression: an open case series. *Pharmacopsychiatry* **34**: 137–141.

Popoli M, Gennarekki M, Racagni G (2002) Modulation of synaptic plasticity by stress and antidepressants. *Bipolar Disorders* **4**: 166–182.

Reid IC, Stewart CA (2001) How antidepressants work: new perspectives on the pathophysiology of depressive disorder. *Br J Psychiatry* **178**: 299–303.

Riemann D, Berger M, Voderholzer U (2001) Sleep and depression—results from psychological studies: an overview. *Biol Psychology* **57**: 67–103.

Rowan MJ, Anwyl R, Xu L (1998) Stress and long-term synaptic depression. *Mol Psychiatry* **3**: 472–464.

Rupniak NMJ, Kramer MS (1999) Discovery of the antidepressant and anti-emetic efficacy of substance P receptor (NK1) antagonists. *TIPS* **20**: 485–490.

Santarelli L, Gobbi G, Debs PC, et al (2001) Genetic and pharmacological disruption of neurokinin 1 receptor function decreases anxiety-related behaviors and increases serotonergic function. *Proc Natl Acad Sci USA* **98**: 1912–1917.

Sapolsky RM (2000) The possibility of neurotoxicity in the hippocampus in major depression: a primer on neuron death. *Biol Psychiatry* **48**: 755–765.

Sheline Y, Sang M, Mintum M, et al (1999) Depression duration but not age predicts hippocampal volume loss in medical healthy women with recurrent major depression. *J Neurosci* **19**: 5034.

Shors T, Gallegos R, Breindl A (1997) Transient and persistent consequences of acute stress and long-term potentiation (LTP), synaptic efficacy, theta rhythms and bursts in area CA 1 of the hippocampus. *Synapse* **26**: 209–217.

Smith GS, Dewey SL, Brodie JD (1997) Serotonergic modulation of dopamine measured with (11C)raclopride and PET in normal human subjects. *Am J Psychiatry* **154**: 490–496.

Smith GS, Reynolds CF, Pollock B, et al (1999) Cerebral glucose metabolic response to combined total sleep deprivation and antidepressant treatment in geriatric depression. *Am J Psychiatry* **156**: 683–689.

Stout SC, Owens MJ, Nemeroff CB (2001) Neurokinin1 receptor antagonists as potential antidepressants. *Annu Rev Pharmacol Toxicol* **41**: 877–906.

Szegedi A, Hillert A, Wetzel H, et al (1997) Pramipexole, a dopamine agonist, in major depression: antidepressant effects and tolerability in an open-label study with multiple doses. *Clin Neuropharmacol* **20**: S36–S45.

Weninger SC, Dunn AJ, Muglia LJ, et al (1999) Stress-induced behaviors require the corticotropin-releasing hormone (CRH) receptor, but not CRH. *Proc Natl Acad Sci USA* **96**: 8283–8288.

Winsberg ME, Sachs N, Tate DL, et al (2000) Decreased dorsolateral prefrontal N-acetyl aspartate in bipolar disorders. *Biol Psychiatry* **47**: 475–481.

Wolkowitz OM, Reus VI, Chan T, et al (1999) Antiglucocorticoid treatment of depression: double-blind ketoconazole. *Biol Psychiatry* **45**: 1070–1074.

Xu L, Anwyl R, Rowan MJ (1997) Behavioral stress facilitates the induction of long-term depression in the hippocampus. *Nature* **387**: 497–500.

Zangen A, Nakash R, Overstreet DH, et al (2001) Association between depressive behavior and absence of serotonin-dopamine interaction in the nucleus acumbens. *Psychopharmacol* **155**: 434–439.

Zobel AW, Yassouridis A, Frieboes RM, et al (1999) Cortisol response to the combined dexamethasone-CRH test predicts medium-term outcome in patients with remitted depression. *Am J Psychiatry* **156**: 949–951.

Zobel AW, Nickel T, Kunzel HE, et al (2000) Effects of the high-affinity corticotropin-releasing hormone receptor 1 antagonist R121919 in major depression: the first 20 patients treated. *J Psychiatr Res* **34**: 171–181.

chapter 3

Genetics of unipolar depression

Subodh Dave, Ian Jones and Nick Craddock

Introduction

Depression is a common psychiatric disorder with a lifetime prevalence as high as 12% in men and 25% in women. A recent review by the World Bank has suggested that by 2020 depression is likely to be second only to ischaemic heart disease as a cause of global health burden (Murray and Lopez, 1996). Depression has been known to run in families since ancient times. Hippocrates, in ancient Greece, had noted the parent-to-child transmission of melancholia. More recent family studies have provided further evidence for this fact. Twin studies and adoption studies have helped to clarify the relative contribution of genetic and environmental factors in the causation of unipolar depression and recent advances in molecular genetics now provide the tools needed to identify genes influencing susceptibility.

Identifying susceptibility genes for depression will pinpoint biochemical pathways involved in pathogenesis, facilitate development of more effective, better targeted treatments and offer opportunities for improving the validity of diagnosis and classification. As is the case for all common familial disorders, there are a number of challenges for genetic investigations—these include: (a) integrating lifetime experience of illness into meaningful diagnostic categories (or dimensions)—attention must be paid to validity as well as reliability, (b) variable age at onset of illness, (c) uncertainty over mode of inheritance, (d) variation in the (poorly understood) non-genetic risk factors, (e) possible secular changes in illness (eg birth cohort effects) (Gershon et al, 1987; Klerman, 1988), and (f) the requirement for large samples. However, clinical and statistical methods have been, and continue to be, developed that address all of these issues. The interested reader will find a more detailed discussion in Jones et al (2002) and Craddock and Owen (1996).

To date, many fewer molecular genetic linkage and association studies have been conducted for unipolar depression than is the case for bipolar disorder and schizophrenia. In this review, we first present the extensive empirical evidence for an important genetic contribution to unipolar depression. We go on to outline the molecular work to date and then consider the way forward in the future and the likely implications.

Classical studies

Epidemiology

Depression is characterized by low mood, anhedonia and disturbances in sleep and appetite. Depression has been classified in a number of ways, such as (a) endogenous and reactive, (b) psychotic and neurotic and, (c) primary (arising *de novo*) and secondary (occurring secondary to another disorder). Current classification systems such as ICD-10 or DSM-IV, however, use the bipolar/unipolar dichotomy to distinguish manic-depressive illness from depression. The current review deals exclusively with unipolar depression. Readers interested in the genetics of bipolar disorder will find extensive reviews in Craddock and Jones (1999) and Jones et al (2002).

Incidence and prevalence

Annual incidence of unipolar depression has been estimated to be 0.2–0.5% for women and 0.08–0.2% for men. Prevalence rates vary according to diagnostic criteria, methodology and sample employed. The large US multicentric Epidemiological Catchment Area (ECA) study reported a lifetime prevalence of DSM-IIIR major depression of 6%. The US National Comorbidity Survey, however, estimated a higher lifetime prevalence of 17.1%, with 10.3% of the population experiencing a major depressive episode in the preceding 12 months (Kessler et al, 1994).

Gender differences in prevalence
One consistent finding revealed by epidemiological studies is the gender difference in prevalence rates. The rate of unipolar disorder for women is about twice that for men—21.3% and 12.7%, respectively, in the US National Comorbidity Survey (Kessler et al, 1994). This high prevalence rate in the face of a low incidence rate is indicative of the chronicity of depression.

Affective disorder patients form a high proportion of users of mental health services and display high morbidity and mortality, with up to 15% of patients eventually committing suicide. Treatments, although generally effective, have been associated with undesirable side-effects and are not effective in all patients. Moreover, pathogenesis remains poorly understood. Identification of underlying genetic mechanisms promises not only a better understanding of aetiology but also safer and more effective treatments.

Family studies of unipolar disorder
Demonstration of familial aggregation by family studies is necessary but not sufficient to provide evidence of genetic causation. Family studies also help in understanding the mode of transmission based on observed patterns of disease expression in the family (eg autosomal dominant or recessive, etc). One can also compare the degree of heterogeneity in the expression of the disease—important in a complex and heterogeneous disorder such as depression.

Relative risk
Essentially, family studies estimate the relative risk among relatives of an affected proband compared to the population from which they were selected or compared to the relatives of a suitable control. Most recent studies of depression have defined relative risk as the ratio of risk of illness in first degree relatives of unipolar probands, to the risk in first degree relatives of controls.

Evidence of familial aggregation was provided even by the earliest family studies of mood disorder, which did not make the bipolar/ unipolar distinction (Tsuang and Faraone, 1990). More recent studies have looked at affective disorders in the relatives of depressed probands. Earlier studies, although supporting the familial aggregation of major affective disorders did not employ control groups. In the past 25 years, there have been 10 rigorous studies using controls. All these studies have demonstrated an increased relative risk in first degree relatives of probands with depression. There is no evidence, however, to suggest that first degree relatives of unipolar probands are at substantially increased risk of bipolar illness (McGuffin and Katz, 1989).

The relative risk has been reported to vary from 1.5 to 20 but most studies support a figure of 1.5 to 3. Figure 3.1 shows the distribution of estimates of relative risk of unipolar depression in first degree relatives of unipolar probands for the controlled family studies of unipolar depression. These studies varied in their methodology, which may account for some of the variation in the results. For example, studies have employed either Feighner, DSM-III, or SADS-RDC diagnostic criteria; only some used age correction procedures and some employed screened (ie 'super-normal') controls.

Gershon et al's earlier (1975) study reported a very high relative risk of 20. This study consisted of only 16 unipolar probands and reported a rather low prevalence of 0.7% for unipolar depression in the relatives of controls. A later sample from the same group (Gershon et al, 1982) reported a prevalence rate of 5.8% for depression in the relatives of controls, resulting in a much-reduced relative risk of 2.9. Farmer et al's (2000) elegant study reports a relative risk of 10. Again, the high relative risk in the Farmer study reflects the very low rate of depression in the controls, which in turn probably reflects the ascertainment through siblings screened for health (ie a 'supernormal' control group).

Age of onset
Family studies of unipolar depression reveal another consistent finding—that earlier onset is associated with increased familiality. This finding shown in earlier studies reviewed by Tsuang and Faraone (1990)

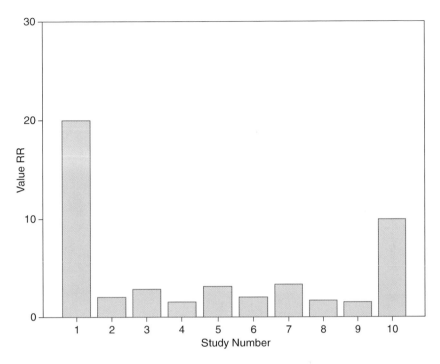

Figure 3.1 *Controlled family studies of unipolar disorder.*
'Value RR' refers to the value of the estimated relative risk in each study. All
studies have a relative risk of greater than one and therefore provide evidence
of familial aggregation of unipolar disorder. Study numbers: (1) Gershon et al,
1975, (2) Tsuang et al, 1980, (3) Gershon et al, 1982, (4) Winokur et al,
1982, (5) Weissman et al, 1984a, (6) Maier et al, 1993,
(7) Heun and Maier, 1993, (8) Winokur et al, 1995, (9) Kendler et al, 1998
(10) Farmer et al, 2000.

has been replicated in most, albeit not all modern controlled studies
that have examined the effect of age of onset in probands and the risk of
unipolar depression in relatives. Sullivan et al (2000) provide a comprehensive review of these studies.

Gershon et al (1975) reported a trend, that did not reach significance,
for an early age of onset to be associated with a greater risk of depression
in relatives, which was later supported by Weissman et al (1984b),
whereas Weissman et al (1982) reported no age effect. A recent controlled
family history study demonstrated increased familiality in childhood

onset depression compared with adult onset (Kovacs et al, 1997). However, the age relationship is not simple and there is evidence that *prepubertal* (ie very early) onset depression may have a distinct, perhaps less genetic aetiology (Harrington et al, 1997).

Gender effect

Family studies have also revealed a gender effect in the risk of unipolar depression. Most studies report a much higher rate of depression in women than for men (reviewed in McGuffin and Katz, 1989). Winokur et al (1982) reported that female relatives of both unipolar probands and controls were significantly more likely to have depression than male relatives. Similarly, Weisman et al (1984a) reported a higher rate of depression in female relatives. The usual multiplier (for women compared to men) is $\times$ 2 and seems to appear at puberty (Angold and Worthman, 1993). The reason for this disparity is unclear and could be due to biological or psychosocial factors, or indeed, both. Part of the difference may be artefactual—men may be less likely to admit to having depressive symptoms and also more likely to forget previous symptoms that they have experienced. The sex of the *proband*, however, does not appear to affect rates of affective illness amongst the relatives of probands with unipolar depression (Heun and Maier, 1993).

The depressive spectrum

Another explanation for the gender difference in risk has been the concept of depressive spectrum and pure depressive disease put forth by Winokur et al (Winokur, 1997). Winokur has explained the lower prevalence in men by suggesting that they may have depressive spectrum disease, for example, alcohol dependence, which is considered to be a depressive equivalent. However, the division of families into those with 'pure' depressive disease and depressive spectrum disease has not been supported by other family studies (Merikangas, 1990).

Twin studies

Although family studies can demonstrate familiality, the cause of this familial aggregation can only be determined by twin and adoption studies. Early twin studies did not distinguish between bipolar and unipolar illness but supported the involvement of genes in broadly defined mood disorders (reviewed by Tsuang and Faraone, 1990). Comparisons between studies of unipolar disorder are hampered by the lack of common ascertainment criteria and diagnostic methodologies. Despite this, most studies agree that although the genetic basis for unipolar depression is not as strong as that for bipolar disorder, there remains substantial evidence of a major genetic contribution to causation (reviewed by McGuffin and Katz, 1989). Most, but not all, point to a substantial genetic effect.

Unipolar depression is much more common than bipolar disorder and larger twin samples are relatively more straightforward to assemble. The use of twin registries and biometrical model fitting to twin data (Kendler, 1993) are important advances in methodology and the interesting recent developments include examination of subtypes of depression, such as puerperal (Treloar et al, 1999), premenstrual (Kendler et al, 1998), or seasonal depression (Madden et al, 1996).

Concordance rates

Reported concordance rate estimates have been in the region of 20% for dizygotic twins and 40% for monozygotic twins, consistent across studies such as McGuffin's hospital-based case register study and Kendler's Swedish population-based study (McGuffin et al, 1996; Kendler et al, 1993a). A duration of longest episode of less than 13 months, multiple episodes and an endogenous rather than neurotic pattern of symptoms tended to predict a higher monozygotic:dizygotic concordance rate (McGuffin et al, 1996). Heritability estimates have been in the range of 37–75%. Genetic and unique environmental factors have been reported to contribute substantially to this heritability while the role of shared environment appears to be negligible. Sullivan et al (2000) in their metanalysis of five twin studies estimated the heritability of unipolar depression to be 37% (95% CI = 31–42%) with a minimal contribution of environmental effects common to siblings (point estimate = 0%, 95% CI = 0–5%) and substantial individual specific environmental effects (point estimate = 63%, 95% CI = 58–67%).

McGuffin et al, in their Maudlsey Hospital Twin Register study, obtained much higher estimates of heritability between 48% and 75% depending on the assumed population risk. Kendler's *community*-based study, however, revealed much lower heritability rates (33–45%). Hospital-based samples are more likely to be severe and therefore, possibly more familial. Furthermore, reliability of diagnoses may be higher in clinical than in community ascertained samples. (In standard twin model studies, poor reliability is known to confound with higher estimates of unique environment effects.) Interestingly, when the reliability of assessment in the community-based Virginia twin registry was corrected for by multiple assessments of twins, estimates of the heritability of major depression increased substantially from around 40% to approximately 70% (Kendler et al, 1993b).

Twin studies and comorbidity
Depression shows significant comorbidity with other psychiatric disorders, especially anxiety disorders, alcohol dependence, etc. Observed correlation between two or more disorders can be due to a variety of factors, such as additive gene effect, unique environment or familial environment. The relative contributions of each of these factors can be determined using multivariate twin models. Kendler et al's Virginia Twin Registry studies (1992) found that the vulnerability to depression and generalized anxiety disorder could be explained by shared genetic mechanisms similar to depression and phobias while the vulnerability factors for alcohol dependence seemed to be disorder-specific and distinct to those for depression. Similarly, Thapar and McGuffin (1997) examined the comorbidity of maternally rated depressive and anxiety symptoms in a sample of twin pairs aged 8 to 16 years and found evidence of shared genetic vulnerability. Part of the comorbidity, however, was explained by unique environmental factors thus demonstrating the influence of specific genetic effects on depressive symptomatology

Gender effect in twin studies
Twin studies have also looked at gender effects. Three studies (Kendler et al, 1995, 1999; McGuffin et al, 1996) have examined the genetic risk

factors for major depression separately in men and women and are consistent in suggesting that they are of equal importance. Two studies, however, have included opposite sex pairs, thus allowing examination of the issue of whether the genes themselves are the same in both sexes. Kendler et al's moderate sized Swedish twin study employed a questionnaire-based assessment. They found that the best fitting model estimated the genetic risk factors to be the same in both sexes (Kendler et al, 1995). A larger study, however, employing the direct interview of probands suggested that men and women share some *but not all* of their genes for major depression (Kendler et al, 1999).

Subtypes of depression and twin studies
Studies employing twin samples have also begun to address issues regarding clinical subtypes of depression. Kendler and colleagues (1996) employed latent class analysis in the identification of three clinically significant depressive syndromes (mild typical depression, atypical depression and severe typical depression) that were at least partially distinct from a clinical, longitudinal and familial genetic perspective. There is evidence that the melancholic or endogenous form of depressive illness identifies a subset of individuals with a particularly high familial liability to depressive illness (McGuffin et al, 1996). Multiple episodes may indicate stronger genetic vulnerability (McGuffin et al, 1996) but in the Virginia Twin sample the best-fitting model indicated an inverted U-shaped function with greatest genetic determination for those with seven to nine lifetime episodes of major depression. (Kendler et al, 1999).

Adoption studies

Adoption studies provide a useful design in distinguishing between genetic and environmental contributions to causation. However, there have been very few adoption studies of depression. Cadoret (1978) showed that 38% of adopted away offspring of patients with affective illness developed mood disorder as opposed to only 9% of controls' adopted away children. The study of Wender et al (1986) from Denmark, again demonstrated the involvement of genetic factors in the aetiology of affective disorder. It found an increased risk of both unipolar depression and suicide in the biological relatives of adoptees with affective illness compared to both their adoptive relatives and the relatives of matched control adoptees. The Swedish study of von Knorring and colleagues (1983) investigated four groups, the biological and adoptive parents of probands with affective disorder and the biological and adoptive parents of matched control adoptees. In complete contrast to the findings of other studies, no significant differences in the rates of affective illness were found between any of the groups. However, the diagnoses of depression in this study were based on indirect sources, such as evidence of clinical treatment, which may underestimate the true prevalence.

Mode of inheritance

Although the above studies point to a significant genetic role in the aetiology of depression, the mode of transmission remains unclear. Unlike bipolar disorder, there have been few claims of probable 'single gene' families. Model fitting and segregation analyses have also focused primarily on bipolar disorder. Consistent findings have not emerged—although a recent study using complex segregation analysis of 50 pedigrees that include a proband with early onset recurrent depressive disorder suggested a major transmissible effect (Marazita et al, 1997). However, caution is required in interpreting the report because this methodology has important limitations when applied to complex phenotypes, such as depression, as it is usually unable to distinguish between single major gene effects and more complex oligogenic epistatic models (Craddock et al, 1997).

Gene–environment interaction

It is *unlikely* that two subtypes of depression exist—one mainly genetic and the other mainly non-genetic (Andrew et al, 1998). In practice, most researchers have adopted the multifactorial model, which assumes an interaction and/or co-action of multiple genes and environmental factors. This model has the advantages of being simple and easy to use with observed data. However, being so loosely defined makes formal testing rather difficult. This interaction may be non-linear (those with pre-existing genetic vulnerability develop the disorder when exposed to the relevant environment). Alternatively, genes may act more subtly by altering, in a linear graded manner, one's sensitivity to depressogenic stressful life events (Kendler, 1998). Kendler et al's (1995) study provides some support for the latter hypothesis. In this study of female twins, they found that, consistent with the model of 'genetic control of sensitivity to the environment', those so genetically predisposed were twice as likely to develop depression when faced with a severe life event than those with low genetic risk.

Another genetic mechanism may be the control of exposure to a depressogenic environment so that those who are genetically vulnerable are more likely to experience depressogenic life events! This hypothesis is supported by McGuffin's study (1988) which found not only an increased rate of depression among relatives of depressed probands but also an increased reporting of life events. A number of subsequent twin or family studies have suggested that familial and/or genetic factors can influence an individual's risk for being exposed to severe adverse life events. Farmer et al's study (2000), however, found that high correlation between sibs for life events was explained by shared events, such as death or illness of a parent. This is an area that is receiving increasing attention as it is now appreciated that a complete account of the aetiology of a complex disorder, such as depression, cannot be obtained without an understanding of the complex interaction of genetic and environmental factors.

Summary of classical genetic studies of unipolar depression

Family studies provide consistent evidence for the adage that 'depression runs in families'. Twin and adoption studies point to genes as an important cause of this familiality. These studies also demonstrate a graduation of risk for depression between various classes of relatives with the monozygotic co-twin showing highest risk, through first degree relative to unrelated member of the general population showing the lowest risk.

Table 3.1 Approximate lifetime rates of unipolar depression in various classes of relatives of unipolar probands

Degree of relationship to unipolar proband	Lifetime risk of unipolar depression
Monozygotic twin	30–50%
First degree relative (including dizygotic twin)	10–30%
General population/unrelated	5–15%

The above figures must be considered as 'ball park' estimates—there are wide variations reported in the literature. These variations result from differences in definition of affection status, population studied, sampling frame and study design. Heritability estimates vary in the range of 35–75% with higher estimates for illnesses that are more severe and more reliably diagnosed.

Table 3.1 shows the approximate relative risk in different classes of relatives of a person with unipolar disorder. These figures only provide a general guide, as producing exact figures for depression is extremely difficult considering the wide variation in estimates in different studies and populations.

Molecular genetic studies

Molecular genetic approaches have achieved great success in discovering the mutations which lead to simple (Mendelian) genetic diseases. The challenge that remains is to develop methodologies that will uncover susceptibility genes for *complex* diseases. Conceptually, molecular genetic studies can be divided into linkage and association studies. The two main corresponding approaches are positional and candidate gene approaches. Both approaches involve the use of genetic markers. Genetic markers are DNA variants that have a specific known chromosomal location and are polymorphic, that is, have at least two alleles with a gene frequency of at least 1% in the population. They are used to track the chromosomal location of putative disease-susceptibility genes.

Linkage is based on the principle that two genes or loci that lie in close proximity on a chromosome are likely to be transmitted to the offspring together. Linkage studies are thus based on an association between alleles at a genetic marker and putative disease genes *within families*. The genetic marker need not be aetiologically related to the disease. This is a *positional* method—an approach that assumes no knowledge of disease pathophysiology but determines the broad chromosomal locations of susceptibility genes, usually by linkage studies.

Association studies, in contrast, are usually used to compare the prevalence of a genetic marker (alleles at a polymorphism in a gene of interest usually identified on the basis of postulated pathophysiology eg monoamine oxidase-A gene in depression) in those with depression and depression-free matched controls. Thus, unlike linkage studies, which are carried out within families, association studies are usually population-based. The candidate gene approach, thus involves the investigator making educated guesses at what genes may be involved in the pathophysiology of a condition and then testing the involvement of these genes by linkage, or more commonly, association studies. In practice, both positional and candidate approaches are often combined (Collins, 1995; Craddock and Owen, 1996).

Linkage studies

There have been few linkage studies of unipolar disorder alone—far fewer than for bipolar disorder. In the premolecular era, several small linkage studies were reported using classical markers, such as blood groups or HLA type, but there were no consistent positive findings (reviewed in Tsuang and Faraone, 1990). Very few linkage studies have been reported using DNA markers and those that have been done have been hampered by small sample size and an unsystematic approach restricted to usage of a few genetic markers often confined to candidate regions. Positive findings have not yet emerged. A key problem has been the likely sample size required—considering that genetic effect sizes are far smaller compared to bipolar disorder, larger samples will be needed to identify genes of pathogenic relevance. Our centre is currently engaged in a large international multicentre sibling pair linkage study of 1200 siblings affected by recurrent depressive disorder which will, it is hoped, address this issue.

Association studies

Association studies have a significant advantage over linkage studies—they are generally able to detect much smaller effect sizes and are also more robust with respect to genetic heterogeneity (Risch and Merikangas, 1996). They provide a powerful tool in the investigation of complex genetic traits, both to follow up regions of interest from linkage studies (by systematic linkage disequilibrium mapping and positional candidate studies) and for pure positional candidate studies. The candidate gene approach is potentially very powerful, particularly when used within the context of a VAPSE (Variation Affecting Protein Sequence or Expression) paradigm. This is a two-stage process in which systematic polymorphism detection is first conducted across the gene of interest followed by association studies in disease comparison samples.

However, as in any case–control study, problems can arise from inadequate matching due to sampling errors or population stratification. Family-based association methods overcome this problem to an extent. A number of statistical approaches have been developed to be used in this design but the transmission disequilibrium test (TDT) is perhaps the most popular. Methodological issues relating to association studies are discussed in Craddock et al (2001).

Candidate genes examined to date

Although problems of population stratification receive considerable attention, perhaps the major problem with candidate gene association studies involves the choice of candidates. Good candidate gene studies depend critically on the choice of good candidates—this inevitably depends on the current understanding of disease pathophysiology, which for depression is relatively underdeveloped. To date, most candidate gene studies have focused on neurotransmitter systems that are influenced by medications used in clinical management of the disorders such as polymorphisms within genes encoding receptors or proteins and enzymes involved in the metabolism, reuptake or action of dopamine, serotonin (5-HT) and noradrenaline (Jones et al, 2001).

Several candidate genes involved in neurotransmitter systems have been examined in unipolar depression including MAOA (monoamine oxidase-A), tyrosine hydroxylase, COMT (catechol-*o*-methyl transferase) and 5-HTT (serotonin transporter or SERT). No consistent findings have emerged, although some studies have suggested that serotonin transporter gene polymorphisms may be associated with depression—see for example, Collier et al (1996) and Ogilvie et al (1996).

Candidate genes for future study

The search is now being widened to more novel candidate genes based on hypothesized involvement in pathogenesis. This will allow testing of more sophisticated models of pathogenesis than has been the case to date. To illustrate this point, we briefly discuss some areas of developing interest.

Interferon

One area of interest is psychoneuroimmunology. Immune dysfunction has been well documented in major depression (Maes, 1999). Interferon (IFN) is a cytokine produced by lymphocytes and macrophages. IFN-induced depression has been reported in a range of conditions, such as hepatitis B and C, leukaemia and melanoma, with rates ranging from 0% to 50% (Bonaccorso et al, 2000, 2001; Zdilar et al, 2000). IFN modulates the expression of cytokines, depletes tryptophan by inducing indoleamine 2,3-dioxygenase (Taylor and Feng, 1991) and also affects binding at serotonin receptors (Abe et al, 1999). IFN may also increase the expression of SERT. It is postulated that IFN, by augmenting SERT activity, may lead to the depletion of synaptic serotonin and thus cause depression. Genes coding for IFN or IFN-receptor genes are therefore interesting candidates.

Oxytocin and vasopressin

Another major area of interest is the stress–mood interface and the psychoneuroendocrine systems. There is compelling evidence from a variety of studies that implicates early life stress in the genesis of depression in adult life (Heim and Nemeroff 1999, 2001). Preclinical animal studies have shown that adverse early environment, such as maternal separation, is associated with persistent behavioural and neurobiological changes that may contribute to increased vulnerability to depression and anxiety disorders. Oxytocin and vasopressin are key neurotransmitters mediating attachment and social bonding, and genes involved in their action may thus prove to be significant candidates for depression.

Candidates may be selected for phenotypic subtypes of depression

A depressive subphenotype that has been receiving attention is seasonal affective disorder (SAD). With its demonstrated familial aggregation (Allen et al, 1993) and possible involvement of SERT and serotonin receptor 2A gene (Sher, 2001), it may be an ideal phenotype to focus on. Plausible candidates for study in this subphenotype include the genes involved in biological rhythms, such as clock genes. Similarly, focusing on treatment-responsive depression, or perhaps more specifically, lithium-responsive depression, may be a promising strategy providing opportunities to examine a more homogeneous phenotypic subtype and investigate a restricted set of focused hypotheses regarding genetic susceptibility.

Implications for the future

Research implications

1 *Better understanding of pathogenesis*   Identification of susceptibility markers can be expected in the near future following recent developments in molecular genetics, in particular the Human Genome Project. Further developments in laboratory and statistical methodology and collaborations with disciplines, such as endocrinology, immunology and neuropsychology, will enhance our understanding of the pathophysiology of depression.

2 *Better diagnostic validity*   The promised availability of genetic markers of susceptibility raises the tantalizing prospect of a biologically driven classification with better diagnostic validity.

3 *Better animal models*   Identification of susceptibility genes will help

devise gene 'knock-out' and other models of depression that will aid development of novel treatments.

4 *Neuropsychopharmacology* Identification of susceptibility genes for depression will lead to the development of targeted treatments. Moreover, identification of genes that predispose to specific side-effects will also lead to the design of safer drugs and more individualized treatments. Identification of specific subtypes of depression will also lead to earlier recognition and better treatment.

5 *Identification of the role of environmental factors* A common misconception about molecular genetics is that it is likely to lead to improvements only in biological treatments. By identifying vulnerable genotypes it will be also possible to identify negative environmental factors that precipitate or even predispose to depression. This holds out the promise of preventative and therapeutic *environmental* treatments in vulnerable individuals.

6 *Better understanding of 'normal' emotions* Depressive symptoms show considerable overlap with everyday human emotions. A better understanding of depression also promises a better understanding of 'normal emotions', such as happiness, which has been shown to be genetically influenced (Lykken and Tellegen, 1996).

Ethical implications

The rapidity of developments in the field of molecular genetics has raised concerns about ethical and psychosocial issues. Important issues (which are encountered in *all* fields of medicine in the developing molecular age) include:

1 *Confidentiality* Current concerns include issues of confidentiality in research and clinical practice especially when dealing with large families.

2 *Discrimination* Lingering fears from the eugenic movement have caused concern about identifying genetic susceptibility markers. Indeed, it raises complex issues about insurance and discrimination at work (Long, 2002). The potential availability of crude commercial self-testing genetic kits has further muddied the waters. It is however, important to point out that modern genetic research is well regulated

and follows strict ethical guidelines. This is an evolving area and doubtless needs continuing societal debate.

3 *Altered doctor–patient relationship* Knowledge of genetic (and other familial) risk factors about an individual patient provide information about risk of illness in other members of the patient's family. This raises issues as to what (if any) responsibility the physician has towards communicating such risks, and offering potentially beneficial interventions, to family members who did not originally seek medical advice or help.

Clinical implications

In addition to the obvious and direct consequences that follow from several of the issues mentioned in the preceding two sections, clinical implications include:

1 *Family history* A substantial and robust body of evidence demonstrates familial aggregation of depression and the importance of genes in influencing susceptibility. In clinical practice care should be taken to elicit a thorough family history and obtain as much detail as possible about the illness in relatives of the patient. This will inform diagnosis and management and set the context for discussions with the patient and family.

2 *Genetic counselling* Currently, empirical estimates of risk derived from previous family and twin studies can be used to provide information and counselling to those concerned about the risks to offspring and other family members—Figure 3.1 offers a useful albeit an approximate guide to the risks. At present, DNA tests are not helpful but it can be expected that they will become useful clinically when the most important susceptibility genes (and environmental risk factors) have been identified.

3 *Diagnosis and management* As the field develops, it can be expected that DNA testing will become a standard part of the clinical assessment procedure—as an adjunct to, *not a replacement for,* clinical examination. Such tests are likely to make direct and useful contributions to the diagnostic process and to targeting treatments.

Conclusion

Family, twin and adoption studies provide a compelling body of evidence that demonstrates the importance of genes in influencing susceptibility to unipolar major depression. The mode of inheritance is complex and almost certainly represents the interaction and/or co-action of multiple genes and environmental risk factors. Molecular genetic linkage and association studies are ongoing but no susceptibility gene has yet been robustly identified. It can be expected that genes that influence susceptibility to, and modify the course of, unipolar depression will be discovered over the next several years. This will have the potential to make a major impact in improving our understanding of disease pathogenesis, both genetic and environmental, and will contribute to improvements in diagnosis and risk prediction and to the development of more effective, better targeted treatments. The challenge to psychiatrists in the 21st century is to ensure that a revolution in understanding of the biology of mood disorder is translated into a revolution in clinical care. Our patients deserve nothing less.

References

Abe S, Hori T, Suzuki T (1999) Effects of chronic administration of interferon alpha A/D on serotonergic receptors in rat brain. *Neurochem Res* **24**: 359–363.

Allen JM, Lam RW, Remick, RA, Sadovnick AD (1993) Depressive symptoms and family history in seasonal and nonseasonal mood disorders. *Am J Psychiatry* **150**: 443–448.

Andrew M, McGuffin P, Katz R (1998) Genetic and non-genetic subtypes of major depressive disorder. *Br J Psychiatry* **152**: 775–782.

Angold A, Worthman CW (1993) Puberty onset of gender differences in rates of depression: a developmental, epidemiologic and neuroendocrine perspective. *J Affect Disord* **29**: 145–158.

Bonaccorso S, Meltzer H, Maes M (2000) Psychological and behavioural effects of interferons. *Curr Opin Psychiatry* **13**: 673–677.

Bonaccorso S, Puzella A, Marino V, et al (2001) Immunotherapy with interferon-alpha in patients affected by chronic hepatitis C induces an intercorrelated stimulation of the cytokine network and an increase in depressive and anxiety symptoms. *Psychiat Res* **105**: 45–55.

Cadoret R (1978) Evidence for genetic inheritance of primary affective disorder in adoptees. *Am J Psychiatry* **133**: 463–466.

Collier DA, Stober G, Li T, et al (1996) A novel functional polymorphism within the promoter of the serotonin transporter gene: possible role in susceptibility to affective disorder. *Mol Psychiatry* **1**: 453–460.

Collins FS (1995) Positional cloning moves from periditional to traditional. *Nat Genet* **9**: 347–350.

Craddock N, Jones I (1999) Genetics of bipolar disorder. *J Med Genet* **36**: 585–594.

Craddock N, Owen MJ (1996) Modern molecular genetic approaches to psychiatric disease. *Br Med Bull* **52**: 434–452.

Craddock N, Dave S, Greening J (2001) Association studies of bipolar disorder. *Bipolar Disord* **3**: 284–298.

Craddock N, Van Eerdewegh P, Reich T (1997) Single major locus models for bipolar disorder are implausible. *Am J Med Genet* **74**: 18.

Farmer AE, Williams J, Jones I (1994) Phenotypic definitions of psychotic illness for molecular genetic research. *Am J Med Genet (Neuropsychiat Genet)* **54**: 365–371.

Farmer AE, Harris T, Redman K, Sadler S, Mahmood A, McGuffin P (2000) Cardiff depression study: a sib-pair study of life events and familiality in major depression. *Br J Psychiatry* **176**: 150–155.

Gershon ES, Mark A, Cohen N, Belizon N, Baron M, Knobe KE (1975) Transmitted factors in the morbid risk of affective disorders: a controlled study. *J Psychiat Res* **12**: 283–299.

Gershon ES, Hamovit J, Guroff JJ, et al (1982) A family study of schizoaffective, bipolar I, bipolar II, unipolar, and normal control probands. *Arch Gen Psychiatry* **39**: 1157–1167.

Gershon ES, Hamovit JH, Guroff JJ, Nurnberger JI (1987) Birth-cohort changes in manic and depressive disorders in relatives of bipolar and schizoaffective patients. *Arch Gen Psychiatry* **44**: 314–319.

Harrington R, Rutter M, Weissman M, et al (1997) Psychiatric disorders in the relatives of depressed probands. I: comparison of pre-pubertal, adolescent and early adult onset cases. *J Affect Disord* **42**: 9–22.

Heim C, Nemeroff C (1999) The impact of early adverse experiences on brain systems involved in the pathophysiology of anxiety and affective disorders. *Biol Psychiatry* **46**: 1509–1522.

Heim C, Nemeroff C (2001) The role of childhood trauma on the neurobiology of mood and anxiety disorders in preclinical and clinical studies. *Biol Psychiatry* **49**: 1023–1039.

Heun R, Maier W (1993) The distinction of bipolar II disorder from bipolar I and recurrent unipolar depression: results of a controlled family study. *Acta Psychiat Scand* **87**: 279–284.

Jones I, Kent L, Craddock N (2001) Clinical implications of psychiatric genetics in the new millennium—nightmare or nirvana? *Psychiat Bull* **25**: 129–131.

Jones I, Kent L, Craddock N (2002) Genetics of affective disorders. In: McGuffin P, Owen M, Gottesman II M (eds), *Psychiatric genetics and genomics*. Oxford University Press.

Kendler KS (1993) Twin studies of psychiatric illness. Current status and future directions. *Arch Gen Psychiatry* **50**: 905–915.

Kendler KS (1998) Major depression and the environment: a psychiatric genetic perspective. *Pharmacopsychiatry* **31**: 5–9.

Kendler KS, Neale MC, Kessler RC, Heath AC, Eaves LJ (1992) Major depression and generalized anxiety disorder: same genes, (partly) different environments? *Arch Gen Psychiatry* **49**: 716–722.

Kendler KS, Pedersen N, Johnson L, Neale MC, Mathe AA (1993a) A pilot Swedish twin study of affective illness, including hospital- and population-ascertained subsamples. *Arch Gen Psychiatry* **50**: 699–706.

Kendler KS, Neale MC, Kessler RC, Heath AC, Eaves LJ (1993b) The lifetime history of major depression in women. Reliability of diagnosis and heritability. *Arch Gen Psychiatry* **50**: 863–870.

Kendler KS, Kessler RC, Walters EE, et al (1995) Stressful life events, genetic liability and onset of major depression in women. *Am J Psychiatry* **152**: 833–842.

Kendler KS, Eaves LJ, Walters EE, Neale MC, Heath AC, Kessler RC (1996) The identification and validation of distinct depressive syndromes in a population-based sample of female twins. *Arch Gen Psychiatry* **53**: 391–399.

Kendler KS, Karowski LM, Corey LA, Neale MC (1998) Longitudinal population based twin study of retrospectively reported premenstrual symptoms and lifetime major depression. *Am J Psychiatry* **155**: 1234–1240.

Kendler KS, Gardner CO, Prescott CA (1999) Clinical characteristics of major depression that predict risk of depression in relatives. *Arch Gen Psychiatry* **56**: 322–327.

Kessler RC, McGonagle KA, Zhao S, et al (1994) Lifetime and 12-month prevalence of DSM IIIR psychiatric disorders in the United States: results from the National Comorbidity Survey. *Arch Gen Psychiatry* **51**: 8–19.

Klerman GL (1988) The current age of youthful melancholia: Evidence for increase in depression among adolescents and young adults. *Br J Psychiatry* **152**: 4–14.

Kovacs M, Devlin B, Pollock M, Richards C, Mukerji P (1997) A controlled family history study of childhood-onset depressive disorder. *Arch Gen Psychiatry* **54**: 613–623.

Long K (2002) Genetic tests at work poses ethical dilemma. *San Francisco Chronicle* 3 March.

Lykken D, Tellegen A (1996) Happiness is a stochastic phenomenon. *Psychol Science* **7**: 186–189.

Madden PAF, Heath AC, Rosenthal NE, Martin NG (1996) Seasonal changes in mood and behavior—the role of genetic factors. *Arch Gen Psychiatry* **53**: 47–55.

Maes M (1999) Major depression and activation of the inflammatory response system. *Adv Exp Med Biol* **461**: 25–46.

Maier W, Lichtermann D, Minges J, et al (1993) Continuity and discontinuity of affective disorders and schizophrenia. Results of a controlled family. *Arch Gen Psychiatry* **50**: 871–883.

Marazita, ML, Neiswanger K, Cooper M, et al (1997) Genetic segregation analysis of early-onset recurrent unipolar depression. *Am J Hum Genet* **61**: 1370–1378.

McGuffin P, Katz R (1989) The genetics of depression and manic-depressive disorder. *Br J Psychiatry* **155**: 294–304.

McGuffin P, Katz R, Bebbington P (1988) The Camberwell Collaborative Study. III: Depression and adversity in the relatives of depressed probands. *Br J Psychiatry* **152**: 775–782.

McGuffin P, Katz R, Watkins S, Rutherford J (1996) A hospital-based twin register of the heritability of DSM-IV unipolar depression. *Arch Gen Psychiatry* **53**: 129–136.

Merikangas KR (1990) The genetic epidemiology of alcoholism. *Psychol Med* **20**: 11–22.

Murray CJL, Lopez AD (eds) (1996) *The global burden of disease: A comprehensive assessment of mortality, injuries, and risk factors in 1990 and projected to 2020.* Harvard School of Public Health and the World Health Organization.

Ogilvie AD, Battersby S, Bubb VJ, et al (1996) Polymorphism in serotonin transporter gene associated with susceptibility to major depression. *Lancet* **347**: 731–733.

Risch N, Merikangas K (1996) The future of genetic studies of complex human diseases. *Science* **273**: 1516–1517.

Sher L (2001) Genetic studies of seasonal affective disorder and seasonality. *Comprehen Psychiatry* **42**: 105–110.

Sullivan PF, Neale MC, Kendler KS (2000) Genetic epidemiology of major depression: review and meta-analysis. *Am J Psychiatry* **157**: 1552–1562.

Taylor MW, Feng G (1991) Relationship between interferon-gamma, indoleamine 2,3, dioxygenase and tryptophan catabolism. *FASEB J* **5**: 2516–2522.

Thapar A, McGuffin P (1997) Anxiety and depressive symptoms in childhood—a genetic study of comorbidity. *J Child Psychol Psychiatry* **38**: 651–656.

Treolar SA, Martin NG, Bucholz KK, Madden PAF, Heath AC (1999) Genetic influences on post-natal depressive symptoms: findings from an Australian twin sample. *Psychol Med* **29**: 645–654.

Tsuang MT, Winokur G, Crowe RR (1980) Morbidity risks of schizophrenia and affective disorders amongst first degree relatives of patients with schizophrenia, mania, depression and surgical conditions. *Br J Psychiatry* **137**: 497–504.

Tsuang MT, Faraone SV (1990) *The genetics of mood disorders.* Baltimore, MA: The Johns Hopkins University Press.

Von Knorring AL, Cloninger CR, Bohman M, Sigvardsson S (1983) An adoption study of depressive disorders and substance abuse. *Arch Gen Psychiatry* **40**: 943–950.

Weissman MM, Kidd KK, Prusoff BA (1982) Variability in rates of affective disorders in relatives of depressed and normal probands. *Arch Gen Psychiatry* **39**: 1397–1403.

Weissman MM, Gershon ES, Kidd KK, et al (1984a) Psychiatric disorders in the relatives of probands with affective disorders. *Arch Gen Psychiatry* **41**: 13–21.

Weissman MM, Wickramaratne P, Merikangas KR, et al (1984b) Onset of major depression in early adulthood. *Arch Gen Psychiatry* **41**: 1136–1143.

Wender PH, Kety SS, Rosenthal D, Schlusinger F, Ortmann J, Lunde I (1986) Psychiatric disorders in the biological and adoptive families of adopted individuals with affective disorders. *Arch Gen Psychiatry* **43**: 923–929.

Winokur G (1997) All roads lead to depression: clinically homogeneous, etiologically heterogeneous. *J Affect Disord* **45**: 97–108.

Winokur G, Tsuang MT, Crowe RR (1982) The Iowa 500—affective disorder in relatives of manic and depressed patients. *Am J Psychiatry* **139**: 209–212.

Winokur G, Coryell W, Keller M, Endicott J, Leon A (1995) A family study of manic-depressive (bipolar I) disease. Is it a distinct illness separable from primary unipolar depression? *Arch Gen Psychiatry* **52**: 367–373.

Zdilar D, Franco-Bronson K, Buchler N, Locala JA, Younossi Z (2000) Hepatitis C, interferon alpha and depression. *Hepatology* **31**: 1207–1211.

chapter 4

Developments in antidepressants

Stephen M Stahl, Meghan M Grady and Robert Niculescu

1 What, if any, are the advantages of dual mechanisms of action over single mechanism of action in the treatment of depression?
2 What are the differences in efficacy and side-effect profiles between specific types of antidepressants and how can these differences be exploited?
3 Are herbal and natural products effective treatments for depression?
4 How can treatment be modified to suit women across the life cycle?
5 What new mechanisms of action are being explored for the treatment of depression?

Classical antidepressants: MAOIs and TCAs

Classically, pharmacological treatment of depression has consisted of agents that affect neurotransmission involving three monoamines: serotonin, norepinephrine, and/or dopamine. From the 1950s through the 1980s, two classes of agents, the monoamine oxidase inhibitors (MAOIs) and the tricyclic antidepressants (TCAs), dominated the treatment of depression. MAOIs increase levels of serotonin (5-HT), norepinephrine (NE) and dopamine (DA) by blocking their metabolism by monoamine oxidase (MAO). Thus, they are non-selective. The original MAOIs also have irreversible effects, that is, they bind permanently to MAO, inactivating the enzyme until it is metabolized. TCAs exert their therapeutic actions through blockade of norepinephrine and/or serotonin reuptake.

While these two classes of agents are clearly effective in reducing depressive symptoms, including in those patients experiencing severe depression, their side-effect profiles include serious and potentially lethal effects on the cardiovascular system, as well as less dangerous but still troublesome side-effects such as sedation, dry mouth and weight gain. Newer agents, while not shown to be more efficacious than the classical drugs, are nonetheless more widely used primarily due to their less serious adverse effects and better tolerated day-to-day side-effect profiles.

SSRIs

In the 1980s, a new class of agents called the serotonin selective reuptake inhibitors (SSRIs) was introduced. These agents, unlike the classical drugs, selectively target the serotonin system, increasing 5-HT levels with little direct effect on other neurotransmitter systems. There are five individual drugs within this class: fluoxetine, sertraline, paroxetine, fluvoxamine, and citalopram. A sixth SSRI, escitalopram, has recently been approved in the US and is pending worldwide approval. This antidepressant is the *S* stereoisomer of racemic citalopram. These agents appear to be as efficacious as the older drugs in controlled studies, and offer advantages in terms of simplicity of dosing and side-effect profiles. MAOIs and TCAs are lethal in overdose, while the SSRIs generally are not as single agents. Furthermore, SSRIs do not have powerful anticholinergic effects and do not cause cardiac toxicity. The SSRIs have also been shown to be useful for the treatment of many disorders as well as major depression, such as anxiety disorders (generalized anxiety disorder, post-traumatic stress disorder, obsessive-compulsive disorder, social anxiety disorder and panic disorder), bulimia, premenstrual dysphoric disorder (PMDD), migraine, and dysthymia. These drugs may have such a wide therapeutic profile because they are selective *to* the serotonin system but not selective *within* the serotonin system, meaning that they affect serotonin levels at receptors in all parts of the body, not just specific brain regions. Thus, disinhibition (ie 'turning on') of serotonin release in one part of the brain may be responsible for therapeutic actions for one disorder, while inhibition of serotonin release in another part of the brain may improve symptoms of a different disorder. The ability of SSRIs to work on various serotonin pathways thus has advantages in terms of the breadth of disorders that they can treat. However, actions at unwanted serotonin receptors can contribute to the side-effect profiles of SSRIs.

The most prominent adverse effects of SSRIs include agitation, akathisia, anxiety, panic attacks, insomnia, sexual dysfunction, gastrointestinal effects and headaches. These side-effects, while generally not as troublesome as the cardiac toxicity and anticholinergic effects of the older agents, are nonetheless disagreeable and may lead to non-compliance. Most appear to be mediated by actions on 5-HT_{2A}, 5-HT_{2C} or 5-HT_3 receptors in various neuronal pathways and tissues throughout the body.

Sexual dysfunction appears to occur as the result of stimulation of 5-HT_{2A} receptors in at least two pathways, the mesolimbic dopamine pathway in the brain and the pathway projecting from the brainstem down the spinal chord. The mesolimbic dopamine pathway seems to mediate the anticipation of pleasure. Stimulation of 5-HT_{2A} receptors in this pathway leads to reduced output of dopamine, and may thus lead to decreased libido, pleasurability, and arousal. The pathway extending from the brainstem down the spinal chord controls parts of the sexual response such as orgasm and ejaculation. Inhibition of these spinal reflexes through stimulation of 5-HT_{2A} or 5-HT_{2C} receptors in this pathway may account for the inability of some SSRI patients to achieve orgasm or ejaculation.

Anxiety, sleep disturbances, akathisia and agitation also appear to be caused by stimulation of 5-HT_{2A} or 5-HT_{2C} receptors. 5-HT_{2A} and 5-HT_{2C} receptors in the serotonin pathway that extends to the hippocampus and limbic cortex may be responsible for symptoms of anxiety and even induction of panic attacks. Insomnia is most likely mediated by 5-HT_{2A} receptors in sleep centres in the brainstem, and akathisia and agitation may occur because of stimulation of 5-HT_{2A} receptors in the serotonin pathway leading to the basal ganglia.

Stimulation of 5-HT_3 receptors probably causes the gastrointestinal side-effects of SSRIs. These effects may occur because of stimulation of $5-HT_3$ receptors in the brainstem vomiting centre, in the serotonin pathway from brainstem to hypothalamus, and in the gut itself.

The SSRIs share the same basic therapeutic and side-effect profiles. However, each SSRI has unique secondary characteristics that could potentially allow these agents to be selected based on patient profile (Figure 4.1). Fluoxetine, which blocks $5-HT_{2C}$ receptors, and sertraline, which inhibits dopamine reuptake, may be more effective at restoring energy and motivation in depressed patients. Fluvoxamine has actions at sigma receptors and paroxetine has mild anticholinergic effects, which may make these agents more effective for relief of insomnia and anxiety (Figure 4.2). However, these differences may only be seen during the first several weeks of treatment, after which the effects of the different SSRIs may be indistinguishable.

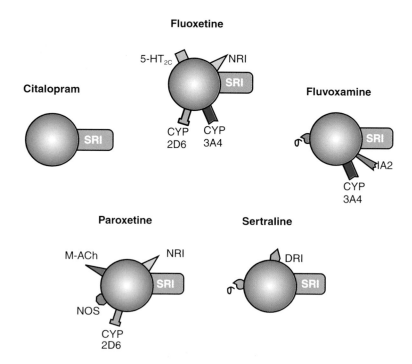

Figure 4.1 Secondary properties of SSRIs.

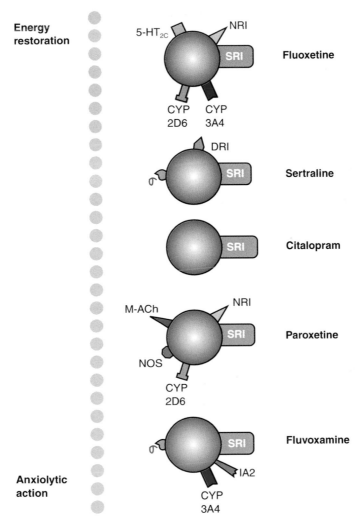

Figure 4.2 SSRI spectrum.

Newer dual-action antidepressants

Although selective drugs have safer and more tolerable side-effects than older multiple mechanism agents, they may not be as effective in severe or refractory cases. Furthermore, remission rates are higher for some dual-action agents than for single action agents (Thase et al, 2001). It may be that agents that combine synergistic mechanisms of action will prove to be the most effective treatments for depression. In fact, developments of new antidepressant treatments have shown a return to the dual mechanisms of action characteristic of the older agents, but with the improved side-effect profiles of the SSRIs. In addition to the MAOIs, TCAs and SSRIs, four other classes of antidepressants are currently on the market, and are distinguished, like the older drugs, by their mechanisms of action. These include a norepinerphine and dopamine reuptake inhibitor (NDRI), a dual serotonin and norepinephrine reuptake inhibitor (SNRI), serotonin-2 antagonist/reuptake inhibitors (SARIs), and noradrenergic and specific serotonergic antidepressants (NaSSAs).

Bupropion, an NDRI, is the only current antidepressant that has no direct actions on the serotonergic system. Thus, the therapeutic and side-effect profiles of bupropion differ from those for the SSRIs and classical antidepressants. This agent may be useful for patients who do not respond to SSRIs, or as an adjunct for those who have lingering symptoms suggestive of a norepinephrine or dopamine deficiency such as psychomotor retardation, anhedonia, hypersomnia, cognitive slowing, inattention, and food craving. However, the noradrenergic actions of bupropion may also lead to adverse effects, including agitation, insomnia, nausea and seizures. The risk of seizure is significantly increased when bupropion is administered as an immediate-release formulation at doses greater than 450 mg/day. However, therapy with the controlled-release formulation (300–400 mg/day) does not appear to raise the risk of seizure above that for any other antidepressant.

Although an inhibitor of only serotonin reuptake at low doses, venlafaxine inhibits both serotonin and norepinephrine reuptake at medium to high doses, and even inhibits dopamine reuptake at very high doses. Thus, venlafaxine at moderate doses has the same therapeutic mechanisms of action as TCAs such as amitriptyline or clomipramine. However, venlafaxine has virtually no effects on cholinergic, histaminergic, or α-adrenergic receptors. Thus, in essence, it has the therapeutic benefits of TCAs without the adverse effect profile. The side-effects that do occur with venlafaxine are generally similar to those of the SSRIs. Some side-effects tend to increase as dose increases (eg dizziness, increased blood pressure, dry mouth), possibly reflecting the addition of side-effects characteristic of increases in norepinephrine and dopamine. Venlafaxine is generally well tolerated, and has shown superiority to SSRIs in terms of response and remission rates (Thase et al, 2001). The recent meta-analysis of Smith et al (2002) extends these findings in a larger group of studies.

Nefazodone, a SARI, weakly and transiently inhibits reuptake of serotonin. However, it is best distinguished from the SSRIs by its effects on the 5-HT_{2A} receptors. While increased levels of serotonin caused by SSRIs lead to stimulation of 5-HT_{2A} receptors, nefazodone acts as an antagonist and blocks the stimulation of these receptors. Because many side-effects of the SSRIs are caused by stimulation of 5-HT_{2A} receptors (eg sexual dysfunction, anxiety), nefazodone is less likely to cause these symptoms. In particular, while SSRIs tend to cause transient insomnia and anxiety at the start of treatment, nefazodone may actually reduce these symptoms. Recently, rare cases of hepatic toxicity have been reported with nefazodone treatment, requiring increased vigilance for symptoms of hepatic disorders during treatment with this agent. Until this relationship is better understood, many experts recommend not using nefazodone for treatment of patients with liver disease.

Mirtazapine, a NaSSA, has actions on both norepinephrine and serotonin systems, but it is not a reuptake inhibitor. Its therapeutic effect is thought to be exerted mainly through antagonism of α_2 receptors, which leads to increased serotonin and norepinephrine release. Mirtazapine's side-effect profile is influenced by its antagonism of 5-HT_{2A}, 5-HT_{2C} and 5-HT_3 receptors. Unlike SSRIs, which stimulate these receptors, mirtazapine blocks them, and thus avoids the majority of the side-effects of SSRIs such as sexual dysfunction, anxiety and gastrointestinal effects. However, mirtazapine also has antihistamine properties, which may cause sedation and weight gain.

New antidepressants: Extensions of existing mechanisms

Antidepressant agents in development or only recently introduced to the market have built on the existing mechanisms of action, retaining the therapeutic actions while attempting to weed out those mechanisms responsible for adverse effects. Some agents that are currently available in Europe and Asia, but not on the market in the US are now being developed in the US. Other pending drug treatments include active enantiomers or isomers and MAOIs that are being developed worldwide (Table 4.1).

Resurrected agents

Two selective norepinephrine reuptake inhibitors (NRIs), reboxetine and atomoxetine, are currently being developed. However, in the US, reboxetine or its active enantiomer may no longer be developed for treatment of depression, but rather for chronic pain. Similarly, atomoxetine is being developed for treatment of attention deficit disorder but not depression in the US. Reboxetine appears to have similar efficacy to the SSRIs, but because it affects norepinephrine instead of serotonin, it has different side-effects. In particular, noradrenergic agents may actually cause side-effects that mimic anticholinergic symptoms, because

Table 4.1 New antidepressants: Extensions of existing mechanisms of action

- Reboxetine
- Atomoxetine
- Duloxetine
- Milnacipran
- S-citalopram
- Gepirone-ER
- Selegiline (MAOB) transdermal
- RIMA (befloxatone, toloxatone, moclobemide, brofaramine)

increasing norepinephrine at α_1 receptors outside the brain reduces acetylcholine at muscarinic receptors. Thus, patients may experience more constipation, dry mouth and urinary retention.

Meta-analysis has shown that SSRIs and NRIs seem to have comparable efficacy in terms of response rates (Nelson, 1999). However, not all patients will respond to a serotonin-selective drug, nor will all patients respond to a norepinephrine-selective drug. Dysfunction of serotonergic systems is hypothetically associated with symptoms such as depressed mood, anxiety, panic, phobia, obsessions and compulsions, food craving and bulimia (Table 4.2). Norepinephrine deficiency is hypothetically associated with impaired attention and concentration, deficiencies in working memory, slowed information processing, depressed mood, psychomotor retardation, and fatigue (Table 4.3). It may be that patients with symptoms consistent with 5-HT dysfunction will respond best to an SSRI, while those whose symptoms reflect a norepinephrine

Table 4.2 Dysfunction of serotonergic systems

- Depressed mood
- Anxiety
- Panic
- Phobia
- Obsessions and compulsions
- Food craving; bulimia

Table 4.3 Norepinephrine dysfunction

- Impaired attention
- Problems concentrating
- Deficiencies in working memory
- Slowness of information processing
- Depressed mood
- Psychomotor retardation
- Fatigue

dysfunction will respond best to an NRI. Furthermore, patients who do respond to an SSRI may have lingering symptoms characteristic of norepinephrine dysfunction, while the opposite may be true of patients who respond to an NRI. Such patients may benefit from treatment with a dual-action agent or from combination therapy. However, it is important to remember that these are hypothetical points: there is currently little evidence available to determine which drug will be most effective based on symptom profile. Still, the growing availability of drugs with different mechanisms of action affords more treatment options that, through knowledge derived from research and clinical practice, may ultimately be selected for an individual patient based on both symptom and side-effect profile.

Other agents that are being resurrected include two SNRIs, duloxetine and milnacipran. Some evidence pertaining to both drugs suggest superior efficacy to SSRIs in attaining remission from depression (Puech et al, 1997; Fukuchi and Kanemotok, 2002; Goldstein et al, 2002; Nemeroff et al, 2002). There is also some evidence that SNRIs may be effective in treating the physical symptoms of depression, which may prove to be an advantage over SSRIs (Detke et al, 2002; Nemeroff et al, 2002). These agents are also being studied in chronic pain states such as fibromyalgia and neuropathic pain.

One more older drug that may be introduced soon is gepirone, a 5-HT_{1A} agonist, in the same class as the currently marketed buspirone. Although there may be no additional efficacy with this drug compared to SSRIs, it is likely that it will have a different side-effect profile than some other agents (ie little sexual dysfunction). However, currently there are limited data on the use of gepirone to treat depression. If approved, it will come to the market as an extended release formulation —gepirone-ER.

Modifying current agents

Isomers of some current serotonin agents are being developed as antidepressant treatments. In particular, the *S* enantiomer of citalopram, *S*-citalopram or escitalopram, has been filed for approval in some countries and has received approval in others. Citalopram consists of a racemic mixture of two enantiomers; the *R* enantiomer has little effect on 5-HT reuptake sites. It has been suggested that the inactive enantiomer may be responsible for some of the behavioural and sexual side-effects of citalopram although this remains to be established. Thus, isolating the *S* enantiomer may improve the side-effect profile without reducing efficacy. A 10 mg per day dose of escitalopram appears to be comparable to 20 mg or even 40 mg of racemic citalopram in terms of antidepressant efficacy (Burke et al, 2002).

Efforts have also been made to modify MAOIs to avoid both the non-selectivity and the irreversibility of these agents. There are two forms of the enzyme MAO: MAOA and MAOB. Both of these enzymes metabolize monoamines and thereby render them inactive. However, MAOA is more selective for norepinephrine and serotonin, while MAOB is more selective for dopamine and phenylethylamine (Bentue-Ferrer, 1996). Selegiline, a MAOB-specific inhibitor, may enter the market as an antidepressant in an innovative formulation—a transdermal patch. Selegnine is already available in tablet form as an approved treatment for Parkinson's disease. Reversible inhibitors of MAOA, or RIMAs, may also be introduced eventually to the market in the US. One RIMA, moclobemide, is already available in many countries. However, there is evidence that moclobemide may be less effective than the older MAOIs (Lotufo-Neto et al, 1999). One advantage of these agents over the older MAOIs is that MAOB-specific inhibitors and RIMAs do not require dietary restrictions, whereas non-selective and irreversible MAOIs generally do.

Mood stabilizers, atypical antipsychotics

Anticonvulsants and atypical antipsychotics may also be able to play a role in the treatment of depression. Data show that lamotrigine and some other agents are effective in bipolar depression (Calabrese et al, 1999, 2000; Thase and Sachs 2000). However, the data on the use of anticonvulsants in unipolar depression are much less compelling. Still, these agents are sometimes used to treat more labile or treatment-resistant unipolar depression in clinical practice.

Atypical antipsychotics, including specifically olanzapine, risperidone, quetiapine and ziprasidone, also may ultimately be used to treat depression (Thase, 2002). Olanazapine, which blocks 5-HT$_2$ receptors and enhances release of NE and 5-HT in the prefrontal cortex, has been shown to significantly enhance fluoxetine response in a small but influential recent study (Shelton et al, 2001a). Ziprasidone inhibits reuptake of norepinephrine and serotonin, and also has actions at 5-HT$_{1D}$ and 5-HT$_{1A}$ receptors. Thus, it uniquely shares properties in common with many of the current antidepressants. Importantly, the benefit of these medications as antidepressant adjuncts does not appear to be limited to psychotic depression.

New antidepressants: Herbs and natural products (Table 4.4)

Herbal and natural products are now beginning to be used to treat depression. St John's Wort is an herbal preparation that has been used to treat depression. However, two recent large multicentre studies did not find any difference between response rates for St John's Wort and those for placebo (Shelton et al, 2001b; Hypericum Depression Trial Study Group, 2002). Further studies on the efficacy of St John's Wort for depression are currently being conducted and may clarify whether or not this agent is in fact an appropriate treatment for depression, especially mild depression or dysthymia. Until then, reserved use is suggested, not only because it may be ineffective, but also because its

Table 4.4 New antidepressants: Herbs and natural products

- St John's Wort (*Hypericum perforatum* L)
- Chromium
- Folate
- Fish oils (omega-3 fatty acids; docosahexanoic acid; eicosopentanoic acid)
- SAMe
- Oestrogen
- RU486

classification as an herbal preparation may mislead some people into thinking that it has no significant drug interactions, which is certainly not true.

Natural substances may be utilized as adjunctive treatments for depression. Two nutritional substances that may have antidepressant properties are chromium and folate. S-adenosylmethionine, or SAMe, has some preliminary data to support its use as an adjunct to antidepressant treatment. The omega-3 fatty acids docosahexanoic acid (DHA) and eicosapentanoic acid (EPA) have also been tested for antidepressant efficacy. Preliminary data have not shown DHA to be effective; however, an ongoing study of depression during pregnancy may show EPA to be efficacious. However, like St John's Wort, none of these supplements have been established as safe and effective treatments for depression. If patients are using any of these supplements, it is important that the practitioner be aware of this, so that potential drug interactions can be avoided.

Currently, the most compelling natural treatment for depression in women is oestrogen replacement therapy. Earlier studies have had mixed results, in part due to lack of controls (eg included perimenopausal and postmenopausal women, or women with both major depression and minor mood fluctuations). However, recent well-controlled studies on oestradiol treatment in perimenopausal women with major depression have shown significant antidepressant effects (Schmidt et al, 2000; Soares et al, 2001). Other well-controlled studies performed recently have shown efficacy of transdermal or sublingual oestradiol treatment in severe premenstrual syndrome, postpartum depression and postpartum psychosis (see, eg Ahokas et al, 1998, 1999). In addition, several multicentre studies have shown that oestrogen replacement therapy may enhance response to SSRIs (Schneider et al, 1997; Amsterdam et al, 1999; Kornstein et al, 2000). This is particularly interesting because there is documented evidence that women over 50 have lower response and remission rates with SSRIs than women under 50. This difference is not seen with venlafaxine, a SNRI (Kornstein et al, 2002). Thus, both oestrogen and norepinephrine may be synergistic with serotonin in women across the life cycle. However, this does not mean that all women should necessarily receive serotonin/oestrogen or serotonin/norepinephrine treatment. In fact, younger women generally do not respond as well to TCAs as they do to MAOIs or SSRIs (Thase et al, 2000; Kornstein et al, 2001). Furthermore, while some women respond well to oestrogen replacement therapy alone, others respond best to antidepressant treatment, and still others do best with both. Nonetheless, oestrogen replacement therapy appears to be a viable option for some women with depression.

New antidepressants: New mechanisms of action

Further developments in antidepressants extend beyond medications that affect the actions on monoamines, which currently dominate the treatment of depression. While most antidepressants on the market in the US work primarily by affecting reuptake of monoamines or by blocking their metabolism, newer mechanisms of action are now being explored, including not only agonist or antagonist actions at serotonin receptors, but also such actions within other neurotransmitter systems. (Table 4.5).

Flibanserin is a 5-HT_{1A} agonist and 5-HT_{2A} antagonist which has mixed data regarding efficacy and side-effects. A selective 5-HT_{1D} antagonist is in early clinical testing, but flibanserin has recently been dropped from further development at this time.

While most focus is placed on the roles of the monoamines in

Table 4.5 New antidepressants: Possible new mechanisms of action

- Flibanserin (5-HT_{1A} agonist, 5-HT_{2A} antagonist)
- 5-HT_{1D} antagonist
- NK-1, -2, -3 (substance P) antagonists
- CRF-1 antagonists
- Nemifitide (novel injectable pentapeptide)

depression, other neurotransmitter systems may be involved as well. In particular, it appears that neurokinins, especially neurokinin-1, also known as substance P, affect emotional functioning (Kramer et al, 1998). Substance P is a neuropeptide previously considered to be involved in the pain response, yet antagonists to substance P's receptors (NK-1 receptors) do not appear to reduce neurogenic inflammation or pain. They have been shown, however, to be associated with improved mood in depressed patients in some but not all early clinical trials (Argyropoulis and Nutt, 2000). The other neurokinins, NK-A and NK-B, may also have beneficial effects on mood.

Corticotrophin-releasing factor (CRF) antagonists are also being studied for their effects on depressed mood (Nemeroff, 1996). Inhibiting the release of CRF in turn inhibits release of cortisol, a stress hormone. Animal studies have shown that CRF antagonists are anxiolytic and stress-relieving (Nemeroff, 1996). Study of these compounds in depressed humans, however, is still quite preliminary.

The so-called 'morning-after pill', RU486, is also being considered as a potential treatment for depression. This drug blocks the actions of cortisol at central and peripheral glucocorticoid receptors, and may thus be analogous to CRF antagonists. Whether or not RU486 will actually demonstrate efficacy in treating depression remains to be established. It is also plausible that glucocorticoid antagonists may only be effective for patients with an elevated hypothalamic-pituitary-adrenocortical function.

A novel treatment on the horizon is nemifitide, a pentapeptide that seems to have a rapid onset of action in depressed patients (Feighner et al, 2001). The mechanism of action of this and other pentapeptides in treating depression is not currently understood. However, the preliminary data suggest that it is both an effective and safe treatment. Netamiftide is administered via injection for five days out of a two-week period, with patients appearing to stay well in between injections. Thus, it represents an entirely new approach to the treatment of depression.

Conclusion

Although the older antidepressants were not surpassed in efficacy by the SSRIs, they are no longer used as first-line treatment for depression because of their potentially dangerous side-effects. SSRIs are currently the most widely prescribed antidepressants on the market. However, newer dual-action agents appear to be nearly comparable to SSRIs in terms of side-effects, but may have advantages in terms of efficacy (Thase et al, 2001; Smith et al, 2002). In particular, dual-action agents appear to be more effective in severe and treatment refractory depression, and may also produce higher remission rates and be useful for painful physical symptoms. The patient profile may also affect the response to drugs with different mechanisms of action. Although little evidence currently exists, it may be that symptom and side-effect profiles can ultimately be used to determine whether SSRIs, dual-action agents, or even NRIs are used.

In addition to symptom and side-effect profiles, the characteristics of the actual patient may affect response to treatment. Specifically, women and men respond differently to antidepressants, as do women over 50 versus women under 50. An important consideration when treating women for depression is whether or not to attempt oestrogen replacement therapy, either as an adjunct or as a monotherapy. Evidence now exists that depressive symptoms may be improved by oestrogen replacement therapy in some women during the postpartum and the perimenopausal periods.

Finally, potential treatments are now being examined that explore mechanisms of action beyond direct effects on monoamine systems. While data are still preliminary, there are some promising methods that may change the face of antidepressant treatment within the next decade.

References

Ahokas AJ, Turtianen S, Aito M (1998) Sublingual oestrogen treatment of postnatal depression. *Lancet* **351**: 109.

Ahokas A, Kaukoranta J, Aito M (1999) Effect of oestradiol on postpartum depression. *Psychopharmacology (Berlin)* **146**: 108–110.

Amsterdam J, Garcia-Espana F, Fawcett J, et al (1999) Fluoxetine efficacy in menopausal women with and without estrogen replacement. *J Affect Disord* **55**: 11–17.

Argyropoulos SV, Nutt DJ (2000) Substance P antagonists: novel agents in the treatment of depression. *Expert Opin Invest* **9**: 1871–1875.

Bentue-Ferrer D (1996) Monoamine oxidase B inhibitors: current status and future potential. *CNS Drugs* **6**: 217–236.

Burke WJ, Gergel I, Bose A (2000) Fixed-dose trial of the single isomer SSRI escitalopram in depressed outpatients. *J Clin Psychiatry* **63**: 331–336.

Calabrese JR, Bowden CL, McElroy SL, et al (1999) A double-blind placebo-controlled study of lamotrigine monotherapy in outpatients with bipolar I depression. Lamictal 602 Study Group. *J Clin Psychiatry* **60**: 79–88.

Calabrese JR, Suppes T, Bowden CL, et al (2000) A double-blind, placebo controlled, prophylaxis study of lamotrigine in rapid-cycling bipolar disorder. Lamictal 614 Study Group. *J Clin Psychiatry* **61**: 841–850.

Detke MJ, Lu Y, Goldstein OH, et al (2002) Duloxetine, 60 mg once daily, for major depressive disorder: a randomized double-blind, placebo-controlled trial. *J Clin Psychiatry* **63**: 308.

Feighner JP, Ehriensing RH, Kastin AJ, et al (2001) Double-blind, placebo-controlled study of INN 00835 (netamiftide) in the treatment of outpatients with major depression. *Int Clin Psychopharmacol* **16**: 1–8.

Goldstein CJ, Mallinckrodt C, Lu Y, et al (2002) Duloxetine in the treatment of major depressive disorder: a double-blind clinical trial. *J Clin Psychiatry* **63**: 225.

Hypericum Depression Trial Study Group (2002) Effect of Hypericum perforatum (St John's Wort) in major depressive disorder: a randomized controlled trial. *JAMA* **287**: 1807–1814.

Kornstein SG, Schatzberg AF, Thase ME, et al (2000) Gender differences in treatment response to sertraline versus imipramine in chronic depression. *Am J Psychiatry* **157**: 1445–1452.

Kornstein SG, Sloan DME, Thase ME (2002) Gender specific differences in depression and treatment response. *Psychopharmacol Bull* **36**: 99–112.

Kramer MS, Cutler N, Feighner J, et al (1998) Distinct mechanism for antidepressant activity by blockade of central substance P receptors. *Science* **281**: 1640.

Lotufo-Neto F, Trivedi M, Thase ME (1999) Metaanalysis of the reversible inhibitors of monoamine oxidase type A moclobemide and brofaromine in the treatment of depression. *Neuropsychopharmacology* **20**: 226–247.

Nelson JC (1999) A review of the efficacy of serotonergic and noradrenergic reuptake inhibitors for treatment of major depression. *Biol Psychiatry* **46**: 1301–1308.

Nemeroff CB (1996) The cortico-releasing factor (CRF) hypothesis of depression: new findings and new directions. *Mol Psychiatry* **1**: 336–342.

Nemeroff CB, Schatzberg AF, Goldstein DJ, et al (2002) Duloxetine for the treatment of major depressive disorder.

Puech A, Montgomery SA, Prost JF, et al (1997) Milnacipran, a new serotonin and norepinephrine reuptake inhibitor: an overview of its antidepressant activity and clinical tolerability. *Int Clin Psychopharmacol* **12**: 99.

Schmidt PJ, Nieman L, Danaceu MA, et al (2000) Estrogen replacement in perimenopause-related depression: a preliminary report. *Am J Obstet Gynecol* **183**: 414–420.

Shelton RC, Keuer MB, Gelenberg A et al (2001a) Effectiveness of St John's Wort in major depression. A randomized controlled trial. *JAMA* **285**: 1978–1986.

Shelton RC, Tollefson GD, Tohen M, et al (2001b) A novel augmentation strategy for treating resistant major depression. *Am J Psychiatry* **158**: 131–134.

Smith D, Dempster C, Glanville J, Freemantle N, Anderson I (2002) Efficacy and tolerability of venlafaxine compared with selective serotonin reuptake inhibitors and other antidepressants: a meta-analysis. *Br J Psychiatry* **180**: 396–404.

Soares CN, Almeida OP, Joffe H, et al (2001). Efficacy of estradiol for the treatment of depressive disorders in perimenopausal women: a double-blind, randomized, placebo-controlled trial. *Arch Gen Psychiatry* **58**: 529–534.

Thase ME, et al (2002) What role do atypical antipsychotic drugs have in treatment-resistant depression? *J Clin Psychiatry* **63**: 95–103.

Thase ME, Frank E, Kornstein S, Yonkers KA. Gender differences in response to treatments of depression. In: E Frank (ed) Gender and its effects on Psychopathology. Washington DC, American Psychiatric Press, Inc, 2000: pp 103–129.

Thase ME, Sachs GS (2000) Bipolar depression: Pharmacotherapy and related therapeutic strategies. *Biol Psychiatry* **48**: 558–572.

Thase ME, Entsuah AR, Rudolph RL (2001) Remission rates during treatment with venlafaxine or selective serotonin reuptake inhibitors. *Br J Psychiatry* **178**: 234–241.

chapter 5

Other antidepressant therapies: Light therapy, ECT, TMS, VNS

Mark S George and F Andrew Kozel

Introduction

The majority of modern treatments for depression (talking therapies and psychopharmacology) arise from two historical schools in medicine and psychiatry. Modern western medicine largely descends from the *allopaths*—who used medicinal compounds in large doses as treatments (other competing schools were the homeopaths and osteopaths.) Talking therapies emerged from Freudian theory and modern cognitive psychology. The area of surgical treatments descends from the barber surgeons. In contrast to these forms of treatment, reviewed elsewhere in this book, there is a newly emerging class of antidepressant therapies which involve stimulation of the brain through physical methods short of ablative surgery. As a class, these treatments are sometimes referred to as 'physical treatments' or somatic therapies. Modern psychiatrists are quite familiar with one of these treatments—electroconvulsive therapy, or ECT. These new treatments include as well, in order of increasing invasiveness, light therapy, transcranial magnetic stimulation (TMS), vagus nerve stimulation (VNS), and to a lesser degree, deep brain stimulation (DBS).

There is much new interest in this class of antidepressant therapies. In part, this interest is spurred on by new knowledge, provided by functional brain imaging, about the specific brain regions involved in depression, mania, normal mood regulation and emotion processing. The ability to stimulate these areas in awake and alert adults without neurosurgery (or at least open craniotomy) is a real advance that clinicians and neuroscientists have long dreamed for. This chapter provides an overview and update of these minimally invasive brain stimulation (MIBS) techniques and their emerging research and therapeutic use in depression.

Background

The rapid development of psychopharmacology during the past 50 years has revolutionized standard methods for treating clinical psychiatric disorders. Although these methods are useful for many psychiatric patients, they are not effective in all cases, and are associated with various side-effects. Thus, for some patients at least, there is a need for new and safe therapies to treat psychiatric illnesses. Additionally, if psychiatric illnesses derive from faulty chemical transmission in certain brain regions or circuits, then taking a medication by mouth is a highly inefficient method for delivering needed compounds to these regions. Only a portion of a pill taken by mouth is absorbed in the gut, with only a smaller portion passing into the brain. Within the brain, only a small amount goes to the defective region.

Although somatic treatments such as insulin coma therapy, electro-convulsive therapy (ECT) and prefrontal leucotomy have been used in treating some psychiatric conditions, high risks, limited therapeutic efficacy and side-effects have limited their clinical utility in most areas. Successful treatment in some psychiatric disorders is believed to be achieved by modifying neuronal activity at a systems or circuit level. Thus, clinical and research neuroscientists have long been interested in the development of methods for stimulating the brain directly without great risk. The ability to excite or inhibit local areas of the brain has raised the possibility of whether these techniques might be novel therapeutic tools in the field of psychiatry. With this background, several novel and minimally invasive techniques to stimulate the brain have recently emerged.

Light therapy for seasonal affective disorder

Background and theory

Light therapy for seasonal mood disorders has been shown to be effective in several large randomized control trials (RCTs) comparing light therapy to plausible placebos (Eastman et al, 1998; Terman et al, 1998). Response usually occurs within two to three weeks and the response rate for non-treatment-resistant seasonal affective disorder (SAD) is between 60% and 90% (Lee and Chan, 1999). Efficacy of light therapy in non-SAD depression is not fully established.

New advances in light therapy

Over the past few years there have been substantial new findings in this area. As is the case for most psychiatric treatments, the basic neurobiology behind light therapy for SAD remains elusive, although there are several good mechanistic theories being tested. In support of the hypothesis that light therapy works by phase shifting individuals, Terman and colleagues (2001) found that the degree of phase advance (eg falling asleep at 10pm rather than 2am) with morning light was associated with clinical response to light therapy in SAD. A different theory about SAD is that the photoperiod in SAD patients is dysregulated. Wehr and colleagues (2001) found that patients with SAD have a longer duration of melatonin release in the winter versus summer, compared with controls. Their results suggest that SAD patients generate a biological signal of change of season that is absent in healthy volunteers. This signal is similar to the signal that mammals use to regulate seasonal changes in their behaviour. This finding is consistent with the hypothesis that neural circuits that mediate the effects of seasonal changes in day length on mammalian behaviour mediate effects of season and light treatment on SAD. The phase shifting and photoperiod hypotheses of SAD and light therapy are not exclusive.

In a controversial study published in *Science* in 1998, researchers used light exposed to the back of the knee to reset circadian rhythms. This study has not been replicated, although a formal failed replication has not been published. Importantly, this non-optical use of light was for resetting circadian rhythms. As a treatment for SAD, the light apparently has to be delivered to the eyes.

Current state of clinical practice

The fluorescent light box remains the gold standard light device. The recommended treatment regimen is 10,000 lux intensity for 30 minutes daily in the early morning, as soon as possible after awakening. Importantly, Avery and colleagues (2001) demonstrated in a large randomized control trial (RCT) that dawn simulation (1.5 hour dawn signal from 4:30 am to 6 am, peaking at 250 lux) was superior to a placebo dawn, and was at least as good as bright light therapy (10,000 lux for 30 minutes, from 6 am to 6:30 am). Of interest in this study, the mean daily hours of sunshine in the week prior to each visit was associated with a significant increase in likelihood of both response and remission. The standard light box should have an ultra violet filter to screen out harmful ultraviolet rays. There is no evidence of ocular damage with proper use of light therapy. Side-effects of light therapy include eye strain, visual disturbances, headache, agitation, nausea, sweating and sedation. These are generally mild and subside with time or with a reduced dose of light. Light therapy can precipitate hypomania or mania in susceptible patients. Many patients experience rapid recurrence of symptoms after discontinuing light therapy. Therefore, patients should continue using light therapy throughout their period of risk for winter depression and discontinue treatment during the asymptomatic summer months. There are few data on long-term or maintenance use of light therapy for SAD or non-seasonal depression.

Important research/clinical questions

More work is needed to understand how light therapy alleviates SAD. This knowledge would help in understanding how and whether to combine light therapy with other medications or devices. It might also provide clues as to methods to improve the efficacy of light therapy for both SAD and other forms of non-seasonal depression.

Electroconvulsive therapy (ECT)

Background and theory

Electroconvulsive therapy (ECT) was first considered as a potential thera-peutic treatment on the basis of the mistaken idea that schizophrenia and epilepsy do not occur together, and following the observation by Meduna in 1932 that patients with schizophrenia showed no gliosis compared with extensive gliosis in epileptic patients (von Meduna, 1935). This 'biological antagonism' was the basis for the development of convulsive therapy. The occurrence of seizures was speculated to protect against the development of schizophrenia. We now know that some patients with epilepsy do develop psychosis. However, based on the 'antagonism theory' generalized seizures were given to patients with psy-chosis, some of whom improved (likely those with psychotic depression or catatonia). Years of clinical ECT use then allowed the refining of applications to its current use profile in mood disorders, and occasion-ally in catatonia, schizophrenia and Parkinson's disease. The history of ECT can be seen as an initial broad application of a powerful brain inter-vention to many conditions. The narrowing of clinical applications has occurred along with substantial refinements in technique, which allow increased efficacy along with decreased side-effects. Thus, ECT was used for 30 years before it was determined that prefrontal application of the electrodes, and not parietal, was necessary for therapeutic effect, regard-less of whether a generalized seizure occurred (Sackeim et al, 1993).

New advances in ECT

There have been several new advances regarding ECT in the areas of: new electrode placements; shorter pulse widths; using neuroimaging to understand ECT effects; relapse following a course of ECT; and using magnetic stimulation to cause seizures.

The standard ECT electrode placement for many years has been prefrontal, either bilateral or unilateral. Bailine and colleagues (2000) recently compared bifrontal (approximately on the forehead above each eye) with bilateral prefrontal ECT (both given at 1.5 times the seizure threshold). They found that the two techniques were equal in efficacy, with bifrontal having a slight cognitive advantage. In other developments, in part stemming from work involving transcranial magnetic stimulation (TMS), there was renewed appreciation that narrower pulses have the advantage of more efficient neuronal excitation at a lower threshold density. Shorter pulses are closer to chronaxie, which describes the relationship between pulse width and threshold current. Briefer pulses are likely safer, more efficient and less toxic. Sackeim and colleagues (2001a) have now shown that ultrabrief pulse ECT is feasible, with lower seizure thresholds and fewer cognitive side-effects. Unfortunately, the machines currently approved for sale in the US are not constructed in order to provide ultrabrief ECT (0.3–1.5 milliseconds).

Nobler and colleagues initially found, using Xenon single photon emission computerised tomography (SPECT), that those patients who go on to respond to ECT have a greater reduction in prefrontal blood flow immediately following ECT. There thus appears to be anatomic specificity to where the ECT stimulus is most needed and is most effective. In 2001, Nobler et al confirmed this specific (although widespread) decreasing metabolism effect of ECT using glucose positron electron tomography (PET). They studied 10 patients immediately before and then 5 days following a course of bilateral ECT. Compared to baseline (before treatment) there were several areas of decreased metabolism, especially in the frontal and parietal cortex, the anterior cingulate, and the temporal cortex (see Figure 5.1).

Also recently, Sackeim and colleagues (2001b) reported on 84 patients who had remitted following a course of ECT. Patients were randomly assigned to receive maintenance placebo, lithium, or lithium and nortriptyline. After 6 months, there was an 84% relapse rate with placebo, 60% with lithium alone, and 39% for the combination of lithium and nortriptyline. These data convincingly show that in a patient group this ill, without active treatment, virtually all remitting patients will relapse within 6 months.

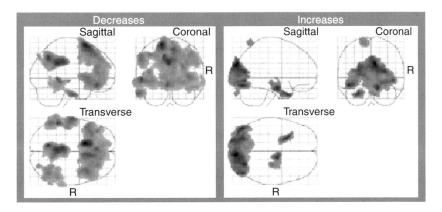

Figure 5.1 *Summary PET images of the brain changes in 10 depressed patients following ECT. Note the widespread areas of decreased activity in the prefrontal and temporal cortex. (From Nobler et al, 2001. Reprinted with permission from the* American Journal of Psychiatry.*)*

Unfortunately, the skull acts as a strong resistor when electrical current is applied to the scalp, so the bulk of the energy of an ECT pulse does not go directly into the brain, and the electrical energy cannot be focused. Recently, Lisanby et al (2001) succeeded in using powerful alternating magnetic fields to cause a seizure in a primate. Unlike electricity, magnetic fields pass unimpeded through skull and soft tissue and can thus be applied in a much more focused fashion. This development opened up the possibility of inducing ECT-like seizures with a magnetic field, hopefully reducing greatly the cognitive side-effects that are probably due to unnecessary passage of electrical current in ancillary brain regions. Lisanby and colleagues, working with Dr Thomas Schlaepfer in Berne, Switzerland, were the first to deliberately induce, using magnets, an ECT-like seizure in a depressed patient. They have called this magnetic seizure therapy (MST). The safety and side-effects of MST are currently being tested in depressed patients who are undergoing a regular course of ECT. Following this safety testing, it will be important to test whether MST has antidepressant efficacy.

Current state of ECT clinical practice

Despite these important research advances, the current practice of ECT has not drastically changed, as the shorter pulse widths and magnetic induction are still being developed at only a few key research sites.

Currently, patients are treated with either prefrontal (unilateral or bilateral) or bifrontal electrode placement, with dose titration and delivery of ECT doses sufficient to induce generalized seizures while under anaesthesia. This is commonly delivered two to four times per week, for 3–5 weeks, depending on clinical response.

Important clinical questions

This is a time of great excitement and rapid change in the field of ECT, with new knowledge developing on several fronts. The major questions revolve around what forms of ECT are the most effective and the least toxic. Perhaps the most important unanswered question is whether there is anything sacred about causing a seizure in a specific region, or whether other forms of brain stimulation, that do not result in seizures, can initiate the same general cascade of events that lead to the treatment of depression.

Transcranial magnetic stimulation (TMS)

Background and theory

Transcranial magnetic stimulation (TMS) uses a powerful hand-held magnet to create a time-varying magnetic field where a localized pulsed magnetic field over the surface of the head depolarizes underlying superficial neurons (George and Belmaker, 2000). High intensity current is rapidly turned on and off in the electromagnetic coil through the discharge of capacitors. TMS, producing powerful but brief magnetic fields that induce electrical currents in the brain, radically differs from the currently popular use of low level static magnetic fields as alternative therapies. If TMS pulses are delivered repetitively and rhythmically, it is called repetitive TMS (rTMS).

Although TMS is able to influence many brain functions, including movement, visual perception, memory, attention, speech and mood, full knowledge of the neurobiological cascade of events triggered by TMS at different settings remains unclear. Numerous animal studies have been important in understanding the modes of action of TMS. Recently, Pope and Keck (2001) have completed a series of studies using focal TMS in rat models. They have largely replicated earlier non-focal TMS animal studies which have shown that TMS has effects in animal models of depression, significantly alters brain monoamines and their receptors in the brain cortex, changes brain function through synaptic changes that are potentially long-lasting, and produces region-specific changes in thyroid stimulating hormone (TSH) and cortisol.

Over the past year, several studies combining TMS with other neuro-physiological and neuroimaging techniques have helped to elucidate how TMS achieves its effects. Our group at MUSC has pioneered and per-fected the technique of interleaving TMS with blood oxygen level-dependent (BOLD) functional magnetic resonance imaging (fMRI), allowing for direct imaging of TMS effects with high spatial (1–2 mm) and temporal (2–3 seconds) resolution. Nahas and colleagues (2001) demonstrated, using the interleaved TMS technique, that prefrontal TMS at 80% motor threshold (MT) produces much less local and remote

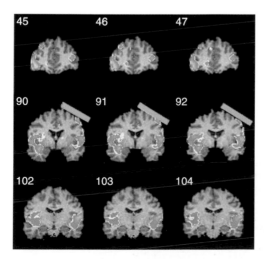

Figure 5.2 Summary of BOLD fMRI data from healthy adults where TMS has been applied at 120% MT over the prefrontal cortex. Note that although TMS initially affects only superficial cortex, cortical-subcortical connections cause changes in deeper limbic regions. (From Nahas et al, 2001. Reprinted with permission from Elsevier Press, Biological Psychiatry.*)*

blood flow changes than does 120% MT TMS (see Figure 5.2). Strafella et al (2001) used PET to show that prefrontal cortex TMS causes dopamine release in the caudate nucleus and has reciprocal activity with the anterior cingulate gyrus.

The notion of using something like TMS as an antidepressant goes back to at least the turn of the 20th century. More recently, there were three open studies in Europe in the early 1990s using round coils to deliver TMS over the vertex to potentially treat depression. Reasoning that prefrontal and limbic regions were more important for mood regulation than the vertex, and that ECT works only when applied over the prefrontal regions (George and Wassermann, 1994), one of us (MSG) in 1995 performed the first open trial of prefrontal TMS as an antidepressant, followed immediately by a crossover blinded study in 1997 (George et al, 1995, 1997). The theory was that chronic, frequent, subconvulsive stimulation of the prefrontal cortex over several weeks would initiate a therapeutic cascade of events both in the prefrontal cortex as well as in connected limbic regions.

New advances in TMS

Since the initial studies, there has been much interest in TMS as an antidepressant. A recent meta-analysis of all TMS antidepressant trials found that TMS was statistically significantly superior to sham TMS, and that this difference was robust (Burt et al, 2002). They found 23 published comparisons for controlled TMS prefrontal antidepressant trials, with a combined effect size of 0.67, indicating a moderate to large antidepressant effect.

There is still large variation in the methods of delivery of TMS. Most, but not all, studies have used focal coils positioned over the prefrontal cortex. The positioning of the coil is done using a rule-based algorithm. This method produced large variation in the particular prefrontal regions stimulated, depending largely on the subject's head size. Most studies have stimulated with approximately the intensity needed to cause movement in the thumb, if delivered over the motor cortex. There is now increasing recognition that higher intensities of stimulation might be needed to reach the prefrontal cortex, especially in elderly patients with prefrontal atrophy (McConnell et al, 2001). There is also emerging data that TMS therapeutic effects take several weeks to build, and that many of the initial trials of only 2 weeks were too short.

The most clinically compelling new TMS information to emerge in the last year are a series of studies from Israel directly comparing TMS to ECT (Grunhaus et al, 2000). In an initial study, the authors compared 40 patients who presented for ECT treatment and were randomized to receive either ECT or TMS. There was similar efficacy between the two treatments. This same group has presented data at international meetings where they have replicated this finding in a larger and independent cohort with an improved design. The two major differences between these studies and the rest of the TMS literature are the patient selection (suitable for ECT), and the length of treatment (3–4 weeks). Unfortunately, neither study explicitly measured differences in cognitive side-effects, although presumably TMS has no measurable cognitive side-effects, wheras ECT has several. In a similar but slightly modified design, Pridmore (2000) reported a most interesting study that compared the antidepressant effects of standard ECT (three times per week), and one ECT per week followed by TMS on the other 4 weekdays. At 3 weeks, they found that both regimens produced similar antidepressant effects. Unfortunately, detailed neuropsychological testing was not performed but one would assume that the TMS and ECT group had less cognitive side-effects than the solely ECT group.

Current state of TMS clinical practice

In summary, TMS is a promising tool for treating depression acutely. Although it is approved in Canada and Israel as a treatment, it is still considered investigational in the US by the Food and Drug Administration. Much work remains to be done to understand the optimal dosing strategy for the antidepressant effect of TMS. It is indeed unlikely that the initial combinations of intensity, frequency, coil shape, scalp location, number of stimuli or dosing strategy (daily, twice daily), are optimal or even close to maximal efficacy.

Several psychiatric antidepressant medications or treatments are also effective antimanic agents (eg anticonvulsants and ECT). One recent clinical trial from Israel found that right prefrontal TMS is antimanic compared to left prefrontal TMS. However, this result is too preliminary to draw any definite conclusions.

Safety issues

Although there is minimal risk of a seizure when TMS is performed within the published safety guidelines, the most critical safety concern with TMS may be inadvertently causing a seizure. In contrast to single pulse TMS, where seizures have not been reported in healthy persons, to date at least eight seizures have been caused by rTMS (none since the safety guidelines were published and adopted in 1996). A muscle tension-type headache and discomfort at the site of stimulation are less serious but relatively common side-effects of TMS. In contrast to ECT, no deleterious cognitive effects of 2 weeks of slow or fast rTMS have been found in two independent studies. Like magnetic resonance imaging (MRI), TMS could cause the movement of paramagnetic objects. For this reason, subjects with paramagnetic metal objects in the head or eye are generally excluded from TMS studies. TMS can cause heating of metallic implants, and the inactivation of pacemaker, medication pumps, or cochlear devices. Although in the US, rTMS is an experimental procedure that requires an investigational device exemption (IDE) from the FDA, substantial experience to date suggests that at least in the short term, TMS at moderate intensity has no clear lasting adverse effects in adults.

Important clinical questions

There are inadequate data concerning how long TMS antidepressant effects might last, or whether repeated TMS over time can be used in a maintenance mode. Moreover, it is not clear with which, if any, medications TMS works well with. However, despite these major unanswered questions, since the first use of prefrontal TMS as an antidepressant in 1995, this tool has clearly opened up new possibilities for clinical exploration and treatment of depression. Many parameters, such as intensity, location, frequency, pulse width, intertrain interval, coil type, duration, numbers of sessions, interval between sessions, and time of day, remain to be systematically explored. Although there is no longer a major debate about whether TMS has antidepressant effects, there are questions about how it might be used in treatment algorithms. It will perhaps always be easier to see a clinician occasionally and take regular medication rather than travelling daily to a treatment facility for TMS. Thus, the ultimate clinical role of TMS in treating depression may be in medication refractory cases, or in patients who are unable to tolerate systemic therapy due to pregnancy or a medical condition. Further work on understanding normal mental phenomena, and how these are effected by TMS, appears to be crucial for advancement. A critically important area that will ultimately guide clinical parameters is to combine TMS with functional imaging to directly monitor TMS effects on brain. Since it appears that TMS at different frequencies has divergent effects on brain activity, combining TMS with functional brain imaging will be helpful to better delineate not only the behavioural neuropsychology of various psychiatric syndromes, but also some of the pathophysiological circuits in the brain.

Vagus nerve stimulation (VNS)

Background and theory

For many years, scientists have been interested in whether and how stimulation of cranial nerves might produce changes in the higher cortex. In 1985, Dr Jake Zabara at Temple University (Philadelphia, USA) demonstrated the anticonvulsant action of VNS on experimental seizures in dogs. These important observations and ideas led to patents, a procedure (NeuroCybernetic Prosthesis: NCP® System), a company (Cyberonics, Inc), and an expanding amount of research in how sensory afferent fibres from the vagus cause brain changes (George et al, 2000).

The vagus nerve (cranial nerve X) has been generally considered as a parasympathetic efferent nerve. However, the vagus is, in fact, a mixed nerve composed of about 80% afferent sensory fibres carrying information to the brain from the head, neck, thorax and abdomen. These sensory afferent vagus fibres relay information to the nucleus tractus solitarii (NTS) and then to many areas of the brain, including the locus coeruleus.

Although the exact mechanisms by which VNS exerts its antiepileptic effect is not fully understood, these important brainstem and limbic neuroanatomical connections are considered the sites of therapeutic effects of this procedure. Studies using functional brain imaging have helped elucidate the mode of action of VNS. SPECT and PET studies suggest that VNS acutely increases synaptic activity in structures directly innervated by central vagal pathways and also acutely alters synaptic activity in multiple limbic system structures bilaterally. At Medical University of South Carolina (MUSC), we have recently succeeded in performing BOLD fMRI studies in depressed patients implanted with VNS generators, and these results show that VNS activates many anterior paralimbic regions, in a dose-dependent fashion that changes over time. Combining VNS with functional imaging offers the promise of better understanding the neurobiology of VNS as a function of the device settings. Ultimately, it may also be used to individually dose VNS patients.

Uses in epilepsy

Initially, VNS was used as an alternative treatment for patients with refractory epilepsy who were unsuitable for epilepsy surgery. However, it is increasingly being used in less severely ill patients. In the past decade, several studies have reported its efficacy and safety in both short- and longer-term follow-up of epilepsy patients. Data from two double-blind controlled studies have suggested that approximately 30% of patients experience more than 50% seizure reduction. The mean overall decline of seizure frequency was about 25–30% compared to baseline. A small number (less than 10%) of patients experience long-term seizure-free intervals. Although clear predictive factors for positive outcome or guidelines for stimulation parameters have not yet been published, a recent reassessment by the American Academy of Neurology concluded that VNS for epilepsy is both 'effective and safe'.

In clinical studies in epilepsy, the efferent peripheral effects of VNS to the left vagus nerve have been minimal, without significant gastrointestinal or cardiac side-effects. In addition, each patient is given a magnet that, when held over the pulse generator, turns off stimulation. When the magnet is removed, normal programmed stimulation resumes.

New advances in VNS

In addition to the neuroanatomical reasoning above, data from several other domains provided the background and rationale for the first VNS implant for treating depression, which was performed in July 1998 at MUSC in Charleston. These hints were: (1) mood effects of VNS observed in epilepsy patients, (2) the role of anticonvulsants (carbamazepine, valproic acid and lamotrigine) and/or ECT (also an anticonvulsant) in treating mood disorders, (3) evidence by brain imaging studies that VNS affects the metabolism of limbic structures relevant to mood regulation, and (4) neurochemical studies indicating VNS effects on brain monoamines.

An initial pilot open study of VNS in 30 adult outpatients with severe, non-psychotic, treatment-resistant major depressive episode reported a 40% response rate after 8 weeks of VNS therapy, using $\geq$ 50% reduction in baseline Hamilton Depression Rating Scale ($HDRS_{28}$) total score to define response (12/30 responders). In this medication-resistant group, there was a 17% complete remission rate (exit $HDRS_{28}$ $\leq$ 10), suggesting efficacy of this technique in depression. This study was extended for longer-term follow-up, and after 6 months of treatment, 17/30 (57%) of the treatment-resistant patients met criteria for response. An additional analysis found that VNS appeared to be most effective in patients with low to moderate, but not extreme, antidepressant treatment resistance. An additional 30 subjects were added to this open trial, with an overall response rate after 8 weeks of therapy (combined in 59 completers) of 30% (Sackeim et al, 2001c). The most common side-effect was voice alteration or hoarseness, occurring in 33/60 patients (55%), which was generally mild and related to the intensity of the output current. History of treatment resistance and intensity of concurrent antidepressant treatment during the acute VNS trial predicted a poorer VNS outcome. Patients who had never received ECT (lifetime) were 3.9 times more likely to respond. None of the 13 patients who had failed more than seven adequate antidepressant trials in the current episode responded, compared to 39.1% of the remaining 46 patients. Thus, VNS as currently delivered, appears to be most effective in patients with low to moderate, but not extreme, antidepressant resistance.

These encouraging initial results served as the basis for the ongoing US multi-site double-blind trial of VNS for chronic or recurrent, low to moderate treatment-resistant depression. The acute phase results of this double-blind study were announced in Spring 2002 by Cyberonics. In this trial, active VNS failed to show a statistically significant difference in acute response from the sham group. The sham response rate was 10%, with the active response being 15%. There are several possible explanations for the differences between the open study 30% response rate and the 15% active acute response found in the later double-blind study. There was probably some placebo response impacting the response rates found in the open study. Additionally, the dose of VNS delivered in the double-blind study was markedly less than in the open study, which was possibly due to the complex nature of the double-blind trial. There is, however, no evidence of a VNS antidepressant dose response relationship—although this does exist for epilepsy and was the basis for the initial double blind epilepsy trials. Finally, an attempt at screening out highly treatment-resistant individuals was not successful.

The one year response rate in the subset of patients with data appeared encouraging, and matched the one year response rate seen in the other open VNS studies (averaging about 50%). The trial is still ongoing, gathering long-term data on these subjects in order to design future studies. Thus, there is no double-blind evidence for VNS as an antidepressant in patients with depression. There are open (Harden et al, 2000) and double-blind (Elger et al, 2000) studies showing that VNS has antidepressant effects in epilepsy patients with comorbid depression.

Current state of VNS clinical practice

Although the general term of VNS refers to several different techniques used to stimulate the vagus nerve, for practically all studies in humans, VNS refers to stimulation of the left cervical vagus nerve using a commercially available device manufactured by Cyberonics Inc, called the NCP® System. This technique has been available for treatment of refractory partial onset seizures in Europe since June 1994 and in the US since July 1997. VNS is now FDA-approved for the treatment of epilepsy and more than 14,000 people worldwide have these generators implanted.

VNS is delivered through an implantable, multiprogrammable, bipolar pulse generator called the NCP® Pulse Generator (the size of a pocket watch) which is implanted in the left chest wall and delivers electrical signals to the left vagus nerve through a bipolar lead. This bipolar lead is wrapped around the left vagus nerve near the carotid artery through a separate incision at surgery and is connected to the generator. The NCP® Programming Wand and Software—along with a portable computer—provides telemetric communication with the pulse generator, which enables non-invasive programming, functional assessments and data retrieval.

Based on the strength of the open pilot data discussed above, VNS has been approved as a treatment for depression in Europe and Canada. It is still considered experimental by the FDA.

Important clinical questions

The most important question regarding VNS and depression is to what extent are the data in the open trials a function of placebo. The placebo response is probably small given the refractory nature of the patients, and the continued long-term improvement. However, the results of the double-blind clinical study will clearly be important in determining the effect size of VNS as a therapy. It is also important to determine any subgroups of patients who are more likely to respond to VNS.

Related questions have to do with which medications are best combined with VNS, and whether some medicines actually have a negative effect on VNS as a therapy. Finally, for a device that requires substantial initial investment and surgery, it will be important to document whether VNS is cost-effective, in the long term, for patients with depression.

Obviously, better understanding of the brain effects of VNS might make VNS a more powerful intervention, especially if ways were found for vagus nerve stimulation that were less invasive than the current method. Different VNS settings probably (intensity, frequency, duty cycle) have varying regional effects. This would imply that finding the VNS settings that maximally affect specific brain regions might be an effective way to dose and guide clinical trials of VNS in different neuropsychiatric conditions.

A note about deep brain stimulation (DBS)

The most invasive of the techniques discussed in this chapter is deep brain stimulation (DBS). This involves creating a small hole in the skull and passing a fine wire, about the width of a human hair, into selected brain regions. This wire has several regions on the distal implanted end, like a stoplight, that can be excited from a pacemaker-like device connected subdermally and implanted in the anterior chest wall. When the DBS is implanted, the wire stimulates at high frequencies and temporarily 'arrests' the function of the region. DBS is thought to be less invasive than ablative surgery as the device can be turned off and the wires removed, with no theoretical long-term damage to the tissue.

DBS in the thalamus was initially approved by the US Food and Drug Administration for the treatment of Parkinson's disease. In January 2002, the FDA approved implanting DBS at the subthalamic nucleus (STN) and the globus pallidus interna (GPI). The model for DBS use in Parkinson's disease involves determining motor regions that act as brakes on movement, and then disabling their braking mechanism with high frequency DBS enabling more fluid movement. There is little to no data on using DBS at low frequencies to temporarily improve function.

DBS has been shown to produce mood effects, although they are in the wrong direction. A striking example was published recently in the *New England Journal of Medicine* where a patient was temporarily made to be depressed with DBS at the STN, and slightly below (Bejjani et al, 1999). Our group at MUSC is actively pursuing whether DBS at different locations or frequencies has mood-improving effects in Parkinson's disease patients.

DBS of the anterior limb of the internal capsule has been studied for the treatment of obsessive-compulsive disorder (OCD). In these open studies, positive mood effects have been reported (Ben Greenberg, pers comm, 16 Dec 2001, Hawaii). Future work in these other disorders is needed before DBS can be rationally considered as a potential treatment for depression.

Conclusion

The ability to non-invasively stimulate the brain in an awake and alert human is a real advance that neuroscientists have long dreamed of. The new techniques described in this overview that allow for the direct stimulation of brain regions with minimal invasiveness are promising tools to investigate regional brain activity and to treat various psychiatric diseases.

Further work is necessary to firmly establish the efficacy and safety of these tools. As functional imaging tools reveal the relevant circuitry involved in several psychiatric diseases, TMS, VNS and DBS offer hope for translating these research findings into novel treatments.

Regardless of their clinical roles as new therapeutic techniques, the capacity of these novel procedures as research tools to focally alter brain activity should lead to important advances in the understanding of brain–behaviour relationships, particularly in the area of mood regulation and depression.

References

Avery DH, Eder DN, Bolte MA, et al (2001) Dawn simulation and bright light in the treatment of SAD: a controlled study. *Biol Psychiatry* **50**: 205–216.

Bailine SH, Rifkin A, Kayne E, et al (2000) Comparison of bifrontal and bitemporal ECT for major depression. *Am J Psychiatry* **157**: 121–123.

Bejjani BP, Damier P, Arnulf I, et al (1999) Transient acute depression induced by high-frequency deep brain stimulation. *N Engl J Med* **340**: 1476–1480.

Burt T, Lisanby SH, Sackeim HA (2002) Neuropsychiatric applications of transcranial magnetic stimulation: a metaanalysis. *Int J Neuropsychopharm* **5**: 73–103.

Eastman CI, Young MA, Fogg LF, Liu L, Meaden PM (1998) Bright light treatment of winter depression: a placebo-controlled trial. *Arch Gen Psychiatry* **55**: 883–889.

Elger G, Hoppe C, Falkai P, Rush AJ, Elger CE (2000) Vagus nerve stimulation is associated with mood improvements in epilepsy patients. *Epilepsy Res* **42**: 203–210.

George MS, Belmaker RH (eds) (2000) *Transcranial magnetic stimulation in neuropsychiatry*. Washington, DC: American Psychiatric Press.

George MS, Wassermann E (1994) Rapid-rate transcranial magnetic stimulation (rTMS) and ECT (Editorial). *Convulsive Therapy* **10**: 251–253.

George MS, Wassermann EM, Williams WA, et al (1995) Daily repetitive transcranial magnetic stimulation (rTMS) improves mood in depression. *Neuroreport* **14**: 1853–1856.

George MS, Wassermann EM, Williams WE, et al (1997) Mood improvements following daily left prefrontal repetitive transcranial magnetic stimulation in patients with depression: A placebo-controlled crossover trial. *Am J Psychiatry* **154**: 1752–1756.

George MS, Sackeim HA, Rush AJ, et al (2000) Vagus nerve stimulation: A new tool for brain research and therapy. *Biol Psychiatry* **47**: 287–295.

Grunhaus L, Dannon PN, Schreiber S, et al (2000) Repetitive transcranial magnetic stimulation is as effective as electroconvulsive therapy in the treatment of nondelusional major depressive disorder: an open study. *Biol Psychiatry* **47**: 314–324.

Harden CL, Pulver MC, Ravdin LD, et al (2000) A pilot study of mood in epilepsy patients treated with vagus nerve stimulation. *Epilepsy Behavior* **1**: 93–99.

Lee TM, Chan CC (1999) Dose-response relationship of phototherapy for seasonal affective disorder: a meta-analysis. *Acta Psychiat Scand* **99**: 315–323.

Lisanby SH, Schlaepfer TE, Fisch HU, Sackeim HA (2001) Magnetic seizure therapy for major depression (Letter). *Arch Gen Psychiatry* **58**: 303–305.

McConnell KA, Nahas Z, Shastri A, et al (2001) The transcranial magnetic stimulation motor threshold depends on the distance from coil to underlying cortex: a replication in healthy adults comparing two methods of assessing the distance to cortex. *Biol Psychiatry* **49**: 454–459.

Nahas Z, Lomarev M, Roberts DR, et al (2001) Unilateral left prefrontal TMS produces intensity-dependent bilateral effects as measured by interleaved BOLD fMRI. *Biol Psychiatry* **50**: 712–721.

Nobler MS, Oquendo MA, Kegeles LS, et al (2001) Decreased regional brain metabolism after ECT. *Am J Psychiatry* **158**: 305–308.

Pope A, Keck ME (2001) TMS as a therapeutic tool in psychiatry: what do we know about neurobiological mechanisms? *J Psychiat Res* **35**: 193–215.

Pridmore S (2000) Substitution of rapid transcranial magnetic stimulation treatments for electroconvulsive therapy treatments in a course of electroconvulsive therapy. *Depress Anxiety* **12**: 118–123.

Sackeim HA, Prudic J, Devanand DP, et al (1993) Effects of stimulus intensity and electrode placement on the efficacy and cognitive effects of electroconvulsive therapy. *New Engl J Med* **328**: 839–846.

Sackeim HA, Prudic J, Nobler MS, Lisanby SH, Devenand DP, Peyser S (2001a) Ultrabrief pulse ECT and the affective and cognitive consequences of ECT. *J ECT* **17**: 77 (abstract).

Sackeim HA, Haskett RF, Mulsant BH, et al (2001b) Continuation pharmacotherapy in the prevention of relapse following electroconvulsive therapy—a randomized controlled trial. *JAMA* **285**: 1299–1307.

Sackeim HA, Rush AJ, George MS, et al (2001c) Vagus nerve stimulation (VNS) for treatment-resistant depression: Efficacy, side effects and predictors of outcome. *Neuropsychopharm* **25**: 713–728.

Strafella AP, Paus T, Barrett J, Dagher A (2001) Repetitive transcranial magnetic stimulation of the human prefrontal cortex induces dopamine release in the caudate nucleus. *J Neuroscience* **21**: 7–10.

Terman M, Terman JS, Ross DC (1998) A controlled trial of timed bright light and negative air ionization for treatment of winter depression. *Arch Gen Psychiatry* **55**: 875–882.

Terman JS, Terman M, Lo ES, Cooper TB (2001) Circadian time of morning light administration and therapeutic response in winter depression. *Arch Gen Psychiatry* **58**: 69–75.

von Meduna LJ (1935) Die konvulsionstherapie der schizophrenic. *Psychatr Neurol Wochscher* **37**: 317–319.

Wehr TA, Duncan WC, Sher L, et al (2001) A circadian signal of change of season in patients with seasonal affective disorder. *Arch Gen Psychiatry* **58**: 1108–1114.

chapter 6

Long-term treatment and prevention

Jon R Nash, Spilios V Argyropoulos and John Potokar

Introduction

Recent advances in the understanding of the nature of depressive disorders have brought about a shift in the concepts of treatment and recovery. Depression is recognized to be a serious disorder with morbidity and mortality comparable to medical conditions such as diabetes and ischaemic heart disease. It is frequently undertreated, has the potential for chronicity, and even when successfully treated carries a high risk of recurrence. Depression causes personal suffering for individuals and families, and inflicts a heavy economic burden on society as a whole.

The findings of large, long-term studies in the 1980s prompted Kupfer and others to define different features of the clinical course of depression (Frank et al, 1991) (Figure 6.1). The aim was to provide a framework within which clinicians could assess the clinical course of a depressive disorder, and researchers could prove and compare the efficacy of new and existing medications or psychological therapies.

Progress in the subsequent ten years has been disappointingly slow. Several new compounds have been licensed as antidepressants, but the majority of clinical trials continue to provide data only on the acute phase of treatment. Significant gaps remain in our evidence base, particularly for maintenance treatment and prevention using medication and psychotherapies. Nevertheless, there is a trend towards engaging patients with depression in longer-term treatments. Here, we present

Illness phases

Response	• The point at which an improvement of sufficient magnitude is observed so that the individual is asymptomatic
Remission	• A period during which an improvement of sufficient magnitude is observed that the individual is asymptomatic, implying that no increase in the intensity of the treatment regime is required
Recovery	• A period of remission of an episode lasting for sufficient time (typically 4–6 months) such that treatment can be discontinued, or further treatment is aimed at prevention of a subsequent episode
Relapse	• The return of symptoms meeting the full syndrome criteria during a period of remission, representing the ongoing course of a single episode
Recurrence	• The appearance of a new episode following recovery from a previous episode

Treatment phases

Acute	• The phase of treatment leading to remission of symptoms
Continuation	• Treatment during the period of remission that aims to achieve a full remission of symptoms and prevents relapse. This period typically lasts for 4–6 months, and during this time the risk of relapse is greatest
Maintenance	• Ongoing treatment following recovery from an episode that aims to prevent a new episode (recurrence). The optimal duration of treatment is not known and is likely to vary among patients

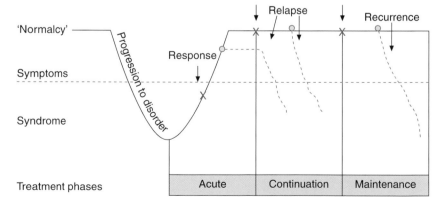

Figure 6.1 *The clinical course of depression (Reprinted with permission of Physicians Postgraduate Press, © 1991, from Kupfer, 1991.)*

the case for the long-term treatment of unipolar depressive disorder and review the evidence available to guide the treating clinician, whilst highlighting the gaps in existing knowledge.

Depression requires long-term management

Depression is increasingly recognized as a disorder with a lifelong potential for recurrence. The major reason for long-term treatment is the prevention of further episodes once a patient has recovered from an initial episode (Kupfer's maintenance phase). However, some cases may require prolongation of the acute and continuation phases of treatment in order to achieve a clinical recovery. This is more likely if the depression is chronic (duration greater than two years), if there is comorbidity with another mental disorder, if a depressive episode occurs on the background of chronic dysthymia (double depression) or if there is a poor initial response to treatment (treatment resistance). A vulnerability to chronic or recurrent depression may be related to various findings of altered biology in the brains of depressed patients.

Recurrence

The prevalence and natural course of depressive disorders have been extensively studied in various settings. It is beyond doubt that depression is a common disorder that is recurrent in the majority of cases. Rates of recurrence have been measured by self-report in cross-sectional surveys (eg recurrence rate of 73.9% among 15- to 24-year-olds in the National Comorbidity Survey (Kessler et al, 1994)), and recorded prospectively in observational cohort studies, mostly following naturalistic treatment regimes, and maintenance treatment studies (Table 6.1). As expected, higher rates of recurrence are seen when the period of follow-up is longer, but most studies with a follow-up of 5 or more years find a recurrence rate in excess of 40–50%. The major study in this group is the US National Institute of Mental Health Collaborative Depression Study, which has followed 431 patients undergoing naturalistic treatment for an index episode of depression from the 1970s, and

Table 6.1 Prospective studies of recurrence of depression

Study	Cohort	Rate of recurrence
Maj et al (1992)	72 outpatients recovered from depression followed for 5 yrs	75% at 5 yrs
Lewinsohn et al (1994)	Community sample of adolescents following recovery from depression	33% at 4 yrs
Angst et al (1995)	406 inpatients with mood disorders followed for up to 25 yrs	>80% at 25 yrs
Ramana et al (1995)	Inpatients followed for 15 months after remission	40% within 10 mths
Goldberg et al (1995)	84 inpatients with unipolar or bipolar affective disorder followed for 4.5 yrs	Equal in unipolar to bipolar disorders
Coryell et al (1996)	787 outpatients with psychotic or non-psychotic depression	Recurrence more likely if psychotic
Kovacs et al (1997)	24 young adults with insulin-dependent diabetes mellitus followed after recovery from depression	47% at 6.5 yrs
Van Londen et al (1998)	Outpatients at university clinic followed for 3–5 yrs	41% at 5 yrs
Mueller et al (1999)	105 recovered outpatients who remained well for 5 yrs	58% at 10 yrs
Mueller et al (1999)	380 recovered outpatients followed for up to 15 yrs	85% at 15 yrs
Solomon et al (2000)	318 recovered outpatients followed for 5–10 yrs	60% at 5 yrs
Brodaty et al (2001)	49 inpatients with depression followed for 25 yrs	88% at 25 yrs

is still ongoing (Keller and Boland, 1998). This study found rates of recurrence following recovery that were thought to be high at the time (60% after 5 years, 87% after 15 years), but have subsequently been supported by other studies. The proportion of patients receiving adequate pharmacotherapy was low (20% of those depressed for at least 6 months

Table 6.2 Factors predicting depressive recurrence

Patient factors	Illness factors
Family history of affective disorder	Previous depressive episodes
Pre-existing dysthymia	Longer or severe index episode
Comorbid anxiety disorder	Residual subsyndromal depression
Comorbid substance misuse	First episode after age 60
Low serum Tri-iodothyronine	Seasonal pattern
(T_3) levels	

received the equivalent of 150 mg or greater of imipramine), but this is consistent with other estimates of antidepressant treatment.

Various factors have been identified as predicting the likelihood of future recurrence (Table 6.2). Important factors are related to the frequency and severity of previous episodes. For clinical and research purposes, individuals at high risk of recurrence have been defined as those suffering three or more episodes, or those suffering two episodes within 5 years. Incomplete remission is also an important prognostic factor, and the Collaborative Depression Study found that the presence of residual subsyndromal depression was actually a stronger predictor of relapse than multiple previous episodes. Recent studies have examined the potential to achieve a full remission of symptoms using a combination of newer antidepressants and psychological therapy.

Chronicity

A proportion of patients experiencing an episode of major depressive disorder do not make a full recovery. Chronic major depression is diagnosed when the full syndrome is present for 2 years without recovery. The National Comorbidity Survey estimated the point prevalence of chronic depression in the US to be approximately 3% (Kessler et al, 1994). The proportion of patients in whom the symptoms of an index episode of depression lasted for more than 2 years was measured at 20% in the Collaborative Depression Study (Keller and Boland, 1998), and

12% of patients remained symptomatic after 5 years of follow-up. Where the depression was recurrent, there was a similar rate of chronicity of 15–20% for each successive episode. Various factors have been shown to increase the risk that an episode of depression will run a chronic course (Table 6.3). Chronic depression is related to an increased risk of suicide, as well as to increased occupational and social impairment.

Several recent studies have increased optimism about the outcome of chronic depression when aggressive treatment strategies are used. Better results are seen using a combination of medication and cognitive behavioural psychotherapy than when either treatment is used alone (Keller et al, 2000). However, response to treatment may be slow, and the risk of relapse is relatively high, suggesting that extended phases of acute and continuation treatment may be required in these patients.

Comorbidity

Depression frequently occurs in the presence of another mental disorder, and this comorbidity predicts a worse prognosis for the depressive episode. The National Comorbidity Survey found that almost 60% of

Table 6.3 Factors predicting chronicity of a depressive episode

Patient factors	*Illness factors*
Strong family history of affective disorder	Early age of onset of illness
Previous hospitalization for depression	Long duration of symptoms at presentation
Poor premorbid functioning	Inadequate or delayed treatment
Previous history of trauma	Triggered by multiple life events
Physical ill-health	
Premorbid neurotic traits	
Low self-esteem	
Social isolation	
Comorbid anxiety disorder	
Comorbid substance misuse	

participants with a history of major depressive disorder (MDD) within the last 12 months could be characterized as having secondary depression, in that they had at least one other disorder within that time period. The frequency of comorbidity with specific disorders is shown in Table 6.4. Episodes of depression may also be comorbid with eating disorders and various personality disorders.

The National Comorbidity Survey found that comorbidity predicted longer and more severe episodes of depression, increased risk of chronicity, interference with life and activities, hospitalization and suicide attempts. Depression also interferes with the course and treatment of the comorbid disorder. The presence of comorbidity is an important factor in the assessment and treatment of a depressed patient.

Double depression

Dysthymic disorder is diagnosed when an individual experiences depressed mood for most of the day, more days than not, for at least

Table 6.4 Comorbidity of depression with other disorders (Kessler et al, 1994)

Disorder	12 mth prevalence in those with MDD within the last 12 mths (%)
Anxiety disorders	51.2
Simple phobia	23.7
Social phobia	20.0
Generalized anxiety disorder	15.4
Post-traumatic stress disorder	15.2
Agoraphobia	12.6
Panic disorder	8.6
Substance-use disorders	18.5
Alcohol dependence	13.0
Other drug dependence	7.5

2 years, along with at least two of the following symptoms: low energy or fatigue, insomnia or hypersomnia, poor appetite or overeating, low self-esteem, poor concentration or indecisiveness and feelings of hopelessness (DSM-IV). It is relatively common (6.4% lifetime prevalence rate in the National Comorbidity Survey), shows a 2:1 female preponderance, is increased where first degree relatives have major depression, has a median duration of approximately 5 years, and is associated with increased lifetime rates of major depression and anxiety disorders. The term 'double depression' is used when an individual with dysthymic disorder develops an episode of major depression (Keller et al, 1997).

The Collaborative Depression Study (Keller and Boland, 1998) found that 26% of a sample of patients with major depression had pre-existing dysthymic disorder. This study found that although recovery from the major depressive episode was good (97% at 2 years), only a minority of the patients recovered from their chronic dysthymia (39% at 2 years). Furthermore, these patients experienced more recurrence of major depression than patients without chronic dysthymia, and the risk of recurrence increased with the duration of chronic dysthymia. The presence of double depression should be considered in the assessment of the depressed patient, as this will have implications for long-term maintenance treatment.

Treatment-resistant depression

A proportion of patients do not respond to conventional treatments for their index episode of depression, and this clearly has implications for prognosis and long-term treatment. The scale of the problem is unclear, as clinical studies in the past have been hampered by a lack of an agreed definition for treatment resistance, and by confounding factors, such as inaccurate diagnosis, inadequate medication regimes, and lack of patient compliance. Treatment-resistant depression has recently been defined as 'failure to respond to two adequate trials of different classes of antidepressants' (Souery et al, 1999). The treatments should be consecutive, and each given in an adequate dosage for a period of 6 to 8 weeks. Estimates of the rate of treatment resistance in clinical samples vary from 10% to 30%, but these may tend to overestimation as they are likely to include some patients who did not tolerate the treatment or did not comply. It is also not always clear whether to classify partial responders as treatment-resistant, and this may depend on the criteria used in the individual study.

Factors contributing to treatment resistance are similar to those leading towards chronicity. The more important are psychiatric comorbidity, concurrent medical disorders (thyroid disease, Cushing's disease) and medications, such as steroids and beta-blockers (Souery et al, 1999). Delay in initiating treatment predicts a poor response, and other factors include older age, female gender, psychotic symptoms, neurotic premorbid personality, family history of affective disorder, multiple loss events and poor social functioning. Treatment resistance may be associated with disturbances of central adrenergic and serotonergic activity, and hypothalamo-pituitary-adrenal axis dysfunction (Souery et al, 1999).

Neurobiological changes in depression

Depression may be associated with structural and functional changes in the brain, and this adds weight to the argument that long-term treatment may be required. A number of possible abnormalities have been suggested. In most cases it is not clear whether the findings represent an underlying pathological process that predisposes to depression, or ongoing adaptation or degeneration related to the abnormal functioning of the brain in the depressed state. A reduction in the volume of the hippocampus and in the density of hippocampal grey matter has been measured using neuroimaging (PET and MRI) and post-mortem studies, and neuropsychological testing has identified specific memory and attention deficits (Greden, 2001). Reductions in neuronal density and cortical thickness have also been described in the prefrontal cortex. A PET study of depressed patients before and after selective serotonin reuptake inhibitor (SSRI) treatment found a global decrease in $5\text{-}HT_{1A}$ receptor density that was not significantly altered by treatment, and it is possible that this may have an effect on serotonergic activity that confers a vulnerability to depression (Sargent et al, 2000). These findings contribute to the view of depression as being, at least in some cases, a chronic disorder requiring long-term treatment.

Therapeutic options for long-term treatment

There is an overwhelming case in favour of the provision of treatment for depression beyond the point at which the patient has appeared to respond. The aim of treatment may be the prevention of relapse (continuation phase) or recurrence (maintenance phase). Although on paper it is tempting to draw clear lines of distinction between these separate phases, in clinical practice things are rarely so clear-cut. Patients may require a prolonged phase of acute treatment to bring about a sustained clinical response, or there may be fluctuations in the severity of symptoms during the first few months of treatment. Most clinicians would take a pragmatic view of treatment with four main treatment goals (Table 6.5).

The body of published research evidence leaves unanswered many questions pertinent to long-term treatment. Most is known about the extension of treatment with antidepressant medication that has been effective during the acute phase. Some studies have looked at long-term treatment with other medications and psychotherapy, and these will be considered later.

Long-term antidepressant therapy

Important factors in the selection of an antidepressant medication for long-term use are efficacy, safety, tolerability and cost. The evidence for

Table 6.5 The four treatment aims in depression

1 To relieve the symptoms of depression
2 To restore normal levels of occupational, domestic and social functioning
3 To reduce the risk of return to the depressed state
4 To minimize the adverse effects of therapy

the suitability of currently available drugs will be considered. Double-blind, randomized controlled trials are required to provide high quality evidence of efficacy. Two distinct study designs have been used: randomized withdrawal studies and extension studies without re-randomization (Storosum et al, 2001).

Randomized withdrawal studies use a cohort of patients responding to acute treatment with medication, often on an open basis. Patients may be selected for an increased likelihood of relapse. Responders are randomized to receive continuation or maintenance treatment with the same medication, or blindly discontinued to receive placebo. In some studies open treatment is given throughout the continuation phase in order to ensure that any return of symptoms is due to a true recurrence. The difference in relapse and recurrence rates between placebo and active treatment groups should give a measure of the effect of the drug in preventing the return of symptoms.

A potential source of bias in these studies is the acute effect of discontinuing medication to placebo, which may falsely increase the rate of recurrence in this group. Tapering doses of medication may be used to minimize this effect. Another criticism is of the heterogeneity of patients at the point of randomization; it is difficult to be sure that a patient has made a full recovery, and therefore to be sure that further symptoms truly represent a recurrent episode. True recurrence prevention could be demonstrated by studying patients who had remained well for a substantial period without medication, and randomizing them to initiate periods of treatment with medication versus placebo, but no studies published so far have used this design.

Extension studies follow patients who respond to double-blind, placebo-controlled treatment in the acute phase, irrespective of whether they responded to medication or placebo. They are continued on the same treatment and the time to relapse or recurrence is measured. These studies tend to conclude that responses to placebo are poorly sustained, but it is doubtful that they truly demonstrate the long-term efficacy of medication. Although the problem of discontinuing medication is removed, the placebo-responders do not represent an adequate control group. They are likely to differ from medication-responders in important ways, and there is evidence from previous studies that placebo response in depression is not robust. These are potential sources of bias that will lead to an overestimation of the effect of medication.

Table 6.6 shows the evidence for efficacy of various antidepressant drugs, as well as information on safety and tolerability. Evidence of maintenance efficacy is assumed if there is a significantly lower rate of recurrence than placebo when randomization occurred at the end of a successful open continuation phase. It is clear from several studies that both continuation and maintenance treatment should be prescribed at the dose of medication required to bring about the acute response. It is not possible to draw conclusions regarding comparative efficacy from these studies, as entry criteria, patient groups and placebo response rates vary so widely. A few studies have directly compared the efficacy of different antidepressants in maintenance treatment, but most have not included sufficient patients to detect a difference. Those studies that do show a difference tend to favour newer drugs, such as SSRIs over tricyclics, and the differences are likely to be related to tolerability. Long-term side-effects of medication are a barrier to compliance, and the more important are sedation, weight gain, sexual dysfunction and increased sweating. An important finding from pharmacoeconomic studies comparing older and newer drugs is that the higher drug costs of newer antidepressants, such as fluoxetine and mirtazapine, are more than offset by improved tolerability and compliance (Holm et al, 2000).

The best guidance for the duration of continuation treatment comes from a study of 839 psychiatric outpatients in the US (Reimherr et al, 1998). These patients had responded to 12 weeks of open-label therapy with fluoxetine 20 mg, and were then randomized into one of four treatment groups, in which fluoxetine was discontinued to placebo at differing fixed points (week 0, week 14, week 38) or continued for a full 50 weeks. It was found that relapse rates were significantly lower when continuation treatment was continued for 38 weeks, but the additional benefit of continuing to week 50 was not significant in this study. The authors calculated that continuation treatment should last for at least 6 months after the remission of symptoms. There is no clear guidance from research studies about the optimal duration of maintenance

Table 6.6 Long-term efficacy, safety and tolerability of antidepressants

Drug	Efficacy in continuation phase vs placebo	Efficacy in maintenance phase vs placebo	Safety	Tolerability
Imipramine	Yes	Yes	Overdose toxicity	Dose-related anticholinergic effects; sedation; weight gain
Dothiepin	No	Yes	Overdose toxicity	Dose-related anticholinergic effects; sedation; weight gain
Amitriptyline	Yes	Yes	Overdose toxicity	Dose-related anticholinergic effects; sedation; weight gain
Nortriptyline	Yes	Yes	Overdose toxicity	Dose-related anticholinergic effects; weight gain
Lofepramine	No	No	Relatively safe in overdose	Mild dose-related anticholinergic effects
Desipramine	No	Yes	Overdose toxicity	Dose-related anticholinergic effects
Phenelzine	No	Yes	Overdose toxicity	Dietary restrictions; sedation; weight gain
Sertraline	Yes	Yes	Safe	Good; causes sexual dysfunction
Fluoxetine	Yes	Yes	Safe	Good; causes sexual dysfunction
Paroxetine	Yes	Yes+	Safe	Good; causes sexual dysfunction

Table 6.6 *continued*

Drug	Efficacy in continuation phase vs placebo	Efficacy in maintenance phase vs placebo	Safety	Tolerability
Fluvoxamine	No	Yes	Safe	Good; causes sexual dysfunction
Citalopram	Yes	Yes	Safe	Good; causes sexual dysfunction
Nefazodone	Yes	No	Safe	Good; low rates of sexual dysfunction
Mirtazapine	Yes	No	Safe	Good; low rates of sexual dysfunction; sedation and weight gain
Venlafaxine	Yes	Yes	Safe	Good; causes sexual dysfunction
Reboxetine	Yes	No	Safe	Good; some sexual dysfunction
Moclobemide	No	No	Safe	Good; low rates of sexual dysfunction

+, 40 mg of Paroxetine compared to 20 mg

therapy, and the advice is that treatment should be maintained for as long as the patient wishes to reduce the risk of new episodes (Montgomery, 1997).

Field studies suggest that in clinical practice only a minority of patients with depression receive medication regimes that would be considered adequate; in fact, the figure has been estimated at less than 10% (Keller and Boland, 1998). Failures in diagnosis and management play a part, but it has been estimated that less than half of patients adhere to the treatment plan agreed with their doctor (Keller and Boland, 1998). Common reasons for early discontinuation include the belief that medication is no longer needed when symptoms improve, side-effects, fear of drug dependence and a dislike of taking medication. The need for thorough assessment, psychoeducation and regular review and compliance monitoring are clear. An enteric-coated once-weekly preparation of fluoxetine 90 mg ('Prozac Weekly') has been shown in some studies to improve compliance. It has recently been licensed in the US for continuation and maintenance treatment of depression, and may provide a useful treatment option for some patients.

Despite the efficacy of antidepressant drugs in the prevention of the relapse or recurrence of depression, a significant proportion of patients taking adequate treatment experience breakthrough symptoms. No trials have been carried out that shed light on this difficult problem, but common strategies include increasing dose, changing medication, adding a second drug, increasing psychological and social support or initiating a specific psychological therapy.

Other drugs

Lithium has been shown in several placebo-controlled studies to be effective in the prevention of depressive recurrence. The optimal blood level is 0.5–0.7 mmol per litre and it is generally well-tolerated at these doses. In a direct comparison with antidepressant medication (imipramine), lithium alone was a less effective prophylactic. It is commonly used to augment antidepressants in refractory cases, and in these patients continuation therapy should also be with a combination of antidepressant and lithium.

Various other medications have been reported in small, open-label studies to have beneficial effects in long-term treatment, and some have substantial use in clinical practice. These include the anticonvulsants carbamazepine and valproate, and the hormones thyroxine, triiodothyronine and oestrogen. St John's Wort, a herbal extract, is effective in the acute treatment of mild to moderate depression, has fewer side-effects than other antidepressant drugs and appears to be safe for long-term use (Barnes et al, 2001). Evidence of its efficacy as a continuation and maintenance therapy is awaited.

Psychological treatments

Psychological therapies for depression have traditionally tended to extend over long periods of time, and it could be argued that psychotherapists, unlike psychopharmacologists, have avoided the pitfall of approaching depression as a disorder with short, discrete and easily treatable episodes. Nevertheless, the drive towards evidence-based medicine has stimulated the development of shorter, focused therapies that are more amenable to measurement in clinical trials. Although only a few long-term studies have been published, it could be that the continuation of therapy that is effective in the acute phase of treatment will reduce the risk of relapse and recurrence, particularly if delivered in combination with medication.

The Pittsburgh Maintenance Study of Depression (Kupfer et al, 1992) took a cohort of depressed patients with a high risk of recurrence, and offered acute treatment with a combination of medication (imipramine) and interpersonal therapy (IPT). This is a structured, one-to-one therapy that focuses on the symptoms of depression and the key roles and relationships in the life of the patient. Those that responded and remained well throughout a continuation phase were randomized to receive one of the following treatment options:

1 monthly IPT alone
2 medication clinic and imipramine
3 monthly IPT and placebo
4 medication clinic and placebo
5 imipramine and monthly IPT.

During the first year, the combination of imipramine and IPT was more effective than medication alone in preventing recurrence, although the rates later converged. In patients taking placebo or no medication, IPT significantly reduced the recurrence rate.

Cognitive behavioural therapy (CBT) is also a structured, one-to-one therapy that has proven efficacy in the acute treatment of major depression. It aims to identify and challenge thinking patterns that perpetuate depressive mood states. In a large study of patients with chronic depression, a combination of nefazodone and CBT was found to be more effective in the acute phase than either treatment alone (Keller et al, 2000), and it is likely that this benefit extends into continuation treatment. The efficacy of CBT as a maintenance therapy was demonstrated in a study of a cohort of patients with recurrent depression who had recovered on medication (Fava et al, 1998). Patients were randomized to receive either CBT aimed at residual depressive symptoms or standard clinical management over 20 weeks, during which time their medication was withdrawn. In the subsequent 2-year follow-up, the rate of recurrence in CBT-treated patients was 25%, compared to 80% in the control group.

The value of other psychological managements is clear from clinical practice, but difficult to quantify in research studies. The roles of psychoeducation and compliance monitoring have been discussed earlier. Recurrence of depression is frequently related to acute or ongoing psychological stresses, such as bereavement or marital conflict, and a supportive psychotherapeutic relationship may be a key factor in coping with such stresses for a patient with a high risk of recurrence. Similarly, for patients with chronic or recurring depression CBT, supportive therapy or occupational therapy may help preserve adequate levels of functioning despite the persistence of symptoms.

Electroconvulsive therapy

Electroconvulsive therapy (ECT) remains an effective and widely used option for the acute treatment of depression, and its use as a continuation and maintenance treatment has been supported by some practitioners for many years. However, the published evidence consists of case reports and retrospective studies, but no prospective randomized controlled trials. Continuation ECT has particularly been used where there is a prior history of antidepressant treatment resistance, severe episodes of depression or a history of relapse despite maintenance medication. Typical regimes continue effective twice-weekly ECT with gradually decreasing frequency, normally maintaining with one treatment per month, but increasing if symptoms return (Wijkstra et al, 2000). Long-term ECT appears to be safe, with the main side-effects being persistent subjective memory loss (generally not confirmed on objective testing). The risk of recurrence is lower if maintenance medication is also continued.

Conclusion

A strong argument is developing that there is a requirement for a widening of the view of the treatment of depression. In a significant proportion of cases it should be considered as a disorder with a risk of chronicity, recurrence or treatment failure, and patients should be engaged in the development of treatment plans that target the full remission of symptoms and the prevention of relapse and recurrence. Although more needs to be known about which patients require long-term treatment, an attempt should be made during assessment of the depressed patient to identify factors that are currently associated with a poor prognosis.

The range of treatment options for the depressed patient continues to increase, and it is to be hoped that more evidence will emerge to clarify the long-term use of existing medical and psychological treatments, and particularly of combination therapies. Some of the newer strategies for the short-term treatment of depression would appear to offer advantages in safety, tolerability and cost if they prove to be effective in the longer term, for example, alternative antidepressants such as St John's Wort, structured exercise therapy and transcranial magnetic stimulation. It seems likely that this field will see significant developments in the coming years.

References

Angst J, Kupfer DJ, Rosenbaum JF (1996) Recovery from depression: risk or reality? *Acta Psychiatr Scand* **93**(6): 413–419.

Barnes J, Anderson LA, Phillipson JD (2001) St John's Wort (*Hypericum perforatum* L.): A review of its chemistry, pharmacology and clinical properties. *J Pharm Pharmacol* **53**: 583–600.

Brodaty H, Luscombe G, Peisah C, et al (2001) A 25-year longitudinal, comparison study of the outcome of depression. *Psychol Med* **31**: 1347–1359.

Coryell W, Leon A, Winokur G, et al (1996) Importance of psychotic features to long-term course in major depressive disorder. *Am J Psychiatry* **153**: 483–489.

Fava GA, Rafanelli C, Grandi S, et al (1998) Prevention of recurrent depression with cognitive behavioural therapy. *Arch Gen Psychiatry* **55**: 816–820.

Frank E, Prien RF, Jarrett RB, et al (1991) Conceptualization and rationale for consensus definitions of terms in major depressive disorder. *Arch Gen Psychiatry* **48**: 851–855.

Goldberg JF, Harrow M, Grossman LS (1995) Recurrent affective syndromes in bipolar and unipolar mood disorders at follow-up. *Br J Psychiatry* **166**:382–385.

Greden JF (2001) The burden of recurrent depression: Causes, consequences and future prospects. *J Clin Psychiatry* **62**(suppl 22): 5–9.

Holm KJ, Jarvis B, Foster RH (2000) Mirtazapine. A pharmacoeconomic review of its use in depression. *Pharmacoeconomics* **17**: 515–534.

Keller MB, Boland RJ (1998) Implications of failing to achieve successful long-term maintenance treatment of recurrent unipolar major depression. *Biol Psychiatry* **44**: 348–360.

Keller MB, Hirschfeld RMA, Hanks D (1997) Double depression: A distinctive subtype of unipolar depression. *J Affect Disord* **45**: 65–73.

Keller MB, McCullough JP, Klein DN, et al (2000) A comparison of nefazodone, the cognitive-behavioural analysis system of psychotherapy, and their combination for the treatment of chronic depression. *N Engl J Med* **342**: 1462–1470.

Kessler RC, McGonagle KA, Zhao S, et al (1994) Lifetime and 12-month prevalence of DSM-III-R psychiatric disorders in the United States. *Arch Gen Psychiatry* **51**: 8–19.

Kovacs M, Obrosky DS, Goldston D, et al (1997) Major depressive disorder in youths with IDDM. A controlled prospective study of course and outcome. *Diabetes Care* **20**: 45–51.

Kupfer DJ (1991) Long-term treatment of depression. *J Clin Psychiatry* **52**(suppl 5): 28–34.

Kupfer DJ, Frank E, Perel JM, et al (1992) Five-year outcome for maintenance therapies in recurrent depression. *Arch Gen Psychiatry* **49**: 769–773.

Lewinsohn PM, Clarke GN, Seeley JR, et al (1994) Major depression in community adolescents: age at onset, episode duration, and time to recurrence. *Am Acad Child Adolesc Psychiatry* **33**: 809–818.

Maj M, Veltro F, Pirozzi R, et al (1992) Pattern of recurrence of illness after recovery from an episode of major depression: a prospective study. *Am J Psychiatry* **149**: 795–800.

Montgomery SA (1997) The need for long-term treatment of depression. *Eur Neuropsychopharm* **7**: S309–313.

Mueller TI, Leon AC, Keller MB, et al (1999) Recurrence after recovery from major depressive disorder during 15 years of observational follow-up. *Am J Psychiatry* **156**: 1000–1006.

Ramana R, Paykel ES, Cooper Z, et al (1995) Remission and relapse in major depression: a two-year prospective follow-up study. *Psychol Med* **25**: 1161–1170.

Reimherr FW, Amsterdam JD, Quitkin FM, et al (1998) Optimal length of continuation therapy in depression: A prospective assessment during long-term fluoxetine treatment. *Am J Psychiatry* **155**: 1247–1253.

Sargent PA, Kjaer KH, Bench CJ, et al (2000) Brain serotonin$_{1A}$ receptor binding measured by positron emission tomography with [^{11}C]WAY-100635. *Arch Gen Psychiatry* **57**: 174–180.

Solomon DA, Keller MB, Leon AC, et al (2000) Multiple recurrences of major depressive disorder. *Am J Psychiatry* **157**: 229–233.

Souery D, Amsterdam J, de Montigny C, et al (1999) Treatment resistant depression: Methodological overview and operational criteria. *Eur Neuropsychopharm* **9**: 83–91.

Storosum JG, van Zwieten BJ, Vermeulen HDB, et al (2001) Relapse and recurrence prevention in major depression: A critical review of placebo-controlled efficacy studies with special emphasis on methodological issues. *Eur Psychiatry* **16**: 327–335.

Van Londen L, Molenaar RP, Goekoop JG, et al (1998) Three- to five-year prospective follow-up of outcome in major depression. *Psychol Med* **28**: 731–735.

Wijkstra J, Nolen WA, Algra A, et al (2000) Relapse prevention in major depressive disorder after successful ECT: A literature review and a naturalistic case series. *Acta Psychiat Scand* **102**: 454–460.

chapter 7

Psychological therapies

Jeremy Holmes and Charles Montgomery

Introduction

Three decades of intensive research have established beyond any doubt the efficacy of psychological therapies in depression (Roth and Fonagy, 1996). Given the equally powerful evidence showing the importance of social disadvantage and loss in the origins of depression—discussed elsewhere in this volume—this is hardly surprising. If loss of a relationship can precipitate depression, as it undoubtedly can, then it follows that the re-establishment of a relationship through therapy may be likely to help in the process of recovery.

That simple formulation guides our approach in this chapter, but of course begs many of the questions that preoccupy researchers and clinicians alike. Which of the several psychological therapies is most appropriate for which type of depression? What is the 'mechanism of action' of psychological therapies in depression? Should psychological therapies be combined with pharmacotherapy, and if so how should that be handled by the clinician? What is the appropriate 'dose' of psychological therapy, and can it be adjusted to prevent relapse? Do psychological therapies have a role to play in resistant depression and in working with the suicidal patient? These are some of the topics we shall review along the way. The chapter is divided into three parts; we start by looking at psychological models of depression as theorized by the various psychotherapeutic modalites; this includes an historical launchpad which is essential in understanding more recent developments. We then go on to describe in some detail techniques used in therapy with depressed patients; and end by looking at the research evidence which can help answer some of the questioned listed above.

Psychological models of depression

The clinical features of depression can conveniently be thought about within a tripartite biopsychosocial framework, each element of which needs to be given due weight in a comprehensive approach to treatment (Table 7.1). The disorder of mood itself—feeling 'low', 'heavy', that 'everything is an effort', together with so-called 'biological' features of weight loss, loss of libido, retardation, sleep disturbance and anhedonia—lend themselves to a biological perspective which takes into account genetic predisposition, neurotransmitter disturbance, and psychopharmacological treatments. Psychological approaches focus on guilt, suppressed anger, low self-esteem, hopelessness, inability to see a

Table 7.1 Biopsychosocial framework for depression

Biological	Psychological	Social
• Low mood	• Guilt	• Loss
• Anhedonia	• Supressed anger	• Disturbance in interpersonal relationships
• Reduced appetite/ weight loss	• Low self-esteem	• Lack of a sense of agency
• Sleep disturbance/ EMW	• Hopelessness	• Deficient social support/roles
• Decreased libido	• Inability to see a future	
• Retardation	• Vision through dark-tinted glasses	

EMW, early morning wakening

future, and the vision through dark-tinted glasses which characterizes the depressive world-view. A social take on depression emphasizes loss as a precipitant; the absence of, or disturbance in, interpersonal relationships; lack of a sense of agency; and deficient social support and roles.

Intriguing links between physiological and psychological models of depression are beginning to emerge. It is likely that morphological changes occur in the human infant's brain in response to early painful events such as separation or loss. Gold et al (1988) suggest that early loss may sensitize receptors leading to vulnerability to depression later in life. The phenomenon of receptor kindling derived from studies of seizure thresholds is a useful paradigm to understand the mechanisms underlying this increased vulnerability (Post, 1992). Repeated early trauma 'sets' limbic system receptors to a state of chronic subthreshold activation; in later life, ideas or images which may appear only distantly connected to the theme of loss might be sufficient to tip the neurochemical system into a depressed state. This model goes some way to explain the psychoanalytic observation that an imagined or a symbolic loss is as potent a stressor in provoking depression as a real loss.

Psychoanalytic models

Psychoanalytic approaches combine the intrapsychic and interpersonal— and indeed might justly claim to have stimulated both trends in thinking about depression. Freud's starting point was psychosocial in that he, like others, saw the parallels between grief and depression (Freud, 1917). He was taken particularly with the self-reproaches that characterize some people's depression. He suggested that this internal criticism could be seen as the internalization of a dialogue with someone from the past by whom the sufferer feels let down or abandoned. From a psychoanalytic perspective current loss triggers these feelings of resentment from the past which constitute an intrinsic vulnerability to depression in the human psyche. The loss of exclusive possession of mother implicit in the Oedipal triangle and the feelings of rage turned inward this sets up are what re-emerge in melancholia in this early psychoanalytic model.

Melanie Klein (1935) also saw depression as part of human development in her notion of psychological movement from 'paranoid-schizoid position' to the 'depressive position' somewhere around the end of the first year of life. Here, depression can be a positive experience in that it represents the moment at which the child begins to realize that the frustrating absent mother is one and the same as the nurturing loving caregiver, and an acknowledgement of guilt that one has hated the person one also loves. This suggests two types of depression. The first is a paranoid-tinged feeling based on splitting in which one is trapped in a world of loss and envy and despair, forever separated from the good things of life. The second is a more mature sense of grounded grief representing a move towards maturity, and is often seen in patients undergoing dynamic psychotherapy as they begin to diminish acting out behaviour and to contain their more difficult emotions. The latter view justifies the psychoanalytic aphorism 'where there's depression there's hope'. Klein developed the important idea of 'reinstatement of the lost object' within the psyche, so that if development is healthy, or therapy successful, the individual feels the object is secure inside their inner world, even though lost in the outer world.

Other authors have added a number of other psychoanalytic angles on depression including:

- The idea of a *harsh super-ego* constantly criticizing sufferers and reinforcing their sense of failure. This may represent the real strictures of controlling and perfectionistic parents, but may also emanate from the depressed person him/herself, as feelings of disappointment and anger are projected onto parental figures.
- A *narcissistic* aspect to depression in which the sufferer becomes increasingly self-preoccupied and withdrawn from relationships with others, this being seen as a response to failure of the caregiving environment. The idea of a 'narcissistic wound' lying at the heart of depression explains some of the phenomena described when considering cognitive approaches (eg taking every slight or loss 'personally').
- The *sado-masochism* or dominance–submission of depressive relationships in which depressed patients appear to seek out a victim role, and to be punishing those around them with their misery and

hopelessness. This can be linked with an attachment perspective in which it is postulated that failure of a more reciprocal type of attachment can lead to a switch into a bullied/clinging pattern in order to maintain some kind of connection to a secure base, however compromised.

- The notion of *disappointment* was developed by Jacobson (1971), in an attempt to account for the pervasive low self-esteem of the depressive. She argues that if loss or disappointment occur in early childhood, before self and object representations have been fully differentiated, this creates a vulnerability to loss in later life, since when the object is lost it feels as though part of the self has been destroyed as well.

The theme of suicide is never far away in working with depressed patients. The therapist will need to be at home with discussion of suicide and its possible consequences. It is important to separate whenever possible the *understanding* of suicidal feelings that is central to psychotherapeutic work, and their *management*, which is part of wider psychiatric care (Holmes, 1996). A full discussion of the psychotherapy of suicide is beyond the scope of this chapter, but a few remarks are in order. Karl Menninger (1933) believed that three wishes might contribute towards a suicidal act—the wish to kill, the wish to be killed and the wish to die. The wish to kill may not only be directed towards an internal object but as in the case of the suicide bomber, is often designed to destroy the lives of the survivors in one final act of revenge, a catastrophic settling of scores. It is sometimes helpful to remind suicidal patients that if they were to kill themselves their mental pain would not disappear altogether, but outlive them, transferred to their loved ones.

Suicide can be viewed as a form of 'acting out'. Hale (1985) introduces the idea of a 'suicide fantasy'. The suicide fantasy, according to Hale, involves an ambivalent relationship between the part of the self which will survive, the 'surviving self', and the body that is identified with an object that has to die. An important part of the fantasy is that of the pleasurable survival of an essential part of the self. Thus, it would be a mistake to overemphasize the role of aggression in suicide. The unbearable loss of a loved one and the fantasy of reunion can in themselves lead to suicide especially where there has been a highly dependent relationship. Many suicidal patients reveal strong and unresolved dependency needs towards a lost object; suicide may be viewed as a regressive wish for reunion with a lost maternal figure. Interestingly, there is a significant correlation between suicide and the anniversary of a parent's death (Bunch and Barraclough, 1971). As Gabbard (1994) comments: 'When an individual's self-esteem and self-integrity depend on attachment to a lost object, suicide may seem to be the only way to restore self-cohesion'.

Cognitive behavioural models

Many sufferers blame their depression on adverse circumstances, and social psychiatric research suggests that they are right to do so, since those suffering from depression are five times more likely to have experienced an adverse loss-like event in the previous year than those who do not become depressed. Nevertheless, the majority of those who experience such losses do not become depressed, which implies that factors other than circumstance also play their part. Moreover, recent research suggests that some individuals may be more prone to adverse life events than others, and that this tendency has, in part at least, a genetic basis.

Cognitive therapy for depression, devised by the former psychoanalyst Aaron Beck (Beck et al, 1979), takes as its starting point the perspective implied in Epictetus' famous statement 'men are troubled not so much by things, as their perception of things'. What we make of what we are made of is what determines whether or not we become depressed in the face of adversity.

Cognitive therapy identifies a particular set of negativistic ideas and attitudes that are characteristic of depression. They are 'cognitive' in that they are the product of faulty reasoning. In Beck's model, depressed mood is the result of negative thinking rather than vice versa, and if faulty logic can be corrected therapeutically, then mood will lift. There are a number of typical patterns of negative thinking that present themselves as 'automatic thoughts' which intrude themselves on depressive sufferers and determine their outlook (Table 7.2).

Table 7.2 Patterns of thought explored in cognitive therapy

- **Arbitrary inference.** This means interpreting an event in a negative way without considering alternative explanations (eg 'the fact that my girlfriend didn't ring me last night proves that she doesn't care about me'). Here, low self-esteem both creates negative inferences but, in a vicious circle, also results from them
- **Selective abstraction.** Taking facts out of context (eg 'my wife goes out with her girlfriends every Wednesday night so she obviously doesn't want to spend time with me') even though she may spend every other evening with her husband
- **Over-generalization.** Taking one negative experience to represent the whole (eg 'when I asked for a date she refused me so I must be totally unattractive')
- **Personalization.** Adverse experiences are interpreted self-referentially (eg 'the fact that my son is doing badly at school must be due to me being a bad parent'). This clearly underlies many of the guilty feelings which dog the depressive
- **Minimization and maximization.** Negative events are blown up out of proportion while successes are diminished in importance
- **Dichotomous thinking.** Things are seen in black-or-white terms (eg 'If I make a mistake, that proves I am a total failure')

Cognitive approaches see mental structures in terms of a hierarchy, summarized in the acronym EARS—*E*xpectations, *A*ssumptions, *R*ules and *S*chemata. These move from relatively superficial and consciousness-accessible expectations and assumptions, to deeply ingrained and less accessible schemata. The latter are not too far removed from the psycho-analytic notion of internal objects and their relationships. Schemata comprise a set of 'meta-rules' which determine one's outlook, and which in the depressed person might take the form of self-statements such as 'whatever you do you are bound to fail', 'you are a waste of space', 'you will never make another person happy', etc. Teasdale et al (1995) argue, that in chronic and severe depression, therapy has to reach and challenge these deeper levels if it is to be successful.

Another influential cognitive theory of depression flows from the work of Seligman (1975) who famously coined the phrase 'learned help-lessness' to describe experimental situations in which dogs, unable to fathom or control a reward–punishment schedule, 'gave up' in a way that was reminiscent of the behaviour of depressed patients. A key assumption here is that self-esteem depends on a sense of mastery and the capacity to influence one's environment. As with the vicious circle of arbitrary inference, the withdrawal and inertia of depression itself reinforces the helplessness/hopelessness which may have initiated the illness in the first place.

Relational/social/attachment models

A social perspective takes it as axiomatic that humans are social animals and that self-esteem depends on feeling part of a network whose members play reciprocally reinforcing roles. Biological and to some extent cognitive models of depression concentrate on the individual and his/her internal workings, be they biochemical or intrapsychic. Social models are essentially *inter*personal. They start from the position that such a patterned behavioural response as depression must have adaptive significance and be comprehensible from an evolutionary perspective. The social ranking theory of depression sees its symptoms as arising out of dominance hierarchies within human groups (Gilbert, 2000). When individuals lose status, for example, through separation from a partner or loss of 'resource-holding potential' (eg bankruptcy), they are intensely vulnerable to aggression and displacement from high ranking position within the group. The depressive response provides a period of with-drawal in which the affected individual can, as it were, slide quietly down the dominance ladder without provoking attack, and, with reduced activity and appetite, consume only modest resources in a way that would not provoke hostility from competitors.

Social models, and in particular Bowlby's attachment theory (Holmes, 1993, 2001), put loss as the central theme of their theorizing about depression. For Bowlby, good self-esteem, and healthy curiosity depend on secure attachment. That attachment provides the necessary secure base which underlies healthy mental functioning and is ideally directed to a trusted other—usually a parent or spouse—but may also be to a particular role, job, social group or skill. If the secure base is lost, for example, through death or divorce or unemployment, then the affected individual will undergo the grief/mourning response. Mourning has many features in common with depression, and if delayed or prolonged, a clinical picture indistinguishable from depression may develop. Conversely, depression may be the presenting manifestation of a mourning that has been suppressed or which the sufferer has failed to overcome.

Depression may also arise in troubled as opposed to lost relationships. Thus, one member of a couple may 'carry' the depression for both of them, through the phenomenon of 'projective identification' in which unwanted psychic experience is unconsciously transmitted from one individual to another. In another equally common systemic scenario there is a vicious circle in which one member of the couple becomes mildly depressed, at which point the spouse takes over his/her role within the family, which then reinforces the sufferer's sense of uselessness and irrelevance.

Specific therapeutic techniques in depression

Psychological approaches to depression can be classified under three headings. First, there are generic therapies such as psychoanalytic or group analytical therapy, applied to depressed patients. Second, there are modified generic therapies, such as mindfulness-based cognitive therapy (Teasdale et al, 1995), or couple therapy (Leff et al, 2000), and psychodynamic interpersonal therapy (Shapiro, 1995) applied to depression. Third, there are therapies devised for depressed patients, of which Klerman and Weissman's (Weissman and Markowitz, 1994) interpersonal therapy (IPT) and Frank's interpersonal–social rhythms therapy (Craighead et al, 1997) are among the best known. We shall consider each of these in turn.

Generic therapies
Psychoanalytic psychotherapy does not specify particular therapeutic techniques for depressed patients. However, certain principles will

govern the evolution of the transference in working with depression. First, as in any therapy, there is the need to form a good working alliance. This will be confounded by three types of counter-transference emotions: despair, irritation, and thwarted desire to nurture the patient. It is the therapist's job to hold onto the hope in the early stages of therapy—in Bion's (1961) terms to 'metabolize' and 'detoxify' feelings of hopelessness. Resentment and anger are often, but not invariably, features of working with depressed patients. Here, it is tempting to bully patients into seeing how distorted their world-view is, and how they neglect or actively destroy the good things about themselves.

This too must be resisted as it recreates the sado-masochistic structure that characterizes the patient's inner world, and substitutes dominance–submission for empathic responsiveness. Equally, the pity and longing to help that some depressed patients evoke have to be tempered with attention to boundaries—it is all too easy to become sucked in to the regressed inner world of the depressive in which the capacity to think and so to rise above pain has been abandoned. In Oedipal terms, there must always be a third term or an external viewpoint from which the depressed feelings can more objectively be viewed. Winnicott's (1965) description of healthy 'hate in the counter-transference' makes a powerful case for both maintaining one's integrity as a therapist at the same time as being able to identify with the patient's distress.

The psychoanalytic psychotherapist working with depressed patients will frequently focus on loss. There will be the precipitating loss which has led to the present depression, but equally important is to seek out prior episodes of loss or abandonment that may well have been suppressed and inadequately grieved. This may centre on a parent who has abandoned the patient, the arrival of a displacing sibling, or the death of a loved grandparent. In each case, the therapist will try to relate the devastating response to the immediate situation to an earlier stage of the patients' lives where their vulnerability was at its greatest and yet their capacity to control their environment was limited. The passivity, helplessness, and feeling of trappedness of depression will be reframed in the light of this regression to an earlier loss.

While focusing in this way on the content of the patient's biography, the therapist will also try to provide a secure, responsive and reliable base from which he/she can begin to work through the grief associated with disappointment. Ultimately, the task of the therapy is to help the patient internalize a more benign version of the abandoning object—to see, for example, that parents whose care was so inadequate were themselves struggling with their own difficulties. Pedder (1982) identifies three situations where this is particularly difficult: when a parent disappears competely during childhood, when a spouse precipitately abandons their partner, and when a therapist 'drops' a patient for no apparent reason. In all three cases it is extremely difficult to internalize a benign version of the abandoning object.

In recovery, a more balanced version of the intense guilt felt by depressed patients will also be found. Patients no longer blame themselves omnipotently for 'everything', while at the same time they begin to take appropriate responsibility for the part they play in the maintenance of their depression, as suggested in the Kleinian idea of the depressive position. Thus, for example, an abandoned spouse may finally be able to look at ways in which he/she has driven the partner away, and, while remaining appropriately angry, to see that there were some happy times as well as miserable ones.

Psychodynamic interpersonal therapy (Margison, 2002) is another generic therapy that has been extensively used to treat mild to moderate depression (Shapiro, 1995). Here, the emphasis is especially on empathic responses by the therapist, and on helping the patient to find metaphors to capture the essence of his/her feelings, however gloomy. Transferential feelings of rejection and loss in relation to the therapy itself (eg at the time of the therapist's holiday breaks) are proactively talked through in the hope that they can be worked through with appropriate sadness and anger, rather than reinforcing depressive affects.

Group analytical techniques can be used effectively in the treatment of depression (McDermut et al, 2001). Of Yalom's (1970) well-known therapeutic factors in group analysis, the instillation of hope, universality, interpersonal learning and group cohesiveness will all in different ways help the depressive to overcome his/her sense of isolation and alienation from society.

Modified generic therapies
Cognitive behavioural therapy (CBT)
Cognitive therapy was originally devised as a treatment for depressed patients, but has now widened greatly in scope. As cognitive *behavioural* therapy (CBT) it also incorporates behavioural techniques which are as important in helping depressed patients as are the strictly cognitive components of the therapy. Some key components of CBT treatment for depression, summarized in Table 7.3, include:

- Keeping a mood diary, so the patient can begin to identify variations in mood through the day, and the triggers which lead to perpetuation of their misery. A mood diary also helps with objectification and distancing from the depressed mood itself, thus creating the beginnings of mastery.
- Identifying 'automatic thoughts' as they arise in relation to difficult everyday situations. The patient, as a 'scientist collaborator', is then helped to question and challenge the basis for these thoughts and to practise substituting alternative versions of events.
- Using estimated percentages for the weight attached to different thoughts. Thus if a girlfriend failed to return a call, the depressed automatic thought might be 'she doesn't care about me'—weight 90%; the alternative might be 'her phone wasn't working'—weight 10%. As therapy progresses the percentages assigned to negative automatic thoughts diminish.
- Reality testing enlarges on the above so that the patient is encouraged to

---

Table 7.3 Components of CBT treatment for depression

- Mood diary
- Identifying automatic thoughts
- Estimating weight attached to different thoughts
- Reality testing
- Activity scheduling
- (Attentional control)

confront his/her negative assumptions and test them out in reality. For example, the patient may equate happiness with reaching the top of his/her chosen career. The patient is then asked to consider whether it is in fact the case that highly successful people are never prone to depression, or, conversely, whether those less ambitious are always miserable.

- The behavioural component of CBT often prescribes 'activity scheduling' as part of the recovery package. Inertia, anxiety and a feeling of emptiness are often part of the depressive's experience of their day. Activity scheduling breaks the day up into manageable parts and makes a plan, however small, for some kind of meaningful activity during each segment.

- In cases of severe depression Teasdale et al (1995) have found that CBT alone is ineffective. They advocate combining CBT with 'attentional control' techniques derived from meditation which, it is claimed, helps sufferers in a more direct way to achieve the detachment from their feelings which is the fundamental aim of CBT.

Couple therapy for depression

A recent study comparing antidepressant medication and couple therapy in depression showed impressive results for couple therapy (Leff et al, 2000). There are many ways in which a systemic approach can help in depression. For example, the couple is asked to consider in detail the spousal behaviour stimulated by the patient's illness. Often an over-attentive spouse may further de-skill an already hopeless depressed partner. Another common pattern is the 'see-saw' of depression in which no sooner does one member of the partnership feel better than the other begins to be miserable, and may do his/her utmost to return to the status quo *ante*. The couple is then set homework tasks that attempt to reinforce positive activity on the part of the patient and encourage the spouse to hold back in his/her attempt to be 'helpful'.

Specifically antidepressant therapies

Interpersonal therapy (IPT)

This is the best known. It is an integrative therapy that draws on psychodynamic, attachment and social-relational models. Devised by Klerman and

Weissman as a manualized therapy that could be incorporated into evaluative research, IPT is a 10-session therapy that starts from the firm view that depression is an illness. Thus, it immediately counteracts the common masochistic cognition that depressives' suffering is their own fault. Depression is seen to arise out of one of four main constellations: unresolved loss, psychosocial transitions, relationship conflict, or social skills deficit.

- Loss is worked on, as in psychodynamic therapy, but using techniques derived from 'guided grief', including encouraging the sufferer to reminisce about good times with their loved one, to bring momentoes to the sessions, and to undergo mourning rituals. These all aim to expose the depressed person to the painful feelings of sadness, to survive the experience, and to move on to reparation and a new beginning.
- Psychosocial transitions include such events as leaving home, marriage, divorce and separation, job changes and retirement. Here, an adult life-cycle perspective is taken, and the sufferer is helped to consider the balance sheet of losses and gains that such changes entail.
- Relationship conflict is dealt with using systemic ideas similar to those described under couple therapy for depression. The couple is seen together and the basic principles of clear communication, owning feelings, acceptance, and conflict resolution inform therapeutic strategies.
- Interpersonal skills deficit is generally thought to be the most problematic of the psychological variables underlying depression. The therapist will use role-play, video-feedback and other methods to help improve basic social skills.

Interpersonal–social rhythm therapy (IPSRT; Frank et al 1994)
This is another tailor-made therapy devised for patients suffering from bipolar disorder. In addition to CBT-type psychological approaches, this therapy tries to address the biological features of severe depression, such as sleep disturbance, poor concentration and disruption of the day's structure. Patients are encouraged to adopt a strict routine as they go through their day, to be meticulous about sleep hygiene, and to follow healthy eating and exercise regimes.

Evidence-based psychotherapy for depression

The past three decades have seen a large number of major trials of psychological therapies for depression throughout the world. In this section we shall see what light this research literature can throw on a number of key questions for clinicians. What is the overall effectiveness of psychological therapies and can this be translated into effectiveness in the clinic? How do psychological therapies compare with pharmacological treatments? What is the role of combined antidepressant and psychological therapy? Are some therapies more effective in some situations than others? How important is therapist skill in influencing outcome? What interventions are best for less severe depression in primary care settings? What is the role of maintenance psychological therapy in preventing relapse? Are different therapies needed for different diagnostic groups, especially bipolar disorder, major depressive disorder, and dysthymia?

The history of psychotherapy research in depression can be divided into a number of phases. The early work comprised small-scale trials, and single case reports. Then came a number of major multicentre studies which form the core data and benchmark for all interested in the field. Next, there have been meta-analytic integration of the major studies, and most recently there has been a number of studies looking as specific aspects, such as combination therapy or therapy in particular settings.

The four 'classical' examples here are the US National Institute for Mental Health multicentre study (Elkin, 1994), the University of Minnesota study (Hollon et al, 1992), the Sheffield Psychotherapy project (Shapiro, 1995) and Frank's Pittsburgh study (Frank and Spanier, 1995). All are based on brief therapy (8–10 sessions), and all use a degree of randomization and comparison methodology—either with placebo or one therapy with another. Sheffield, for instance, compares interpersonal– psychodynamic therapy with CBT. Outcome measures are target symptom reduction and problem resolution. All were based on outpatient samples with mild to moderate severe depression.

Comparison studies and meta-analyses can attempt to answer one of three questions:

1 Is psychotherapy better than no therapy or placebo?
2 Is psychological treatment better than or equal to antidepressant therapy?
3 Is any one form of psychological therapy superior to any other?

The answer to the first question is an unequivocal vote of confidence in psychological therapies. For example, two meta-analytic studies showed that specific psychological therapies were more markedly effective than waiting list controls, with effect sizes varying from 0.74 to 2.15 (Neitzel et al, 1987; Dobson, 1988). However, it should be noted that these early meta-analyses were not intention-to-treat samples, and the effects were partially attenuated once allegiance effects (tendency of researchers to favour their 'own' brand of therapy) were taken into account (Robinson et al, 1990).

There has been a lot of debate about the relative efficacy of psychotherapy and antidepressants. In the US National Institute of Mental Health (NIMH) trial, antidepressants plus clinical management outperformed both IPT and CBT, but Hollon's et al's (1992) study, which included a two year follow-up, found that CBT and antidepressants did significantly better than placebo and clinical management. This study rehabilitated CBT as a front-line psychological therapy in depression, and it has been suggested that the poor performance in the NIMH trial was due to one centre where therapists were poorly trained and supervised. This suggests that therapist skill and 'quality control' (ie good supervision) in psychological therapy is important.

It is probably easier and cheaper to prescribe an antidepressant than for the patient to undergo a course of psychotherapy. On the other hand, there are a significant group of patients who do not want antidepressants, fail to respond to them, or cannot tolerate their side-effects. For these clearly psychological therapy is going to be the first line of treatment. Many patients referred for specialist psychological therapy suffer from chronic or 'double depression' (ie major depressive disorder and dysthymia), have been ill continuously or intermittently for long periods and are already on antidepressants. In this situation there is good evidence that the combination of psycho- and pharmacotherapy produces better results than either alone. In a striking recent study, Keller et al (2000) found that in chronic depression, using an intention-to-treat design and large samples, acute phase remission could be achieved in less than 50% of patients offered monotherapy (antidepressants or a modified form of CBT), but 73% of those given combination therapy. If drop-out were excluded, the figures were for psychotherapy 52%, for antidepressants 55%, but for combination therapy an unprecedented 85%.

It is reasonable to suppose that antidepressants and psychotherapy target different aspects of depression. Thus, those on drugs tended to lose symptoms, such as sleep disturbance more quickly, but social functioning is likely to improve with the help of psychotherapy.

The relative efficacy of different psychological therapies is a controversial subject. Proving that a good treatment is better than no treatment is easy. Proving that a good treatment is better than a slightly less good one is much more difficult. Paykel and Scott (2000) report a meta-analysis of 29 controlled trials showing that CBT and IPT both performed equally well (around 50% in intention to treat design compared with pharmacotherapy's 58%) and seemingly more effective than brief dynamic therapy (35%), which barely outperformed waiting-list controls. Advocates of dynamic therapy (including the present authors) question this finding on the grounds that dynamic therapy is often less easy to manualize and control, and cite studies, such as the Sheffield project (Shapiro, 1995), where the outcome for CBT and dynamic therapy were identical at 16 weeks, although CBT produced a 'smoother' and more rapid initial response. In Paykel and Scott's analysis, IPT was found to be more effective when a significant other was included in the therapy and this is consistent with the findings of the London depression trial (Leff et al, 2000) where couple therapy significantly outperformed antidepressants. The latter study is interesting in that the intended CBT arm had to be discontinued due to a very high drop-out rate in this chronic and very disturbed group of patients.

Maintenance psychotherapy is another important topic. Hollon et al (1992) found that CBT was more effective in relapse prevention than antidepressants, while Frank and Spanier (1995) showed that maintenance IPT (once a month following more intensive acute phase treatment) and pharmacotherapy were roughly equivalent. An interesting finding from the latter study was that 'high quality' therapy was markedly more effective in relapse prevention than less good therapy.

A final topic concerns the role of psychological therapies relative to severity of depression. It seems that in the primary care setting, with presumably relatively less severe disorders, generic counselling, specific therapies such as CBT, and antidepressants have roughly equivalent outcomes (Wagner and Simon, 2001). Patient preference becomes an important issue here since those that preferred counselling did significantly better than those that were simply allocated to it. Given that psychotherapy is essentially a collaborative venture this is hardly surprising.

There is increasing interest in the use of psychological treatments for severe depression and especially bipolar disorder (Porter et al, 2001). An ongoing study of IPSRT (Craighead et al, 1997) showed that those receiving psychological therapy spent more time in an euthymic state than those undergoing clinical management alone.

Conclusion

The scope and toll of depression is so great that it is hard—indeed unethical—to conceive of a management strategy in which psychological approaches do not play a central role. Sensitive clinicians need to adopt a psychological perspective in all aspects of their work with depressed patients, whether it be supportive therapy as an adjunct to pharmacotherapy, or matching a specific psychotherapeutic approach to the needs of the individual patient. The evolution of effective psychological therapies for depression is one of the great success stories of modern psychiatry. The combination of moral hope and good technique that lies at the heart of these treatments bodes well not just for those suffering from depression, but as a beacon for the discipline of psychiatry more generally.

References

Beck A, Rush A, Shaw B, Emery G (1979) *Cognitive therapy of depression*. New York: Wiley.

Bion WR (1961) *Experiences in groups*. London: Tavistock/Routledge.

Bunch J, Barraclough B (1971) The influence of parental death and anniversaries on suicide dates. *Br J Psychiatry* **118**: 621–626.

Craighead W, Miklowitz D, Vajk F, Frank E (1997) Psychosocial treatments for bipolar disorder. In: Nathan P, Gorman J (eds) *A guide to treatments that work*. New York: Oxford Unversity Press, pp. 53–71.

Dobson K (1988) A meta-analysis of the efficacy of cognitive therapy for depression. *J Cons Clin Psychol* **57**: 414–419.

Elkin I (1994) The NIMH treatment of depression collaborative research programme: where we began and where we are now. In: Bergin A, Garfield S (eds) *Handbook of Psychotherapy and Behaviour Change*. New York: Wiley, pp 114–139.

Frank E, Kupfer D, Ehlers C (1994) Interpersonal and social rhythm therapy for bipolar disorder. *Behaviour Therapist* **17**: 143–149.

Frank E, Spanier C (1995) Interpersonal therapy for depression: overview, clinical efficacy and future directions. *Clin Psychol: Sci Practice* **2**: 349–369.

Freud S (1917) Mourning and melancholia. In the *Standard edition of the complete psychological works of Sigmund Freud*. London: Hogarth, Vol 14, pp. 237–260.

Gabbard G (1994) *Psychodynamic psychiatry in clinical practice*. Washington DC: Am Psychiatry Press, 2nd edn.

Gilbert P (2000) *Counselling for Depression*. London: Sage, 2nd edn.

Gold P, Goodwin F, Chrousos G (1988) Clinical and biochemical manifestations of depression: relation to the nuerobiology of stress. *N Eng J Med* **319**: 413–420.

Hale R (1985) Suicide and the violent act. *Bull Br Assoc Psychotherapists* **4**: 1–13.

Hollon S, DuRubeis R, Evans M (1992) Cognitive therapy and pharmacotherapy for depression singly or in combination. *Arch Gen Psychiatry* **49**: 774–781.

Holmes J (1993) *John Bowlby and attachment theory*. London: Routledge.

Holmes J (1996) *Attachment, intimacy, autonomy: Using attachment theory in adult psychotherapy*. New York: Jason Avonson.

Holmes J (2001) *The search for the secure base: Attachment theory and psychotherapy*. London: Routledge.

Jacobson E (1971) *Depression*. New York: International Universities Press.

Keller MB, McCullough JP, Klein DN, et al (2000) A comparison of nefadazone, the cognitive behavioural analysis system of psychotherapy and their combination for the treatment of chronic depression. *N Engl J Med* **342**: 1462–1470.

Klein M (1935) A contribution to the psychogenesis of manic-depressive states. *Love, hate and reparation*. London: Hogarth, pp. 262–289.

Klerman G, Weissman M, Rounsaville B (1984) *Interpersonal psychotherapy of depression*. New York: Basic Books.

Leff J, Vearnals S, Wolff G (2000) The London depression trial. RCT of antidepressants versus couple therapy in patients with depression living with a partner: outcome and costs. *Br J Psychiatry* **177**: 95–100.

Margison F (2002) Psychodynamic-interpersonal therapy. In: Holmes J, Bateman

A (eds) *Integration in psychotherapy: Models and methods.* Oxford: Oxford University Press; pp. 129–156.

McDermut W, Miller IW, Brown RA (2001) The efficacy of group psychotherapy for depression: a meta-analysis. *Clin psychol: Sci practice* **8**: 98–116.

Menninger KA (1933) Psychoanalytical aspects of suicide. *Int J Psychoanalysis* **14**: 376–390.

Neitzel M, Russell R, Hemmings K, Gretter M (1987) Clinical significance of psychotherapy for unipolar depression: a meta-analytic approach to social comparison. *J Cons Clin Psychol* **55**: 156–161.

Paykel E, Scott J (2000) Treatment of mood disorders. In: Gelder M, Lopez-Ibor J, Andreasen N (eds) *New Oxford Textbook of Psychiatry.* Oxford: Oxford University Press; pp. 724–736.

Pedder J (1982) Failure to mourn and melancholia. *Br J Psychiatry* **141**: 329–337.

Porter R, Linsley K, Ferrier N (2001) Treatment of severe depression—non-pharmacological aspects. *Adv Psychiat Treatment* **7**: 117–124.

Post RM (1992) Transduction of psychosocial stress into the neurobiology of recurrent affective disorder. *Am J Psychiatry* **149**: 999–1010.

Robinson LA, Berman JS, Neimeyer RA (1990) Psychotherapy for the treatment of depression: A comprehensive review of controlled outcome research. *Psychol Bull* **108**: 30–49.

Roth A, Fonagy P (1996) *What works for whom?* New York: Guilford Press.

Seligman M (1975) *Helplessness: On depression, development and death.* San Francisco: Freeman.

Shapiro D (1995) Finding out how psychotherapies help people change. *Psychother Res* **5**: 1–21.

Teasdale J, Segal Z, Williams M (1995) How does cognitive therapy prevent depressive relapse and why should attentional control (mindfulness) training help?. *Behav Res Therapy* **33**: 25–39.

Wagner E, Simon G (2001) Managing depression in primary care. *BMJ* **322**: 746–747.

Weissman M, Markowitz J (1994) Interpersonal therapy: current status. *Arch Gen Psychiatry* **51**: 599–606.

Winnicott D (1965) *The maturational processes and the facilitating environment.* London: Hogarth.

Yalom ID (1970) *The theory and practice of group psychotherapy.* New York: Basic Books.

chapter 8

Complementary therapies

David Mischoulon and Andrew A Nierenberg

Although 'complementary' or natural medications have been used for centuries (Schulz et al, 2001), their popularity has increased dramatically over the past decade (Eisenberg et al, 1993; Krippner, 1995; Whitmore and Leake, 1996; Fisher, 1997), with up to 25% of people in the US using some type of alternative treatment (NIHOAM, 1997a).

While there are many different types of complementary remedies available for physical or medical problems, there are relatively fewer such medications for psychiatric disorders (Schulz et al, 2001). Some of these, such as St John's Wort, kava and valerian, are derived from plants and herbs. Others, such as melatonin, are hormones. Additional nutraceuticals include vitamins, such as folic acid and vitamin B_{12}; omega-3 fatty acids such as docosahexanoic acid (DHA); and various homeopathic preparations that are mixtures of nutraceuticals. Despite the growing popularity of these remedies, their actual benefits are not clear, and there is a dearth of well-designed clinical trials to assess their effectiveness and safety.

Many individuals self-medicate with natural over-the-counter (OTC) treatments, sometimes in combination with prescription medications, and often without informing their physician. While this approach entails obvious risks, many people perceive that they benefit from taking a natural medication. As placebo-expectancy factors account for about 75% of the effect of a medication (Kahn et al, 2000), it is not surprising that any so-called medication has perceived therapeutic effects.

Physicians therefore must become familiar with these treatments, so that they may advise their patients appropriately. This chapter will review the indications and mechanisms of the better-known natural psychotropics, review the available data regarding drug-drug interactions, and provide guidelines for clinicians who may be called upon to recommend these remedies. Table 8.1 provides a summary of complementary medications.

Treatments for mood disorders

St John's Wort

The extract of the flower of the plant St John's Wort (*Hypericum perforatum* L) has been used to treat mood disorders since antiquity (Schulz et al, 2001). Physicians in Europe routinely prescribe St John's Wort (SJW) for mild-to-moderate depression with generally positive outcomes. In the US, SJW is sold over the counter at health food stores and pharmacies, and increasing numbers of American physicians are becoming aware of its putative antidepressant effect.

St John's Wort has been reported to have greater efficacy than placebo and equal efficacy to active comparators, based on a number of double-blind placebo-controlled studies (NIHOAM, 1997a); five studies have compared SJW to tricyclic antidepressants (Martinez et al, 1993; Harrer et al, 1994; Vorbach et al, 1994, 1997; Wheatley, 1997). It must be emphasized that, in these European clinical trials, typical doses of imipramine and maprotiline are in the order of 75 mg daily, lower than those considered adequate by most psychopharmacologists. The duration of most of these studies was short (4–6 weeks) and no information about longer-term outcomes was available. However, the placebo response rate appears comparable to that observed in many outpatient studies of antidepressants conducted in the US (Nierenberg, 1998).

St John's Wort has recently been compared against the selective serotonin reuptake inhibitors (SSRIs), sertraline and fluoxetine. In a 6-week double-blind, randomized study with 30 patients, SJW (900 mg/day) and sertraline (75 mg/day) were compared. Clinical response was noted in

Table 8.1 Summary of complementary medications (reproduced from Mischoulon D, Rosenbaum JF (2002) with permission from Lippincott Williams and Wilkins © 2002)

Medication	Active components	Putative indications	Possible mechanisms of action	Suggested dose	Adverse reactions
St John's Wort (*Hypericum perforatum* L)	Hypericin, hyperforin, polycyclic phenols, pseudohypericin	Depression	Cytokine production; decreased serotonin receptor density; decreased neurotransmitter reuptake; MAOI activity	900–1200 mg/day, bid–tid	Dry mouth, dizziness, constipation, phototoxicity, serotonin syndrome when combined with SSRIs; adverse interactions with warfarin, cyclosporin, oral contraceptives, theophylline, fenprocoumon, digoxin and indinavir; mania

Table 8.1 *continued*

Medication	Active components	Putative indications	Possible mechanisms of action	Suggested dose	Adverse reactions
SAMe	S-adenosyl methionine	Depression	Methyl group donation	200–1600 mg/day (sometimes higher)	Mild insomnia, lack of appetite, constipation, nausea, dry mouth, sweating, dizziness, and nervousness. Mania or hypomania
Omega fatty acids	Essential fatty acids (primarily ω-6 and ω-3)	Depression (docosahexanoic acid: ω-3); Mania (ω-3 mixture); Psychosis (ω-3 and ω-6)	Inhibition of membrane signal transduction	200–3000 mg/day	GI upset

Table 8.1 *continued*

Medication	Active components	Putative indications	Possible mechanisms of action	Suggested dose	Adverse reactions
Inositol	Second messenger precursor	Depression, panic, OCD	Second messenger synthesis; sensitization of serotonin receptors	12–18 g/day	GI upset, dizziness, insomnia, sedation, headache
Kava (*Piper methysticum*)	Kavapyrones	Anxiety	Muscle relaxant, anticonvulsant, GABA receptor binding	60–300 mg/day	GI upset, allergic skin reactions, headaches, dizziness, ataxia, hair loss, visual problems, respiratory problems
Valerian (*Valeriana officinalis*)	Valepotriates, sesquiterpenes	Insomnia	Decreased GABA catabolism	450–600 mg/day	Blurred vision, dystonias, hepatotoxicity, headaches, mutagenicity?

Table 8.1 *continued*

Medication	Active components	Putative indications	Possible mechanisms of action	Suggested dose	Adverse reactions
Melatonin	Pineal gland hormone	Insomnia	Circadian rhythm regulation in suprachiasmatic nucleus	0.1–0.3 mg/day (sometimes higher)	Sedation, confusion, inhibition of fertility, decreased sex drive, hypothermia, retinal damage
Ginkgo biloba	Flavonoids, terpene lactones	Dementia	Nerve cell stimulation and protection, membrane/receptor stabilization, free radical scavenging, PAF inhibition	120–240 mg/day, bid–tid	Mild GI upset, headache, irritability, dizziness, haemorrhage in individuals with bleeding disorders or who take anticoagulants

47% of patients receiving SJW and 40% of those receiving sertraline. The difference was not statistically significant (Brenner et al, 2000). In a similar trial against fluoxetine, 240 patients with mild-to-moderate depression were compared. After 6 weeks of treatment, the mean end-point HAM-D scores were comparable for SJW and fluoxetine, but mean clinical global impression (CGI-severity) was significantly superior on SJW, as was the responder rate. The incidence of adverse events was 23% on fluoxetine and 8% on SJW (Schrader, 2000). Although SJW demonstrated a somewhat better responder rate, the authors believed that the main difference between the two treatments was tolerability. A major limitation of these two studies is the lack of a placebo control arm; this makes it difficult to assess the degree of placebo response, which is known to be high (up to 50%) in antidepressant trials.

A recent study by Shelton and colleagues (2001) suggested that SJW was not an effective treatment for more severe episodes of major depression. A total of 200 depressed adults received SJW for 12 weeks, up to 1200 mg/day, or placebo. Response rates did not differ between groups, although the remission rate was higher for the SJW group. Despite the discouraging data in the context of a well-designed trial, several caveats must be noted. The placebo remission rate was unusually low, and there appeared to be no discontinuations because of non-response, both of which are unusual in depression trials. The mean duration of patients' depressive episodes was longer than 2 years, which indicates that many in the study group had chronic depression. Similarly, the severity of depression was higher than that reported in most other SJW trials; SJW may therefore be less effective for more severe depression (an observation that has been suggested in prior trials). Nevertheless, this represents the first large-scale, placebo-controlled trial of SJW for depression.

The results of a second large US trial, conducted under the auspices of the National Institute of Mental Health, were recently published. In that study (Hypericum Depression Trial Study Group, 2002), neither hypericin (900–1500 mg/day) nor sertraline (50–100 mg/day) were significantly more effective than placebo across 8 weeks of double-blind therapy. Response rates were: 53% (sertraline); 43% (SJW); and 50% (placebo). With an *N* of 340, this study had the power to reliably detect moderate-sized drug-placebo differences. In the terminology of the US Food and Drug Administration, this would be considered indicative of a 'failed trial'—an antidepressant with known efficacy was not effective. The failure of sertraline in this trial is not unexpected—fully 50% of the industry-sponsored trials of SSRI therapy failed to yield statistically significant differences. If St John's Wort was being developed by a major pharmaceutical company, perhaps four or five such failed or negative studies would be 'tolerated' before research efforts were shut down.

If effective, the mechanism of action of SJW is not as well understood as that of registered antidepressants. Hypericin, believed to be one of the main active components in SJW, may inhibit monocyte cytokine production of interleukin-6 and perhaps interleukin-1β, resulting in a decrease in corticotrophin-releasing hormone (CRH), thus decreasing the production of cortisol and dysregulating the hypothalamic-pituitary-adrenal (HPA) axis (Thiele et al, 1993) (Figure 8.1). Hypericin is also thought to be a weak inhibitor of reuptake of serotonin, norepinephrine and dopamine (Müller and Rossol, 1993), and chronic treatment may produce downregulation of β-adrenoreceptors and increased $5-HT_2$ and $5-HT_{1A}$ receptor density (Teufel-Mayer and Gleitz, 1997). Finally, SJW may also have affinity for GABA receptors (Schulz et al, 2001).

More recent studies have suggested that hyperforin (a phoroglucinol derivative) is a key component in the antidepressant effect of SJW (Chatterjee et al, 1998; Laakmann et al, 1998; Schellenberg et al, 1998). Laakmann and colleagues (1998) performed a randomized, double-blind, placebo-controlled 6-week study of two different extracts of St John's Wort on a sample of 147 patients. The two extracts varied only in hyperforin content (0.5% vs 5%). Patients who received the SJW extract with 5% hyperforin showed somewhat greater improvement in their HAM-D scores than the group that received the extract with 0.5% hyperforin, and the latter group showed only slightly greater improvement than the placebo group. Chatterjee and colleagues (1998), have demonstrated that hyperforin is a potent uptake inhibitor of serotonin, dopamine, norepinephrine, GABA and L-glutamate.

Other components of St John's Wort, including the flavonoids, are irreversible MAOA inhibitors, but the concentrations of these

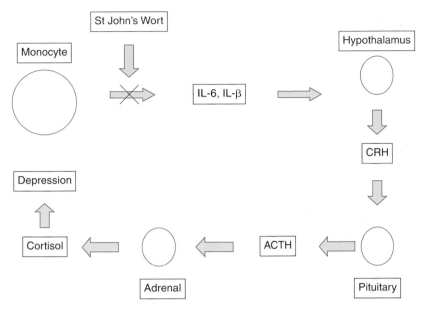

Figure 8.1 *Possible mechanism of St John's Wort (Hypericum perforatum L).*
(IL, interleukin; CRH, corticotrophin-releasing hormone; ACTH,
adrenocorticotrophic hormone.) Reproduced from Nierenberg A (2002) with
permission from Lippincott Williams and Wilkins © 2002.

compounds in the extract are so small that they are unlikely to be involved in the antidepressant mechanism (Bladt and Wagner, 1993). Nonetheless, it is recommended that SJW is not combined with SSRIs, as cases of 'serotonin syndrome' have been reported with this combination (Beckman et al, 2000; Fugh-Berman, 2000; Prost et al, 2000).

Adverse drug events with SJW have generally been mild, and include dry mouth, dizziness, constipation, other gastrointestinal symptoms, and confusion (Schulz et al, 2001). Cases of mania and hypomania resulting from SJW have been reported (O'Breasail and Argouarch, 1998; Schneck, 1998; Nierenberg et al, 1999; Barbenel et al, 2000; Fugh-Berman, 2000; Moses and Mallinger, 2000). Further research will be necessary to clarify the risks and benefits of SJW in bipolar depression, but physicians should warn bipolar patients of the risk of using SJW without supervision and without concomitant mood stabilizers.

Phototoxicity has been associated with SJW in grazing cattle and sheep. It has therefore been suggested that patients who take an overdose of SJW should be isolated from UV radiation for 7 days. However, this caution may not necessarily apply to patients taking typical doses. One study (Brockmoller et al, 1997) found that doses of SJW as high as 1800 mg caused a minor increase in sensitivity to UV light in humans, but no phototoxicity. So far, there are no published data assessing the effects of a SJW overdose (Balfour, 2000).

With regard to drug-drug interactions, hyperforin has been shown to induce CYP-3A4 expression, but has no effect on CYP-2D6 (Moore et al, 2000). Combinations of SJW products with warfarin, cyclosporin, oral contraceptives, theophylline, fenprocoumon, digoxin and indinavir have led to reported interactions and reduced therapeutic activity (Baede-van Dijk et al, 2000; Fugh-Berman, 2000; Moore et al, 2000; Miller, 2000; Piscitelli et al, 2000). Caution is therefore required in sexually active women taking birth control pills and HIV-positive patients receiving protease inhibitors, as well as in transplant recipients taking cyclosporin.

In summary, a number of studies have shown St John's Wort to be either more effective than placebo or comparable to registered antidepressants. Several large negative trials in the US have taken some of the bloom from St John's Wort, but the story is far from settled. St John's Wort has a benign side-effect profile, although care needs to be taken when it is combined with other antidepressants. Potentially harmful drug-drug interactions have been demonstrated, and St John's Wort should therefore be used with caution in patients who are on multiple medications.

S-Adenosyl methionine (SAMe)

SAMe functions by donating methyl groups during synthesis of hormones, neurotransmitters, nucleic acids, proteins and phospholipids (Baldessarini, 1987). Its activity is particularly dependent on levels of folate and vitamin B_{12} in the brain (Figure 8.2). Deficiencies of folate and vitamin B_{12} have been associated with development of depression and/or refractoriness to antidepressant treatment (Smythies et al, 1986).

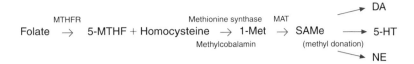

Figure 8.2 *SAMe-related metabolic pathway. (MTHFR, methyltetrahydrofolate reductase; MTHF, methyltetrahydrofolate; 1-Met, methionine; MAT, methionine adenosine transferase; DA, dopamine; 5-HT, serotonin (5-hydroxytryptophan); NE, norepinephrine.) Reproduced from Mischoulon D, Rosenbaum JF (2002) with permission from Lippincott Williams and Wilkins © 2002.*

SAMe has demonstrated a mood elevating effect in depression. Early clinical studies showed that parenteral (IV or IM) SAMe was superior to placebo and comparable to tricyclic antidepressants (TCAs) (Spillman and Fava, 1996). Results of more recent trials of oral SAMe, at doses up to 1600 mg/day (Spillman and Fava, 1996), suggested efficacy comparable to TCAs and superiority to placebo. SAMe may have a relatively faster onset of action than conventional agents. Some patients improve within a few days, and most within 2 weeks (Mantero et al, 1975; Scarzella and Appiotti, 1977; Del Vecchio et al, 1978; Miccoli et al, 1978; Calandra et al, 1979; Monaco and Quattrochi, 1979; Kufferle and Grunberger, 1982; Bell et al, 1988; Janicak et al, 1988). The combination of SAMe and low dose TCA may result in earlier onset of action than TCA alone (Alvarez et al, 1987; Berlanga et al, 1992).

Other psychiatric uses for SAMe include the reduction of cognitive deficits in dementia (Fontanari et al, 1994); relief of puerpueral distress (Cerutti et al, 1993); and the reduction of psychological distress during opioid detoxification (LoRusso et al, 1994). SAMe may also be useful to depressed alcoholics (Agricola et al, 1994), and in medically ill depressed patients for whom conventional agents may be contraindicated (Rocco, 1994).

SAMe is well tolerated, free of adverse effects, and has no apparent hepatotoxicity (Spillman and Fava, 1996). Its side-effects include mild insomnia, lack of appetite, constipation, nausea, dry mouth, sweating, dizziness and nervousness (Spillman and Fava, 1996). There are some reports of increased anxiety, mania or hypomania in bipolar individuals (Spillman and Fava, 1996), and some of the SAMe clinical trials demonstrated a higher rate of switch to mania with SAMe than with placebo (Carney et al, 1983, 1987). In view of the above, SAMe should be used with caution in bipolar individuals, and preferably prescribed in combination with a concomitant mood stabilizer.

Recommended doses of SAMe range from 400–1600 mg/day (Kagan et al, 1990; De Vanna et al, 1992; Salmaggi et al, 1993). Anecdotal evidence suggests that some patients may benefit from even higher doses. So far, there appears to be no evidence of adverse drug-drug interactions, and SAMe can generally be safely combined with other medications. The 'weight' of published evidence favouring SAMe is about 10% of that supporting the typical novel antidepressants. Moreover, there are no large-scale, placebo-controlled trials of SAMe.

Omega fatty acids

The omega-3 and -6 fatty acids are essential polyunsaturated fatty acids (PUFAs) (Lands, 1992; Simopoulos and Robinson, 1999). They are classified according to the position of the first double bond with respect to the methyl (CH_3) end of the molecule (designated as the omega-carbon) (Figure 8.3). The predominant omega-3 fatty acids include docosahexanoic acid (DHA) and eicosapentanoic acid (EPA), which are found primarily in fish (Stensby, 1969), and alpha-linolenic acid (ALA), obtained from land-based plants such as flaxseed (Simopoulos et al, 1992; Stoll et al, 1999). Omega-6 fatty acids include linoleic acid (LA) and arachidonic acid (AA), which are derived primarily from vegetable oils.

The omega-3 fatty acids have been studied primarily as a treatment for bipolar disorder. Stoll and colleagues (1999) reported a 4-month, prospective, double-blind, placebo-controlled trial of omega-3 mixture in a sample of bipolar patients. The omega-3 fatty acid mixture (6.2 g of EPA and 3.4 g of DHA per day) was compared to olive oil (assumed to be an inert placebo) in subjects who had experienced a recent episode of mania or hypomania. The omega-3 fatty acid group performed better than the placebo group (64.3% vs 18.8% sustained remission rate), and this difference was statistically significant. The duration of remission was

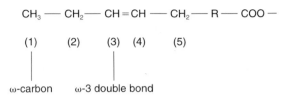

Figure 8.3 *Example of an omega-3 fatty acid. (R represents the variable radical group.)*

also significantly greater in the omega-3 group compared to placebo. Limitations of this study included the lack of control for concomitant pharmacotherapy.

Stoll and colleagues have also reported treating 16 patients with refractory unipolar depression with omega-3 fatty acids (Stoll and Locke, 2001). While only five of these patients responded, this may represent an improvement over spontaneous response rates expected for refractory patients. Omega-3 and -6 fatty acids may also help alleviate psychotic symptoms when added to the antipsychotic regimens of patients with schizophrenia (Fenton et al, 2000). No controlled dose-response studies have yet been performed, and it is not clear at this time whether EPA, DHA, or ALA are psychotropically active.

The mechanism of psychotropic action of the omega-3 fatty acids has been investigated and appears to be multifold. Omega-3 fatty acids are typically incorporated into the phospholipid bilayer membrane surrounding the cells (Lands, 1992), and may help regulate intracellular signal transduction (Sperling et al, 1993) by inhibiting the G-protein and phospholipase C-mediated hydrolysis of phosphatidylinositol (PI). This, in turn, would inhibit formation of the second messenger molecules inositol triphosphate and diacylglycerol, a step in a putative cascade mechanism of antidepressant action (Sperling et al, 1993; Stoll and Severus, 1996). Mood stabilizers, such as lithium and valproate appear to function similarly (Stoll and Severus, 1996). Therefore, the mood-stabilizing action of the omega-3 fatty acids may be related to this effect on signal transduction.

Other putative mechanisms of action of omega-3 fatty acids include regulation of calcium ion influx (Pepe et al, 1994; Xiao et al, 1997) via phospholipase A2-mediated hydrolysis of omega-3 fatty acid-containing phospholipids. Omega-3 fatty acids also decrease secretion of inflammatory cytokines (Maes and Smith, 1998), and may thus decrease hypothalamic secretion of corticotrophin-releasing factor. This would reduce the release of adrenocorticotrophic hormone (ACTH) and corticosteroids (Kling et al, 1989), and, in turn, improve mood abnormalities and stress-related immune responses (Brown et al, 1999) (see also Figure 8.1).

Mild gastrointestinal distress, particularly loose stools, has been reported in some individuals taking omega-3 fatty acids. Otherwise, the treatment appears to be well tolerated (Stoll et al, 1999). There seems to be no toxicity associated with the omega-3 fatty acids, including a lack of teratogenic effects.

The data reviewed here suggest that omega-3 fatty acids may have psychotropic effects, perhaps by multiple mechanisms. So far, omega-3 fatty acids have been studied primarily as augmenting agents, and appear safe to combine with other psychotropics. However, there are not yet enough data to say with certainty whether the omega-3 fatty acids are truly effective antidepressants and/or mood stabilizers.

Inositol

Inositol is a naturally occurring isomer of glucose. It may function as an intermediary of the phosphatidylinositol (PI) cycle, a second-messenger system involving noradrenergic, serotonergic and cholinergic receptors (Benjamin et al, 1995a) (Figure 8.4). Interest in a potential psychotropic role came from several lines of evidence. Specifically, inositol in the cerebrospinal fluid (CSF) may be decreased in depression (Levine et al, 1996); lithium reduces inositol levels; and pharmacological doses of peripheral inositol reverses both the behavioural effects of lithium in animals and the side-effects of lithium in humans. Inositol's mechanism of action is unclear, but may involve the reversal of desensitization of serotonin receptors (Benjamin et al, 1995a).

Inositol has been studied for various indications, primarily by Belmaker and colleagues, who have published a series of small clinical trials (ie 15–20 patients each) (Benjamin et al, 1995a). In depressed

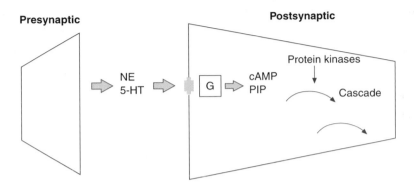

Figure 8.4 *Second messengers. (NE, norepinephrine; 5-HT, serotonin; G, G-protein; cAMP, cyclic AMP; PIP, phosphatidylinositol phosphate.)*

individuals, a 4-week double-blind controlled trial of 12 g/day inositol showed superiority to placebo (Levine et al, 1995a). A related study combining inositol with SSRIs showed no significant difference between groups (Levine et al, 1999). In panic disorder, a 4-week double-blind controlled trial of 12 g/day inositol showed decrease in frequency and severity of panic attacks and agoraphobia (Benjamin et al, 1995b). In obsessive-compulsive disorder (OCD) a 6-week double-blind controlled trial of 18 g/day inositol resulted in a significant reduction of symptoms (Fux et al, 1996). Similar trials showed no effect in schizophrenia (Levine, 1997), ADHD (Levine, 1997), Alzheimer's (Barak et al, 1996), autism (Levine et al, 1997), or ECT-induced cognitive impairment (Levine et al, 1995b). As of yet, there are no published studies of inositol for bipolar disorder. Most recently, a small double-blind study of inositol treatment of bipolar depression yielded equivocal results (Chengappa et al, 2000).

Inositol has no apparent toxicity and a benign side-effect profile (Benjamin et al, 1995a). Some have complained of the compound's unpleasant taste, particularly in the large doses that appear to be necessary to achieve the clinical effect. Overall, inositol appears to be a promising treatment, particularly compelling because of its safety and multiple possible applications. However, clinical trials so far have been small, and larger patient samples are required for a better understanding of this drug's safety and effectiveness.

Treatments for anxiety and sleep disorders

Kava

Medicinal use of the roots and leaves of the pepper plant (*Piper methysticum* Forst) originated in the Polynesian islands. Natives typically drank a kava beverage reported to have a calming and relaxing effect (Singh, 1992). Kava (also called kava-kava) has become increasingly popular in the US during the past few years.

Controlled double-blind studies indicate that kava may be effective for mild anxiety (Schulz et al, 2001). A 25-week multicentre, randomized placebo-controlled double-blind study of a special extract of kava assessed 101 outpatients suffering from different types of anxiety disorders including agoraphobia, specific phobia and generalized anxiety disorder. There was a significant superiority of kava over placebo from week 8 onwards (Volz, 1997).

In a second randomized, placebo-controlled double-blind study, two groups of 29 anxious patients were treated for 4 weeks with kava extract 100 mg tid or a placebo preparation. Improvement in anxiety symptomatology occurred in the active drug group after only 1 week of treatment, and the difference between drug and placebo increased over the course of the study (Kinzler et al, 1991).

A third randomized, placebo-controlled double-blind study treated two groups of 20 patients with climacteric-related symptoms for 8 weeks with kava extract 100 mg tid or a placebo preparation. Those who received kava showed more improvement in anxiety and depression than did the placebo group (Warnecke, 1991).

Kava's anxiolytic effect appears to be due to kavapyrones, which act centrally as muscle relaxants (Singh, 1983; Seitz et al, 1997a) and anticonvulsants (Gleitz et al, 1996). Kava is proposed to reduce the excitability of the limbic system, perhaps as effectively as benzodiazepines, but without evidence of physical or psychological tolerance or dependency

(Duffield and Jamieson, 1991). For this reason, kava has been recommended for individuals with mild anxiety, as well as for those who abuse or cannot tolerate standard agents (Laux, 1997). Postulated mechanisms include GABAA receptor binding (Jussofie et al, 1994), but this is controversial (Davies et al, 1992; Holm et al, 1991). Three kava-pyrones, (+)-methysticine, (+)-kavain and the synthetic racemate (±)-kavain, were shown to inhibit uptake of [^{3}H]-noradrenaline in the cerebral cortex and hippocampus of rats (Seitz et al, 1997b). This mechanism may, at least in part, contribute to the psychotropic properties of kavapyrones. Other studies (Walden et al, 1997) suggest that kawain and dihydromethysticin may enhance the effects of the anxiolytic 5-HT$_{1A}$ agonist ipsapirone and that activation of NMDA receptors and/or voltage-dependent calcium channels may be involved in the mechanism of action of some kavapyrones.

Suggested doses of kava are between 60 mg and 120 mg daily. There are reports of sedation when kava is taken together with benzodiazepines (Schulz et al, 2001) or with alcohol (Jamieson and Duffield, 1990). Side-effects from kava are uncommon but may include gastrointestinal (GI) upsets, allergic skin reactions, headaches and dizziness (Suss and Lehmann, 1996; Schulz et al, 2001). Toxic reactions with high doses have occurred; ingestion of up to 300–400 g per week of kava (ie at least 100 times typical doses) may result in anorexia and subnormal weight, ataxia, hyperreflexia, facial oedema, rash, hair loss, yellowing of the skin, abnormal liver function tests, haematuria, abnormal blood indices, redness of the eyes, problems with visual accommodation and respiratory problems associated with tall P waves on a resting electrocardiogram, suggesting possible pulmonary hypertension (Mathews et al, 1988; Hansel et al, 1994; Schulz et al, 2001). Because of concern about long-term toxicity, the duration of kava therapy is not recommended to exceed 3 months (Schulz et al, 2001).

In summary, kava may be more effective than placebo for the treatment of mild anxiety. However, given the various medical complications that may result from its use, particular care needs to be taken with patients who are on multiple medications, or have underlying medical illness. Research comparing kava and conventional anxiolytics, alone and in combination, are needed to determine if this herbal therapy has a place in the pharmacological armamentarium.

Valerian

The root of *Valeriana officinalis* has been used around the world for over 1000 years as a sedative and mild hypnotic (Houghton, 1988; Cott, 1995). It is particularly popular among the world's Hispanic population (Mischoulon, 2001).

The CNS activity of valerian has been attributed to its valepotriates and sesquiterpene constituents, and its mechanism may be similar to that of benzodiazepines or barbiturates (Hendriks et al, 1985; Leuschner et al, 1993). EEG studies suggest that valerian results in minor but significant changes in sleep architecture (Gessner and Klassner, 1984; Balderer and Borbely, 1985; Schultz and Jobert, 1995), although polysomnographic studies have not yet conclusively demonstrated therapeutic efficacy. *In vitro* studies suggest that valerian may decrease the catabolism of GABA (Reidel et al, 1982), increasing its concentration at the synapse (Santos et al, 1994).

A number of controlled trials have been performed, with various types of valerian preparations, some of which are not specified in the published reports (Schulz et al, 2001). Some studies were performed on healthy subjects and others on symptomatic individuals. One three-armed trial examined non-symptomatic individuals who received valerian, placebo, or another natural product, for three non-consecutive nights (Leathwood et al, 1982). Valerian was found to improve sleep quality without significant daytime sleepiness, particularly for those self-described as poor sleepers.

A small placebo controlled trial with symptomatic patients showed that 450 mg per night of valerian significantly decreased sleep latency compared to placebo. Doses of 900 mg had no statistically significant advantage over 450 mg (Leathwood and Chauffard, 1985). Valerian has been found to be comparable to flunitrazepam in efficacy, but with fewer adverse effects on cognition (Gerhard et al, 1996). Vorbach et al (1996) performed a placebo-controlled double-blind study in 121 patients with significant sleep disturbance. Initially, there was little difference between valerian and placebo, but after 4 weeks the valerian-treated group showed a statistically significant advantage in response. Valerian has been combined with propranolol with no significant adverse effects (Kohnen and Oswald, 1988).

The main limitations of these valerian trials are the relatively short duration and small sample sizes. Another major limitation to a valid double-blind clinical trial valerian is the powerful and distinctive smell of the medication, due to isovaleric acid, a breakdown product of vale-potriates (Schulz et al, 2001).

Recommended doses of valerian are 450–600 mg, approximately 2 hours before bedtime. Valerian appears to be benign in overdose (Willey et al, 1995). Adverse effects may include headaches or gastrointestinal complaints. Rare toxic reactions may include blurred vision, dystonias and hepatotoxicity (MacGregor et al, 1989), although some have argued against such an association (Farrel and Lamb, 1990; Chan et al, 1995). Products based on Mexican or Indian valerian are not recommended, as they contain higher levels of valepotriates (up to 8%) and baldrinals, which may be carcinogenic (Braun et al, 1982, 1985; Schulz et al, 2001).

The reviewed studies suggest that although valerian may not be ideal for active treatment of insomnia, its value may be in the promotion of natural sleep after several weeks of use with no risk of dependence or residual daytime somnolence (Schulz et al, 2001). It can probably be combined safely with other psychotropics.

Melatonin

Melatonin is a hormone derived from serotonin, and manufactured in the pineal gland. It is involved in the organization of circadian rhythms (Sack et al, 1997), and many use it to reset their biological clocks when travelling across time zones. However, studies have disagreed on the degree of efficacy of melatonin compared to placebo, and there is limited consensus as to the appropriate dose, which may range from 0.5 mg to 10 mg/day (Arendt, 1999).

Melatonin appears to be an effective hypnotic, which works within 1 hour of administration regardless of time of day. It may be more effective for people with insomnia due to circadian disturbances (Monti and

Cardinali, 2000; Sack et al, 2000). Its mechanism of action may involve interaction with the suprachiasmatic nucleus, by which it resets the circadian pacemaker, and attenuates alerting process (Vanecek and Watanabe, 1999). It may also have a direct soporific effect (Cajochen et al, 1997).

Doses as small as 0.25–0.30 mg/day have been shown to decrease sleep latency, but many preparations have as much as 10 mg of melatonin. Interestingly, a recent randomized double-blind study of 257 Norwegian physicians suggested lack of efficacy for jet lag. No significant differences were found between placebo and three different regimens of melatonin (doses varied from 0.5 mg to 5.0 mg) (Spitzer et al, 1999).

High doses may cause daytime somnolence or confusion (Dollins et al, 1993). Serious adverse effects, although rare, may include inhibition of fertility and decreased sex drive (Partonen, 1999), hypothermia (Mishima et al, 1997) and retinal damage (Wiechmann and O'Steen, 1992; Lehmann and Johnson, 1999). Because of potential interactions with the HPA axis and the thymus, which may result in immunosuppression, it should be used with caution in individuals taking steroids (Persengiev et al, 1991; Raghavendra and Kulkarni, 2000).

In summary, melatonin is a promising hypnotic, which is generally accepted as safe and effective. There appear to be no adverse interactions in combination with other drugs, except perhaps with immunosuppressants. It is likely safe to combine with antidepressants and other psychotropics.

Treatments for symptoms of dementia

Ginkgo biloba

Ginkgo biloba, the seed from the ginkgo tree, has been used therapeutically in Eastern Asia for at least 2000 years (Schulz et al, 2001). The primary indication for ginkgo is the treatment of cognitive deficits found in brain diseases such as Alzheimer's and vascular dementia. Its active components are flavonoids, such as quercetin, kaempferol and isorhamnetin and terpene lactones including ginkgolides, bilobalide and ginkgolic acids (Schulz et al, 2001).

Ginkgo is believed to stimulate populations of functional nerve cells, protecting them from pathological influences such as hypoxia, ischaemia, seizure activity and peripheral nerve damage. Its mechanism of action is thought to be multifold, and may involve membrane stabilization (Hoyer, 1995), free radical scavenging which decreases capillary fragility (Smith et al, 1996), inhibition of age-related decline in muscarinic choline receptors and α_2 adrenergic receptors, and promotion of choline uptake in the hippocampus (Schulz et al, 2001). Ginkgo also inhibits platelet-activating factor, and for this reason, it should be avoided in patients with bleeding disorders (Smith et al, 1996).

Over 30 placebo-controlled double-blind trials of ginkgo have been conducted since 1975 in patients with cognitive deficits (Schulz et al, 2001). Results suggest that dementia symptoms and their progression ameliorate with ginkgo treatment. The standards for testing the efficacy of ginkgo and other nootropic drugs, however, have changed over the years. In 1991, the German Federal Health Agency required that nootropic (cognition enhancing) therapy must ameliorate not only dementia symptoms (such as memory, abstract thinking and psychomotor function), but also enhance the patient's functioning in daily activities and need for care (Schulz et al, 2001). Most of the older studies would hence not meet adequate methodological criteria, and despite evidence for cognitive improvement, they do not show conclusively that overall functioning in daily activities improves or that need for daily care is reduced.

A study by LeBars and colleagues (1997) assessed the efficacy and safety of ginkgo in Alzheimer's disease and multi-infarct dementia. In this year-long, randomized double-blind, placebo-controlled study, 309 outpatients with Alzheimer's disease or multi-infarct dementia were treated with ginkgo (120 mg/day) or placebo. Of the 202 completers, those treated with ginkgo achieved a modest but statistically significant improvement on various cognitive scales, and no significant adverse events were reported compared with placebo. The changes in daily function were also observable by the caregivers of the study subjects.

Gingko has been compared with synthetic nootropic drugs such as piracitam, pyritinol, ergot alkaloids, nicergoline and nimodipine. While they all appear to be comparable in efficacy (Riederer et al, 1993), ginkgo demonstrates a lower incidence of side-effects (1.69% vs 5.42%) (Burkard and Lehrl, 1991), and for this reason, many physicians favour it over the synthetic nootropics (Stoppe et al, 1996).

The suggested daily dose of ginkgo is 120–240 mg, bid or tid. A minimal 8-week course is recommended in patients with dementia, and the patient should be re-evaluated every 3 months to determine if continuation is appropriate. Assessment of the impact of ginkgo on social functioning may require at least one year of observation (Schulz et al, 2001). Side-effects are rare, and may include mild gastrointestinal upset, headache, irritability, dizziness, or allergic reactions. Its toxicity is very low, and there are no significant interactions with other drugs (Stoppe et al, 1996), although care needs to be taken in patients on anticoagulants. There is no evidence of carcinogenic or genotoxic effects from ginkgo (Hansel et al, 1994).

Recent studies have suggested a role for ginkgo in the treatment of antidepressant-induced sexual dysfunction (Cohen, 1996). In an open trial of ginkgo in 63 patients with sexual dysfunction secondary to various antidepressants of different classes (SSRIs, SNRIs, TCAs, MAOIs) (Cohen, 1997), 91% of women and 76% of men reported improvement in all aspects of the sexual cycle (desire, excitement, orgasm and resolution). Effective doses were between 60 mg and 180 mg bid. The mechanism for this improvement may involve ginkgo's interaction with platelet-activating factor (PAF), prostaglandins, peripheral vasodilatation or central serotonin and norepinephrine receptor activity.

Overall, ginkgo therapy appears to result in a modest but measurable improvement in dementia symptoms, with a benign side-effect profile. The full extent of its role in the attenuation or prevention of dementia, as well as its role in the reversal of antidepressant-induced sexual side effects, remain to be clarified. Apart from the risk of haemorrhage in people who take anticoagulants, ginkgo appears to be safe to combine with other medications.

Conclusions

Natural medications represent a growing field in the pharmacology of mental disorders, and may eventually prove to be a valuable addition to the psychopharmacological armamentarium. But given the uncertainty about the efficacy and safety of these medications, well-designed, controlled studies on larger, rigorously diagnosed patient populations are needed.

In the absence of additional data, psychiatrists who recommend natural medications to their patients should proceed with caution (Eisenberg, 1997). The best candidates for these treatments may be those for whom a delay in adequate treatment would not be devastating, specifically the mildly symptomatic patient with a strong interest in natural remedies. At the other end of the clinical spectrum, patients who have failed multiple trials of conventional medications (because of non-response or side-effects) may also benefit from natural remedies. This population, however, is often the most difficult to treat, and natural agents appear to be most suitable for mild-to-moderate illness (Schulz et al, 2001).

Clinicians must be aware that many patients are engaging in over-the-counter pharmacotherapy, adding natural medications to their prescribed treatments, often without informing their health providers (Smith and Buckwalter, 1992; Corcoran, 1997; Barat et al, 2000). Although outcomes of combining alternative with registered medications is still not well documented, anecdotal evidence and preliminary studies suggest usefulness for some difficult to treat patients. But, again, given the limited efficacy data, and reported adverse interactions with registered medications, clinicians should routinely ask their patients about natural medication use, and discuss the risks and benefits of these remedies, alone or in combination with other medications. Finally, because of the lack of data regarding safety in pregnancy, it is not advisable for pregnant women to use these remedies.

The National Institutes of Health and National Institute of Mental Health have acknowledged the need for systematic research on the effectiveness and safety of natural medications (NIHOAM, 1997a,b), and academic institutions are now undertaking multicentre studies on herbal medications, such as St John's Wort, kava and other complementary therapies. It is hoped that these studies will clarify questions about natural medications. For the time being, a reasonable recommendation is to treat these medications with the same respect given to registered medications.

Acknowledgements

Parts of this chapter have been reproduced from: D Mischoulon. Polypharmacy of alternative and herbal medications. In: SN Ghaemi. *Polypharmacy in Psychiatry*. Marcel Dekker, 2002, with kind permission from Marcel Dekker, Inc.

References

Agricola R, Dalla Verde G, Urani R, et al (1994) S-Adenosyl-L-methionine in the treatment of major depression complicating chronic alcoholism. *Curr Therapeut Res* 1994; **55**: 83–92.

Alvarez E, Udina C, Guillamat R (1987) Shortening of latency period in depressed patients treated with SAMe and other antidepressant drugs. *Cell Biol Rev* **S1**: 103–110.

Arendt J (1999) Jet-lag and shift work: 2. Therapeutic use of melatonin. *J Roy Soc Med* **92**: 402–405.

Baede-van Dijk PA, van Galen E, Lekkerkerker JF (2000) Drug interactions of *Hypericum perforatum* (St. John's wort) are potentially hazardous. *Ned Tijdschr Geneeskd* **144**: 811–812.

Balderer G, Borbely AA (1985) Effect of valerian on human sleep. *Psychopharmacology* **87**: 406–409.

Baldessarini RJ (1987) The neuropharmacology of S-adenosyl-L-methionine. *Am J Medicine* **83**: 95–103.

Balfour P (2000) Use of hypericum as antidepressant. Safety in overdose needs to be established *BMJ* **320**: 1142–1143.

Barak Y, Levine J, Glasman A, et al (1996) Inositol treatment of Alzheimer's disease: a double blind, cross-over placebo controlled trial. *Prog Neuropsychopharmacol Biol Psychiatry* **20**: 729–735.

Barat I, Andreasen F, Damsgaard EM (2000) The consumption of drugs by 75-year-old individuals living in their own homes. *Eur J Clin Pharmacol* **56**: 501–509.

Barbenel DM, Yusufi B, O'Shea D, et al (2000) Mania in a patient receiving testosterone replacement postorchidectomy taking St John's wort and sertraline. *J Psychopharmacol* **14**: 84–86.

Beckman SE, Sommi RW, Switzer J (2000) Consumer use of St. John's wort: a survey on effectiveness, safety, and tolerability. *Pharmacotherapy* **20**: 568–574.

Bell KM, Plon L, Bunney WE, Jr, et al (1988) S-adenosylmethionine treatment of depression: a controlled clinical trial. *Am J Psychiatry* **145**: 1110–1114.

Benjamin J, Agam G, Levine J, et al (1995a) Inositol treatment in psychiatry. *Psychopharmacol Bull* **31**: 167–175.

Benjamin J, Levine J, Fux M, et al (1995b) Double-blind, placebo-controlled, crossover trial of inositol treatment for panic disorder. *Am J Psychiatry* **152**: 1084–1086.

Berlanga C, Ortega-Soto HA, Ontiveros M, et al (1992) Efficacy of S-adenosyl-L-methionine in speeding the onset of action of imipramine. *Psychiat Res* **44**: 257–262.

Bladt S, Wagner H (1993) MAO inhibition by fractions and constituents of hypericum extract. *Nervenheilkunde* **12**: 349–352.

Braun R, Dittmar W, Machut M, et al (1982) Valepotriate mit Epoxidstruktur-beachtliche Alkylantien. *Dtsch Apoth Z* **122**: 1109–1113.

Braun R, Dittmar W, von der Hude W, et al (1985) Bacterial mutagenicity of the tranquilizing constituents of valerianaceae roots. *Naunyn-Schmiedeberg's Arch Pharmacol* (Suppl 329): R28.

Brenner R, Azbel V, Madhusoodanan S, et al (2000) Comparison of an extract of hypericum (LI 160) and sertraline in the treatment of depression: a double-blind, randomized pilot study. *Clin Ther* **22**: 411–419.

Brockmoller J, Reum T, Bauer S, Kerb R, Hubner WD, Roots I (1997) Hypericin and pseudohypericin: pharmacokinetics and effects on photosensitivity in humans. *Pharmacopsychiatry* **30**(Suppl 2): 94–101.

Brown ES, Khan DA, Nejtek VA (1999) The psychiatric side effects of corticosteroids. *Ann Allergy Asthma Immunol* **83**: 495–503.

Burkard G, Lehrl S (1991) Verhaltnis von Demenzen vom Multiinfarkt- un vom Alzheimertyp in arztlichen Praxen. *Münch Med Wschr* **133**(Suppl 1): 38–43.

Cajochen C, Krauchi K, Wirz-Justice A (1997) The acute soporific action of daytime melatonin administration: effects on the EEG during wakefulness and subjective alertness. *J Biol Rhythms* **12**: 636–643.

Calandra C, Roxas M, Rapisarda V (1979) Azione antidepressiva della SAMe a paragone della clorimipramina. Ipotesi interpretative del meccanismo d'azione. *Minerva Psychiatrica* **20**: 147–152.

Carney MWP, Martin G, Bottiglieri T, et al (1983) Switch mechanism in affective illness and s-adenosylmethionine. *Lancet* i: 820–821.

Carney MWP, Chary TNK, Bottiglieri T (1987) Switch mechanism in affective illness and oral S-adneosylmethionine (SAM). *Br J Psychiatry* **150**: 724–725.

Cerutti R, Sichel MP, Perin M, et al (1993) Psychological distress during puerperium: a novel therapeutic approach using S-Adenosylmethionine. *Curr Therapeut Res* **53**: 707–716.

Chan TY, Tang CH, Critchley JA (1995) Poisoning due to an over-the-counter hypnotic, Sleep-Qik. *Postgrad Med J* **71**: 227–228.

Chatterjee SS, Bhattacharya SK, Wonnermann M, et al (1998) Hyperforin as a possible antidepressant component of hypericum extracts. *Life Sci* **63**: 499–510.

Chengappa KNR, Levin S, Gershon S, et al (2000) Inositol as an add-on treatment for bipolar depression. *Bipolar Disorders* 2: 47–55.

Cohen A (1996) Treatment of antidepressant-induced sexual dysfunction: a new scientific study shows benefits of ginkgo biloba. *Healthwatch* 5.

Cohen A (1997) *Ginkgo biloba for drug-induced sexual dysfunction* (abstract 35). In: Syllabus and Proceedings Summary, American Psychiatric Association Annual Meeting, San Diego, p 15.

Corcoran ME (1997) Polypharmacy in the older patient with cancer. *Cancer Control* 4: 419–428.

Cott JM (1995) Natural product formulations available in Europe for psychotropic indications. *Psychopharmacol Bull* 273: 607–609.

Davies LP, Drew CA, Duffield P, et al (1992) Kava pyrones and resin: studies on GABAA, GABAB and benzodiazepine binding sites in rodent brain. *Pharmacol Toxicol* 71: 120–126.

De Vanna M, Rigamonti R (1992) Oral S-adenosyl-L-Methionine in depression. *Curr Therapeut Res* 52: 478–485.

Del Vecchio M, Iorio G, Cocorullo M, et al (1978) Has SAMe (Ado-Met) an antidepressant effect? A preliminary trial versus chlorimipramine. *Rivista Sperimentale Freniatria* 102: 344–358.

Dollins AB, Lynch HJ, Wurtman RJ, et al (1993) Effect of pharmacological daytime doses of melatonin on human mood and performance. *Psychopharmacology (Berlin)* 112: 490–496.

Duffield PH, Jamieson D (1991) Development of tolerance to kava in mice. *Clin Exp Pharmacol Physiol* 18: 571–578.

Eisenberg DM (1997) Advising patients who seek alternative medical therapies. *Ann Intern Med* 127: 61–69.

Eisenberg DM, Kessler RC, Foster C, et al (1993) Unconventional medicine in the United States: prevalence, costs, and patterns of use. *N Engl J Med* 328: 246–252.

Farrel RJ, Lamb J (1990) Herbal remedies. *BMJ* 300: 47–48.

Fenton WS, Hibbeln J, Knable M (2000) Essential fatty acids, lipid membrane abnormalities, and the diagnosis and treatment of schizophrenia. *Biol Psychiatry* 47: 8–21.

Fisher P (1997) The wheat and chaff in alternative medicine. *Lancet* 349: 1629.

Fontanari D, DiPalma C, Giorgetti G, et al. (1994) Effects of S-adenosyl-L-methionine on cognitive and vigilance functions in elderly. *Curr Therapeut Res* 55: 682–689.

Fugh-Berman A (2000) Herb-drug interactions. *Lancet* 355: 134–138.

Fux M, Levine J, Aviv A, et al (1996) Inositol treatment of obsessive-compulsive disorder. *Am J Psychiatry* 153: 1219–1221.

Gerhard U, Linnenbrink N, Georghiadou CH, et al (1996) Effects of two plant-based sleep remedies on vigilance. *Schweizerische Rundschau für Medizin* 85: 473–481.

Gessner B, Klassner M (1984) The effect of harmonicum much on human sleep— A polygraphic EEG investigation. *EEG-EMG Zeitschrift für Elektroenzephalographie Elektromyographie und verwandte Gebeite* 15: 45–51.

Gleitz J, Friese J, Beile A, et al (1996) Anticonvulsive action of (+/−)-kavain estimated from its properties on stimulated synaptosomes and Na+ channel receptor sites. *Eur J Pharmacol* 315: 89–97, 1996.

Hansel R, Keller K, Rimpler H, et al (eds) (1994) *Hagers Handbuch der Pharmazeutischen Praxis, ed 6, Drogen E-O.* Berlin/Heidelberg/New York: Springer, 1994, pp 201–221, 268–292.

Harrer G, Hubner WD, Podzuweit H (1994) Effectiveness and tolerance of the hypericum preparation LI 160 compared to maprotiline: a multicenter double-blind study. *J Geriat Psychiat Neurol* 7(Suppl 1): 524–528.

Hendriks H, Boss R, Woerdenbag HJ, et al (1985) Central nervous system depressant activity of valerennic acid in the mouse. *Planta Medica*: 28–31.

Holm E, Staedt U, Heep J, et al (1991) The action profile of D,L-kavain. Cerebral sites and sleep-wakefulness rhythm in animals. *Arzneimittel-Forschung* 41: 673–683.

Houghton PJ (1988) The biological activity of valerian and related plants. *J Ethnopharmacol* 22: 121–142.

Hoyer S (1995) Possibilities and limits of therapy of cognition disorders in the elderly. *Zeitschrift für Gerontologie und Geriatrie* 28: 457–462.

Hypericum Depression Trial Study Group (2002) Effect of *Hypericum perforatum* (St John's Wort) in major depressive disorder. *JAMA* 287: 1807–1814.

Jamieson DD, Duffield PH (1990) Positive interaction of ethanol and kava resin in mice. *Clin Exp Pharmacol Physiol* 17: 509–514.

Janicak PG, Lipinski J, Davis JM, et al (1988) S-Adenosylmethionine in depression: a literature review and preliminary report. *Alabama J Med Sci* 25: 306–313.

Jussofie A, Schmiz A, Hiemke C (1994) Kavapyrone enriched extract from *Piper methysticum* as modulator of the GABA binding site in different regions of rat brain. *Psychopharmacology* 116: 469–474.

Kagan BL, Sultzer DL, Rosenlicht N, et al (1990) Oral S-adenosylmethionine in depression: a randomized, double-blind, placebo-controlled trial. *Am J Psychiatry* 147: 591–595.

Kahn A, Warner HA, Brown WA (2000) Symptom reduction and suicide risk in patients treated with placebo in antidepressant clinical trials. An analysis of the Food and Drug Administration database. *Arch Gen Psychiatry* 57: 311–317.

Kinzler E, Kromer J, Lehmann E (1991) Effect of a special kava extract in patients with anxiety, tension, and excitation states of non-psychotic genesis. Double blind study with placebos over 4 weeks. *Arzneimittel-Forschung* 41: 584–588.

Kling MA, Perini GI, Demitrack MA, et al (1989) Stress-responsive neurohormonal systems and the symptom complex of affective illness. *Psychopharmacol Bull* 25: 312–318.

Kohnen R, Oswald WD (1988) The effects of valerian, propranolol, and their combination on activation, performance, and mood of healthy volunteers under social stress conditions. *Pharmacopsychiatry* 21: 447–448.

Krippner S (1995) A cross cultural comparison of four healing models. *Alternative Therapies Hlth Med* 1: 21–29.

Kufferle B, Grunberger J (1982) Early clinical double-blind study with S-adenosyl-l-methionine: a new potential antidepressant. In: Costa E, Racagni G (eds), *Typical and atypical antidepressants.* New York: Raven Press, pp 175–180.

Laakmann G, Schule C, Baghai T, et al (1998) St. John's Wort in mild to moderate depression: the relevance of hyperforin for the clinical efficacy. *Pharmacopsychiatry* 31(Suppl 1): 54–59.

Lands WEM (1992) Biochemistry and physiology of ω-3 fatty acids. *FASEB J* 6: 2530–2536.

Laux G (1997) Pharmacotherapy. *Therapeutische Rundschau* 54: 595–599.

Leathwood PD, Chauffard F (1985) Aqueous extract of valerian reduces latency to fall asleep in man. *Planta Medica* 2: 144–148.

Leathwood PD, Chauffard F, Heck E, et al (1982) Aqueous extract of valerian root (*Valeriana officinalis* L.) improves sleep quality in man. *Pharmacol Biochem Behav* 17: 65–71.

LeBars PL, Katz MM, Berman N, et al (1997) A placebo-controlled, double-blind, randomized trial of an extract of Ginkgo biloba for dementia. North American EGb Study Group. *JAMA* 278: 1327–1332.

Lehman NL, Johnson LN (1999) Toxic optic neuropathy after concomitant use of melatonin, zoloft, and a high-protein diet. *J Neuroophthalmol* 19: 232–234.

Leuschner J, Muller J, Rudmann M (1993) Characterization of the central nervous depressant activity of a commercially available valerian root extract. *Arzneimittel-Forschung* 43: 638–641.

Levine J (1997) Controlled trials of inositol in psychiatry. *Eur Neuropsychopharm* 7: 147–155.

Levine J, Barak Y, Gonzalves M, et al (1995a) Double-blind, controlled trial of inositol treatment of depression. *Am J Psychiatry* 152: 792–794.

Levine J, Pomerantz T, Stier S, et al (1995b) Lack of effect of 6 g inositol treatment of post-ECT cognitive function in humans *J Psychiat Res* 29: 487–489.

Levine J, Kurtzman L, Rapoport A, et al (1996) CSF inositol does not predict antidepressant response to inositol. (Short communication.) *J Neural Transm* 103: 1457–1462.

Levine J, Aviram A, Holan A, et al (1997) Inositol treatment of autism. *J Neural Transm* 104: 307–310.

Levine J, Mishori A, Susnosky M, et al (1999) Combination of inositol and serotonin reuptake inhibitors in the treatment of depression. *Biol Psychiatry* 45: 270–273.

LoRusso A, Monaco M, Pani A, et al (1994) Efficacy of S-Adenosyl-L-methionine on relieving psychological distress associated with detoxification on opiate abusers. *Curr Therapeut Res* 55: 905–913.

MacGregor FB, Abernethy VE, Dahabra S, et al (1989) Hepatotoxicity of herbal medicines. *BMJ* 299: 1156–1157.

Maes M, Smith RS (1998) Fatty acids, cytokines, and major depression. *Biol Psychiatry* 43: 313–314.

Mantero M, Pastorino P, Carolei A, et al (1975) Studio controllato in doppio cieco (SAMe-imipramina) nelle sindromi depressive. *Minerva Medica* 66: 4098–4101.

Martinez B, Kasper S, Ruhrmann B, et al (1993) Hypericum in the treatment of seasonal affective disorders. *Nervenheilkunde* 12: 302–307.

Mathews JD, Riley MD, Fejo L, et al (1988) Effects of the heavy usage of kava on physical health: summary of a pilot survey in an aboriginal community. *Med J Australia* 148: 548–555.

Miccoli L, Porro V, Bertolino A (1978) Comparison between the antidepressant activity of S-adenosyl-l-methionine (SAMe) and that of some tricyclic drugs. *Acta Neurologica* 33: 243–255.

Miller JL (2000) Interaction between indinavir and St. John's wort reported. *Am J Hlth Syst Pharm* **57**: 625–626.

Mischoulon D (2001) Herbal anxiolytics: a review of kava and valerian. *Psychiat Ann.*

Mischoulon D, Rosenbaum JF (eds) (2002) Natural medications for psychiatric disorders: considering the alternatives. London and New York: Lippincott Williams and Wilkins.

Mishima K, Satoh K, Shimizu T, et al (1997) Hypnotic and hypothermic action of daytime-administered melatonin. *Psychopharmacology (Berlin)* **133**: 168–171.

Monaco P, Quattrocchi F (1979) Studio degli effetti antidepressivi di un trans-metilante biologico (s-adenosil-metionina—SAMe). *Rivista di Neurologia* **49**: 417–439.

Monti JM, Cardinali DP (2000) A critical assessment of the melatonin effect on sleep in humans. *Biol Signals Recept* **9**: 328–339.

Moore LB, Goodwin B, Jones SA, et al (2000) St. John's wort induces hepatic drug metabolism through activation of the pregnane X receptor. *Proc Natl Acad Sci USA* **97**: 7500–7502.

Moses EL, Mallinger AG (2000) St. John's Wort: three cases of possible mania induction. *J Clin Psychopharmacol* **20**: 115–117.

Müller W, Rossol R (1993) Effects of hypericum extract on the expression of serotonin receptors. *Nervenheilkunde* **12**: 357–358.

National Institutes of Health Office of Alternative Medicine (NIHOAM) (1997a) Clinical practice guidelines in complementary and alternative medicine. An analysis of opportunities and obstacles. Practice and Policy Guidelines panel. *Arch Fam Med* **6**: 149–154.

National Institutes of Health Office of Alternative Medicine (NIHOAM) (1997b) *General information on sponsored research.* Rockville, MD: NIHOAM.

Nierenberg AA (1998) St. John's Wort: a putative over-the-counter herbal anti-depressant. *J Depress Disord Index & Reviews* **III**: 16–17.

Nierenberg AA, Burt T, Matthews J, et al (1999) Mania associated with St. John's wort. *Biol Psychiatry* **46**: 1707–1708.

Nierenberg A (2002) St. John's Wort as an antidepressant. In: Mischoulon D, Rosenbaum JF (eds), *Natural Medications for Psychiatric Disorders: Considering the Alternatives.* London and New York: Lippincott Williams and Wilkins.

O'Breasail AM, Argouarch S (1998) Hypomania and St John's wort. *Can J Psychiatry* **43**: 746–747.

Partonen T (1999) Melatonin-dependent infertility. *Med Hypotheses* **52**: 269–270.

Pepe S, Bogdanov K, Hallaq H, et al (1994) Omega-3 polyunsaturated fatty acid modulates dihydropyridine effects on L-type Ca^{2+} channels, cytosolic Ca^{2+}, and contraction in adult rat cardiac myocytes. *Proc Natl Acad Sci USA* **91**: 8832–8836.

Persengiev S, Marinova C, Patchev V (1991) Steroid hormone receptors in the thymus: a site of immunomodulatory action of melatonin. *Int J Biochem* **23**: 1483–1485.

Piscitelli SC, Burstein AH, Chaitt D, et al (2000) Indinavir concentrations and St John's wort. *Lancet* **355**: 547–548.

Prost N, Tichadou L, Rodor F, et al (2000) St. John's wort-venlafaxine interaction. *Presse Med* **29**: 1285–1286.

Raghavendra V, Kulkarni SK (2000) Melatonin reversal of DOI-induced hypo-phagia in rats; possible mechanism by suppressing 5-HT(2A) receptor-mediated activation of HPA axis. *Brain Res* **860**: 112–118.

Reidel E, Hansel R, Ehrke G (1982) Hemmung des Gamma-Amino-buttersaureabbaus durch Valerensaurederivate. *Planta Medica* **46**: 219–220.

Riederer P, Laux G, Poldinger W (eds) (1993) *Neuropsychopharmaka: Vol 5. Parkinsonmittel and Nootropika*. Vienna/New York: Springer, pp 161–324.

Rocco PL (1994) Major depression complicating medical illness: utility of S-Adenosyl-L-methionine. *Neuropsychopharmacology* **10**(Suppl pt 2): 99.

Sack RL, Hughes RJ, Edgar DM, et al (1997) Sleep-promoting effects of melatonin: at what dose, in whom, under what conditions, and by what mechanisms? *Sleep* **20**: 908–915.

Sack RL, Brandes RW, Kendall AR (2000) Entrainment of free-running circadian rhythms by melatonin in blind people. *N Engl J Med* **343**: 1070–1077.

Salmaggi P, Bressa GM, Nicchia G, et al (1993) Double-blind, placebo-controlled study of s-adenosyl-l-methionine in depressed post-menopausal women. *Psychother Psychosom* **59**: 34–40.

Santos MS, Ferreira F, Cunha AP, et al (1994) An aqueous extract of valerian influences the transport of GABA in synaptosomes. *Planta Medica* **60**: 278–279.

Scarzella R, Appiotti A (1977) *A double clinical comparison of SAMe versus chlorimipramine in depressive syndromes*. Paper presented at the VIth World Congress of Psychiatry, Honolulu.

Schellenberg R, Sauer S, Dimpfel W (1998) Pharmacodynamic effects of two different hypericum extracts in healthy volunteers measured by quantitative EEG. *Pharmacopsychiatry* **31**(Suppl 1): 44–53.

Schneck C (1998) St. John's wort and hypomania. *J Clin Psychiatry* **59**: 689.

Schrader E (2000) Equivalence of St John's wort extract (Ze 117) and fluoxetine: a randomized, controlled study in mild-moderate depression. *Int Clin Psychopharmacol* **15**: 61–68.

Schultz H, Jobert M (1995) Die Darstellung sedierender/tranquilisierender Wirkungen von Phytopharmaka im quantifizierten EEG (abstract). *Z Phytother Abstractband*: 10.

Schulz V, Hansel R, Tyler VE (2001) *Rational phytotherapy: A physician's guide to herbal medicine*. Berlin: Springer, 4th edn.

Seitz U, Ameri A, Pelzer H, et al (1997a) Relaxation of evoked contractile activity of isolated guinea-pig ileum by (+/−)-kavain. *Planta Medica* **63**: 303–306.

Seitz U, Schule A, Gleitz J (1997b) [3H]-monoamine uptake inhibition properties of kava pyrones. *Planta Medica* **63**: 548–549.

Shelton RC, Keller MB, Gelenberg A, et al (2000) Effectiveness of St John's wort in major depression: a randomized controlled trial. *JAMA* **285**: 1978–1986.

Simopoulos AP, Salem N Jr (1986) Purslane: a terrestrial source of omega-3 fatty acids (letter). *N Engl J Med* **315**: 833.

Simopoulos AP, Robinson J (1999) *The omega diet*. New York: HarperCollins.

Simopoulos AP, Norman HA, Gillaspy JE, et al (1992) Common purslane: a source of omega-3 fatty acids and antioxidants. *J Am Coll Nutr* **11**: 374–382.

Singh YN (1983) Effects of kava on neuromuscular transmission and muscle contractility. *J Ethnopharmacol* **7**: 267–276.

Singh YN (1992) Kava: an overview. *J Ethnopharmacol* **37**: 13–45.

Smith M, Buckwalter KC (1992) Medication management, antidepressant drugs, and the elderly: an overview. *J Psychosocial Nurs Mental Health Services* **30**: 30–36.

Smith PF, Maclennan K, Darlington CL (1996) The neuroprotective properties of the ginkgo biloba leaf: a review of the possible relationship to platelet-activating factor (PAF). *J Ethnopharmacol* **50**: 131–139.

Smythies JR, Alarcon RD, Bancroft AJ, et al (1986) Role of the one-carbon cycle in neuropsychiatry. In: Borchardt RT, Creveling CR, Ueland PM (eds), *Biological methylation and drug design.* Clifton, NJ: Humana Press, pp 351–362.

Sperling RI, Benincaso AI, Knoell CT, et al (1993) Dietary omega-3 polyunsaturated fatty acids inhibit phosphoinositide formation and chemotaxis in neutrophils. *J Clin Invest* **91**: 651–660.

Spillman M, Fava M (1996) S-adenosyl-methionine (ademethionine) in psychiatric disorders. *CNS Drugs* **6**: 416–425.

Spitzer RL, Terman M, Williams JB, et al (1999) Jet lag: clinical features, validation of a new syndrome-specific scale, and lack of response to melatonin in a randomized, double-blind trial. *Am J Psychiatry* **156**: 1392–1396.

Stensby ME (1969) Nutritional properties of fish oils. *World Rev Nutr Diet* **11**: 46–105.

Stoll AL, Severus E (1996) Mood stabilizers: shared mechanisms of action at post synaptic signal transduction and kindling processes. *Harvard Rev Psychiatry* **4**: 77–89.

Stoll AL, Locke CA (2001) Omega-3 fatty acids in mood disorders: A review of neurobiological and clinical actions. In: Mischoulon D, Rosenbaum J (eds), *Natural medications in psychiatric disorders.* Philadelphia: Lippincott Williams & Wilkins.

Stoll AL, Severus E, Freeman MP, et al (1999) Omega-3 fatty acids in bipolar disorder: a preliminary double-blind, placebo-controlled trial. *Arch Gen Psychiatry* **56**: 407–412.

Stoppe G, Sandholzer H, Staedt J, et al (1996) Prescribing practice with cognition enhancers in outpatient care: are there differences regarding type of dementia?—Results of a representative survey in Lower Saxony, Germany. *Pharmacopsychiatry* **29**: 150–155.

Suss R, Lehmann P (1996) Hematogenous contact eczema cause by phytogenic drugs exemplified by kava root extract. *Hautarzt* **47**: 459–461.

Teufel-Mayer R, Gleitz J (1997) Effects of long-term administration of hypericum extracts on the affinity and density of the central serotonergic 5-HT1 A and 5-HT2 A receptors. *Pharmacopsychiatry* **30**(Suppl 2): 113–116.

Thiele B, Ploch M, Brink I (1993) Modulation of cytokine expression by hypericum extract. *Nervenheilkunde* **12**: 353–356.

Vanecek J, Watanabe K (1999) Mechanisms of melatonin action in the pituitary and SCN. *Adv Exp Med Biol* **460**: 191–198.

Volz HP, Kieser M (1997) Kava-kava extract WS 1490 versus placebo in anxiety disorders—a randomized placebo-controlled 25-week outpatient trial. *Pharmacopsychiatry* **30**: 1–5.

Vorbach EU, Hubner WD, Arnoldt KH (1994) Effectiveness and tolerance of the hypericum extract LI 160 in comparison with imipramine. Randomized double blind study with 135 out-patients. *J Geriat Psychiat Neurol* **7**(Suppl 1): S19–S23.

Vorbach EU, Gortelmayer R, Brunning J (1996) Therapie von Insomnien: Wirksamkeit and Vertraglichkeit eines Baldrian-Preparates. *Psychopharmakotherapie* **3**: 109–115.

Vorbach EU, Arnoldt KH, Hubner WD (1997) Efficacy and tolerability of St. John's wort extract LI 160 versus imipramine in patients with severe depressive episodes according to ICD-10. *Pharmacopsychiatry* **30**(Suppl 2): 81–85.

Walden J, von Wegerer J, Winter U, et al (1997) Effects of kawain and dihydromethysticin on field potential changes in the hippocampus. *Prog Neuropsychopharmacol Biol Psychiatry* **21**: 697–706.

Warnecke G (1991) Psychosomatic dysfunctions in the female climacteric. Clinical effectiveness and tolerance of Kava Extract WS 1490. *Fortschritte der Medizin* **109**: 119–122.

Wheatley D (1997) LI 160, an extract of St. John's wort, versus amitriptyline in mildly to moderately depressed outpatients—a controlled 6-week clinical trial. *Pharmacopsychiatry* **30**(Suppl 2): 77–80.

Whitmore SM, Leake NB (1996) Complementary therapies: an adjunct to traditional therapies. *Nurse Practitioner* **21**: 12–13.

Wiechmann AF, O'Steen WK (1992) Melatonin increases photoreceptor susceptibility to light-induced damage. *Invest Ophthalmol Vis Sci* **33**: 1894–1902.

Willey LB, Mady SP, Cobaugh DJ, et al (1995) Valerian overdose: a case report. *Vet Hum Toxicol* **37**: 364–365.

Xiao YF, Gomez AM, Morgan JP, et al (1997) Suppression of voltage-gated L-type Ca^{2+} currents by polyunsaturated fatty acids in adult and neonatal rat ventricular myocytes. *Proc Natl Acad Sci USA* **94**: 4182–4187.

Index